American Diction
STANDARD AMERICAN DICTION FOR SINGERS AND SPEAKERS

By Geoffrey G. Forward With Elisabeth Howard

Published by:
Performing Arts Global Publishing

1909 N. Topanga Canyon Blvd.
Topanga, CA 90290 USA

First Printing 1990
Second Printing 1994 revised
Third Printing 1998
Revised Printing 2000
Printed in the United States of America
Illustrations by Anida Margolis

Performing Arts Global Publishing books are available at **special discounts for bulk purchases**
for sales promotions, premiums, fund-raising, or educational use. For information on seminars and
speakers, please write or call:

Performing Arts Global Publishing
1909 N. Topanga Canyon Blvd.
Topanga, CA 90290 USA
(888) 773-3246
email: spchmastr@earthlink.net
http://www.shakespeare-usa.com/speechmasters

Copyright © MMI by Alfred Publishing Co., Inc.
All rights reserved   Printed in USA.
ISBN 0-7390-1876-0 (Book & CDs)
(Previously published by Speechmasters of America, ISBN 0-944200-00-1)
ISBN 0-7390-1875-2 (Book)
ISBN 0-7390-1920-1 (2 CDs)

Praise for *American Diction for Singers*

"...a remarkable book, a significant contribution to the literature...conversational in style... practical in approach...Profusely illustrated, well researched, rich with practical exercises, this excellent book is one of the most up-to-date and comprehensive manuals of diction for singers available. No less important are the appropriate, utilitarian demonstrations on the two tapes. ...the remarkable set is highly recommended for use in all voice studios."

—Richard Dale Sjoerdsma
National Association of Teachers of Singing (NATS) Journal

"The definitive book that once and for all settles the problems of how to sing in good Standard American English."

—John DeMain
Music Director, Houston Grand Opera

*"**American Diction for Singers** by Geoffrey G. Forward is a most important contribution to the field of singing and the teaching of singing. Both the book and the accompanying tapes offer a clear and practical guide for the singer in an area far too often neglected. We work so hard with our students on their French, German, and Italian and foolishly assume that they face no problems in their native language. Mr. Forward's careful explanation of how the sounds are made and his simple but essential rules will be of inestimable value to all who wish the great texts set by American composers to be clear to their listeners. This work will also be a great help to those who champion the singing of opera in English. Nothing in any way runs counter to healthy singing. Any student's vocal technique will only be enhanced by following those precepts which Mr. Forward advocates. Special bonuses are the history of American speech, the chapter on pop singing by Elisabeth Howard, and the Shakespeare quotations to which every student should be exposed. I recommend **American Diction for Singers** most strongly."*

—Dale Moore
Professor of Music, Indiana University
Past President, National Association of Teachers of Singing

"I am overwhelmed by the thought, research and care that have gone into this book... All the principles are clearly stated and correctly assessed. The ideas and directions are clear. The drawings are great. ... All of your ideas are immediately applicable to other languages, as well... a wonderful book..."

—Maralin Niska
Metropolitan Opera Soprano

*"You have done wonderful work in your book **American Diction for Singers**. I recommend it to students because its clear organization and abundant practice materials provide them with the necessary tools to teach themselves and to make noticeable progress independently. Your books and tapes all give constant emphasis to relaxed articulation so that the student is continually reminded of vocal health and ease. Whoever applies these techniques will not just sing more clearly but will sing with more freedom and expression."*

—John Glenn Paton
Diction and Voice Teacher, USC
Author of *Foundations In Singing*, Editor of *26 Italian Songs and Arias*

*"Teachers and students alike were unanimous in their praise of your concise, informative lecture-demonstration on the use of vowels and consonants.... Your new textbook on diction, **American Diction for Singers**, is an important addition to the resources available for singers and teachers."*

—Kari Windingstad
Adjunct Associate Professor of Voice, UCLA,
President, NATS, Los Angeles Chapter

"American Diction for Singers is highly recommended for every singer who aspires to perform at their very best, whether professionally or personally. Every singing student, every voice teacher, every vocal coach, every theatrical school, music school, and public library should have a copy of American Diction For Singers on their shelves."

—James A. Cox
Editor-in-Chief
Midwest Book Review

Table of Contents

For Liz
without whose patience, love and unflagging support
I could never have finished this project.

Acknowledgments

I am grateful for the help of many people in preparing this book for publication, especially:
Elisabeth Howard, founder and co-director of the Vocal Power Institute, in Los Angeles,
and my wife, who encouraged me to write this book, read the manuscript and discussed
it with me, and whose vast knowledge of singing proved invaluable on many occasions.
John DeMain, Musical Director of the Houston Grand Opera, guest conductor for
opera and musical theatre companies all over the world and an understanding and
supportive friend. He generously shared with me his thoughts and suggestions regarding
American diction gained from his extensive experience conducting singers for whom
English is either their first language or second language.
John Paton, voice teacher at the University of Southern California and former faculty
member for 25 years at the Universities of Wisconsin and Colorado, who discussed
diction with me on many occasions, graciously read portions of the manuscript and
offered numerous valuable suggestions.
Maralin Niska, who read the manuscript and generously offered numerous suggestions
for improvement.
The Huntington Library, in San Marino, CA, where I did much of the writing and
research.
My students, on whom I practiced until I got it right.
To all my sincere thanks.
As to any errors, they are my responsibility and if detected by any reader, I would appreciate
a letter pointing them out to me.

Also by Geoffrey G. Forward

PROSPEECH-book
PROSPEECH-audio tapes
POWER SPEECH-audio tapes

1 Introduction to Diction

This book and CD combination teaches both speaking and singing diction, for professional singers.

What is Diction?

At intermission, those of us who sit out in the dark theatre with the audience hear many things said about a singer. Diction is often mentioned.

Not infrequently we hear someone complain. *"I didn't understand a word he* (or she) *said."* His (or her) companion sagely replies, *"That's just the nature of singing, you never can understand what they say."*

Another, more welcome, but regrettably less frequently heard, comment is, delightedly, *"I could understand everything he (or she) said."* The reply, equally delightedly, *"Yes, he (or she) is a wonderful singer."*

Why does being able to understand a singer make the singer better and the performance more enjoyable?

Let's look at how good diction transforms an ordinary singer into a **wonderful** singer.

The Two Meanings of Diction

If you look up *diction* in a dictionary, you'll find it has two meanings:

(1) How clearly you say your words, that is, your pronunciation, articulation or enunciation.

(2) Your choice of words, especially with regard to whether they are correct, clear and effective in expressing your thought.

On a basic, elementary level, diction means saying and singing your words clearly and correctly, so that the audience can understand what you are saying. This may be referred to as: *pronunciation*, *articulation* **or** *enunciation*.

In general, people use these terms interchangeably, although they have slightly different meanings.

Pronunciation

Pronunciation refers to the way you say a word, with regard to which *vowels*, *diphthongs* and *consonants* you use. For example, whether you say *of_ten* with or without the *t*, or whether you say *get* or *git*.

Pronunciation also refers to the *syllable stress* you give to a word. For a word to be pronounced correctly the stress must be on the correct syllable—**lov**ely, not *love***ly**.

Articulation

Articulation is the movement and placement of your articulators as you make the sounds of speech. (Your articulators are your *jaw*, *lips*, *teeth*, *tongue*, *soft palate*, and *hard palate*.) This is a muscular activity that you learn, like riding a bike or bouncing a ball.

Articulation also involves *linking*, or connecting *sounds*, *syllables* and *words* together for the smooth flow of speech and singing. *Linking* may also be called *liaison*.

Enunciation

Enunciation refers to how clearly you say the vowels, consonants and diphthongs of speech.

As we said, these terms are generally used to refer to how you say your words, without being too precise about their meanings. A person may use "pronunciation" when technically he means "articulation" or "enunciation"—as in, *"You didn't pronounce that 'a' correctly."*

Good articulation is the basis of clear speech.

Good articulation is also the basis of good diction.

The sounds you say are a result of the way you make them. How you move and place your articulators determines how correctly and clearly you say the sounds of speech.

The elements of good diction are studied by all serious singers—not just classical singers. All singers need to be understood—

though not all singing styles have the same kind of pronunciation, articulation and enunciation. We discuss this in the chapter on *Pop Diction*.

Expressive Singing

The second meaning of diction is your choice of words to express your thoughts and emotions.

Of course, in singing you don't choose your own words. You sing the words that the poet, lyricist or librettist has written for you. However, you do have control over how expressively you sing your words, phrases and thoughts.

Singing expressively means singing with meaning and emotion. It is part of your artistic and creative contribution to the performance.

Finding the Emotion In the Words

The great acting coach, Constantin Stanislavski, taught that,

> *Inside each and every word there is an emo-tion, a thought, that produced the word and justifies its being there. Empty words are like nutshells without meat, concepts without content; they are no use, indeed they are harmful. ...Until the actor is able to fill out each word of the text with live emotions, the text of his role will remain dead.*
> (*Creating A Role*, p. 94).

In singing, as in acting, the path to the emotions is through the specific meaning and imagery of the words.

The words you sing have emotions locked inside them. When you discover their correct meaning and imagery you release their emotion—in yourself and your audience. If you don't find the right meaning and imagery, the emotion you project to your audience is vague, impotent and boring.

You are the key. *You* must find the specific meaning and imagery in the words and sing them with that feeling.

But just because you feel the emotion, don't think that your audience automatically feels the same emotion. They can't feel what you are feel-ing unless they also understand the words you are saying. Look at the following word— *fatoble*.

What does it mean to you? Do you get any imagery? Or does it leave you puzzled and a little frustrated? (It's a made-up word. It doesn't mean anything.) No matter what kind of emotion is in an actor's voice, as he says *fatoble*, you won't relate to it, or know what to think of it. You don't recognize it and you don't have any memories or associations with the word.

If you were singing a group of sounds that someone told you were words, but you didn't know what they meant, could you be filled with their emotion? No, of course not.

It's the same for your audience. They need to recognize the word before they can relate any specific meaning and imagery to the word.

Of course, the general emotional quality in your voice and in the music gives your audience some idea of what you're feeling, which stimulates some emotional reaction in them. But that only opens the door part way. To fully feel the emotion themselves, they need to understand the words. Their understanding and emotion depends on your diction.

Why Do We Need To Study Diction?

Why should we study diction? Don't we all talk and can't we all be understood?

Not all the time.

Sure, anyone can order from a menu and get what they asked for.

But in a restaurant, if the waiter doesn't understand what you say, he can always ask you to repeat your order.

In a performance, the audience can't stop the show and ask you what you said or sang (no matter how much they would like to).

Diction for Performance

We can compare a singer's diction with the diction of an actor. The actors' speech you hear on stage, film or television is not the same as normal, everyday speech—it's more clear, precise and interesting to listen to. It's controlled, careful and artistic, even when it doesn't appear to be. Let's take a famous example. Marlon Brando's speech in *On the Waterfront* gives the impression of being mumbled, but you can understand every word he says. His artistry is in having control over his speech to get the effect he wants.

All good actors have speech that sounds like ordinary speech. But put someone without speech training on stage or in front of the camera next to someone with speech training and the difference becomes painfully obvious. In fact, in the early years of films, the Hollywood studios provided elocution classes for all their young talent to teach them to speak clearly and beautifully (Barry Norman, *The Story of Hollywood*, p. 48).

Good speech is part of an actor's charisma—as many silent film stars found out to their dismay, when their careers disappeared along with the silent films.

Actors study diction and take care to speak clearly because they know their audience has to easily understand them the first time they say their lines. This is particularly true on stage. In front of the camera, you have a chance to do it over again, either immediately or in dubbing. But that's the point. If the words are not clear, you repeat the scene until they are clear. The words must be understood.

Diction for the Professional Singer

Obviously, singing words that the audience can understand is not the only criterion of a good singer. But, at the same time, it is true that audiences, critics and singers alike, appreciate good diction as one of the marks of professionalism and excellence in singing and miss it when it isn't there.

Enrico Caruso, lamented that,

> *Good diction, or the art of pronouncing the words of a song or opera properly and intelligently, is a matter sadly neglected by many singers.*

And he maintained that,

> *Certainly no singer can be called a great artist unless his diction is good, for a beautiful voice alone will not make up for other deficiencies.* (Caruso and Tetrazzini on the Art of Singing, pp. 61-62)

The great song stylist, Lotte Lehmann, wrote that among singers *"the word is entirely too much neglected"* (p. 12). *"I have listened to many young singers,"* she says,

> *...and have found with ever increasing astonishment that they consider their preparation finished when they have developed a lovely voice, a serviceable technique and musical accuracy. At this point they consider themselves ready to appear before the public...*
> (*More than Singing, The Interpretation of Songs*, p. 10)

But, in her opinion, they are not ready—not without good diction. She makes the point that singers sing both words and music. One cannot be more important than the other. Good diction in singing cannot be left to chance. You must study it, think about it and make it a habit.

But singing with good diction does not mean that you should always sing vowels, diphthongs and consonants the same way, regardless of the language you are speaking or the style of music you are singing. Different languages and different dialects often have slightly, sometimes drastically, different pronunciations, or articulations, of the sounds of speech. You must say the sounds the way they are normally said in the language or dialect you are singing.

Singing English after being trained in classical technique presents a special challenge.

John DeMain, Music Director of the Houston Grand Opera and conductor of numerous English language operas and Broadway musicals, gives the following advice to classical singers singing English:

> *I think it is important for the young students of singing to remember that in the early stages of their vocal development, they were trained on Italian vowels and consonants. After several years of singing five Italian vowels, learning how to deal with double consonants, the Italian **t** and **d**, and all those rules concerning flipped and rolled **r**'s, I have found innumerable examples of young singers inadvertently applying these rules or habits to singing in English, whether it be British or American style. This is an unforgivable*

*oversight that really deprives the listener of the beauty (yes, beauty, I say) of the myriad sounds of the English language; and, after all, doesn't our own language deserve the time and attention we lavish on foreign languages? It is high-time we rediscover the American **t** and **d**, double consonants and other English consonants, as well as the many vowel sounds and how to sing the diphthongs that go with them.*

(Taken from conversations with the author.)

The English language is infinitely beautiful and expressive and deserves the same kind of study, care and effort put into singing and speaking other languages.

The fact that you are able to speak English (even for American-born singers) does not mean that you are automatically qualified to sing it or speak it well enough to perform in public. Stage diction only sounds like normal, everyday speech. In reality, it is not. It is an artistic illusion of ordinary speech.

Good Speech vs. Bad Speech

There has always been a standard of "good" and "bad" speech, which may be described as Daniel Jones does in *The Pronunciation of English*:

'Good' speech may be defined as a way of speaking which is clearly intelligible to all ordinary people. 'Bad' speech is a way of talking which is difficult for most people to understand. It is caused by mumbling or lack of definiteness of utterance. (p. 4.)

This is a practical, common sense definition which must be observed by anyone who wants to communicate clearly and persuasively, but especially by professional speakers and singers.

Notice that the definition for good speech does not mention a special dialect or pronunciation. One dialect is not intrinsically better than another. Nor is good or bad speech defined by differences in pronunciations, in which one vowel may be substituted for another, as in *tom**a**to* or tom**ah**to, or in which the *r* may be dropped or not, as in *p**ar**k* or *p**ah**k*.

The simple criterion for good diction is whether or not you can be understood by your listeners. (However, in some circumstances, such as in a performance, it could be argued that the criterion for good speech should be expanded to include, (1) saying sounds that fit the style of the music and (2) presenting the image and emotion you want to present.)

Some Common Misconceptions About Dialect and Diction

Before we continue discussing diction and dialect, let's take a moment and question some popular misconceptions about diction and dialect in singing:

Question: Is it true that singing with a dialect means you have bad diction?

Answer: Not necessarily. The criterion for judging diction is whether or not you can be understood—not whether or not you use a certain kind of pronunciation.

Question: Is it true that you can't understand most popular (nonclassical) singers, because they have bad diction?

Answer: No. You only need to listen to some of the best to hear that you can understand their words. Most pop singers have good diction. It's just not classical diction.

Question: Is it true that most of the time you can't understand classical singers, even when they sing in English?

Answer: No. There are many professional classical singers who can be easily understood when they sing in English. The fact that you can point to some singers of any style and say that you can't understand them only proves the rule: You can understand the best professional singers of all styles.

What Dialect Should You Sing?

There are many different American dialects and a dialect that is appropriate to use in one situation may not be acceptable in another. This is especially true in singing different styles of music, as can be attested to by anyone who has heard a classically trained singer sing a pop song with classical diction or—not to pick on classical singers— a pop singer singing classical music with pop diction.

But because there are a number of different dialects spoken in America, we should look at how the question of dialect or pronunciation is resolved by professional singers and speakers.

When we speak of a dialect we refer to a type of speech that is characteristic of:

(1) a geographic region or

(2) a certain group of people.

In the United States there are three general geographical dialects, each with a number of subdialects:

(1) New England, or Eastern region

(2) Southern region

(3) General American.

In 1950, J.S. Kenyon, in *American Pronunciation*, estimated that a little less than 9% of the U.S. population spoke the Eastern type of dialect, about 20% spoke the Southern type and nearly 71% spoke the General American dialect (p. 14.)

Which dialect you should sing depends partly upon the kind of music you sing. Theoretically, there are as many singing dialects as there are speaking dialects. Different dialects are used in different styles of music— country/western, rock, blues, pop, musical theatre, classical, and so on. Your singing dialect should be appropriate to the style of music.

The *Pop Diction* chapter, by Elisabeth Howard, will go into this subject in greater detail.

Note that "good diction" does not necessarily mean "classical" diction. Diction in any dialect is good if you can be understood by your audience.

Standard American Stage Dialect

Although there are many dialects in America, there is a particular one, usually described as a non-dialect, used by American singers and actors when they sing or speak non-dialect roles. It is called Standard American Stage Dialect.

Standard American Stage Dialect is not confined to a geographic region. It is a particular kind of speech used by a group of people who perform professionally.

This is a relatively new dialect in American speech and it is worthwhile looking at how it came about.

A Brief History of American Speech

The First American Dialect

The roots of American speech lie deep in 17th and 18th century England. As pointed out by Albert H. Marckwardt, in *American English* (revised by J.L. Dillard, 1980), the first English settlers in the New World had learned their English prior to 1600 and had English accents just like their British counterparts (p. 15.)

Speech in America springs from the speech of the early settlers in three distinct regions—(1) the Puritans of New England, (2) the Quakers of Pennsylvania and (3) the aristocratic plantation owners of the Southern settlements in Virginia and the Carolinas.

The leaders of the colonists were wealthy, educated noblemen and courtiers, who came from the southeastern counties of England, including London, who spoke the prestigious London dialect. This was the dialect of the upper class of England, the speech of Shakespeare and his contemporaries, and the nobles of the Courts of Elizabeth and James.

Most of the rank and file members of these first colonies also came from the southeastern counties, with a few from the western and northern counties. Some were educated, younger sons of wealthy families, who spoke the London dialect. But many were from the middle and poor classes, who spoke their local dialects.

Later settlers spoke a variety of dialects. In *A Word Geography of the Eastern United States*, Hans Kurath, a leading authority on American dialects, notes that "the great majority of the American colonists, whether they came from England, Northern Ireland, or Germany, belonged to the middle class of European society or to the poor" (p. 4).

Obviously, middle class, provincial dialects were an important part of the speech mix of the American colonies. In terms of speech influences, however, it is significant that the colonies had a nucleus of respected leaders, officials, planters, merchants, ministers, teachers and scholars, who set the speech standards. Kurath states that,

> *This small but influential group knew the literary language of England, and those among them who had grown up in London or had been educated at Cambridge or Oxford spoke Standard English or something approximating it.... The standard English spoken and written by the leading personalities became the model for the middle class, whatever their English provenience.* (p. 4)

Kurath's study of modern American dialects concludes,

> *There can be no doubting the fact that the major speech areas of the Eastern states coincide in the main with settlement areas and that the most prominent speech boundaries run along the seams of these settlement areas.* (*Word Geography*, p. 1)

In New England, most of the first colonists came from the Southeastern counties of England. George Philip Krapp, in his extensive study, *The English Language in America*, uses Anders Orbeck's study, *Early New England Pronunciation*, to place their origins. He shows that these early settlers came from a number of counties in England, including the north and the west, but that the majority of them emigrated from the Southeastern counties of Suffolk,

Norfolk, Essex and London. (Orbeck sets the percentage at 67.78%.) The speech of this Southeastern area was the prestigious London dialect, the dialect of the Court and the upper class. This became the dominant dialect of the New England colonists.

The Quakers began settling Pennsylvania in the early 1680s. William Penn, the leader of this settlement, had joined the Society of Friends, or Quakers, while a student at Oxford. His father was the wealthy Admiral Sir William Penn, conqueror of Jamaica, royal creditor and friend to influential people at court. The younger Penn received the Pennsylvania territory from the king to pay off a debt owed to the Penn family.

In 1681 Penn advertised his colony in America as a haven for freedom of thought and worship and it became an immediate success. The Quakers who moved there were an intelligent middle class, cultured, educated, upwardly mobile and the dominating influence for many years.

Albert C. Baugh, notes that in England the Quakers were mostly from the north and north Midlands areas, so that they probably spoke with a northern dialect (*Aspects of American English*, Elizabeth M. Kerr, Ralph M. Aderman, eds., p. 109). However, the Quaker philosophy appealed to more intellectual and educated personalities, such as its founder, William Penn. The speech of these people, educated in the universities and associating with the wealthy upper classes, would have been influenced to some extent by the prestigious London and court dialect. So that the Pennsylvania Quakers spoke with a dialect approximating that of the New England colonists.

In the southern colonies of Virginia and the Carolinas, the dominant group came from the aristocratic families of England. These naturally spoke the dialect of London and the court.

The speech of the three early settlement areas did not differ greatly. The comments of 18th century observers give evidence that by the middle 1700s they and their children had merged their speech into what sounded like the London standard dialect.

The Rev. John Witherspoon, president of Princeton University, writing in 1781, observed that *"there is a greater difference in dialect between one county and another in Britain, than there is between one state and another in America."* (*The Beginnings of American English*, M.M. Mathews, ed., p. 16).

And Noah Webster, in 1806, was of the opinion that, *"before the publication of Sheridan's Dictionary* [in 1780], *the pronunciation of words in the northern states was so uniform, that it is doubtful whether the gentlemen of education differed in fifty words..."* (*A Compendious Dictionary of the English Language*, p. xvi).

George Philip Krapp, in *The English Language in America*, writes that the speech of New Englanders *"agreed in the main with the generally accepted cultivated standard in Great Britain"* and that *"the speech of the New England colonists thus stood in fairly close relations to that of the southern... colonists."* (p. 20.)

It is clear that before the American Revolution, speech in the American colonies—North, Middle and South—sounded much alike and that it sounded like the dialect used by the cultured and educated speakers of Southeastern England, or the London dialect.

Changes in the American Dialect

Some changes in the London dialect during the period up to the American Revolution were reflected in American speech and helped divide modern American speech into its three broad geographical dialects.

The story actually starts in England about 1400, when a speech phenomenon called The Great Vowel Shift began. This dramatically changed the pronunciation of English words and the sound of the English language. We don't need to go into all the details, but basically, the pronunciation of the vowels in words changed.

To illustrate, let's look at two speech sounds that were hallmarks of that change—the sounds represented by the letters *a* and *r*.

First, the sound of the letter *a*, as pronounced in such words as modern American *father* and *fat*.

There were three possible pronunciations of this *a* sound in England and America during the period of American colonization. The modern American speech sound of *a*, in *father*, which we will call the *broad a*), said with unrounded lips and a relaxed tongue. The sound of *a* in *fat*, which we will call the *flat a*, also said with unrounded lips, but with a slightly raised tongue. And an *a* sound in between these two. This intermediate *a* is heard today in the American New England dialect and may be called the **Boston a**, but it was called the *Italian a* in dictionaries of the 17th and 18th centuries.

Polite, refined speakers pronounced words such as *father* and *fat* either with the *flat a* or the *Italian a*. (E.J. Dobson, *English Pronunciation, 1500–1700*, p. 58; and Helge Kokeritz, *Shakespeare's Pronunciation*, p. 162). Both Dobson (p. 58) and Kokeritz (p. 545) compare the *Italian a* to the **French a** sound spoken in Paris.

Less educated speakers used the *broad a*. Exhaustive research by Krapp, Kurath and others have shown that *"during most of the Eighteenth Century... a broad a was regarded in both England and America as a rusticism, and careful speakers commonly avoided it"* (Mencken, *The American Language*, pp. 334-335).

All three *a* sounds (*flat, broad a* and *Italian*) were spoken in various dialects within London and in the outlying areas. However, during the period from 1400 to the late 1700s, the *flat a* gained popularity among educated speakers. It took hold first among the middle and poor classes of England and gradually became accepted in the courtly London speech. By Shakespeare's time, around 1600, which was also the beginning of American settlement, the *flat a* (*fat*) was accepted as proper, educated pronunciation, with holdouts for the *Italian a* only by older, more conservative speakers.

The popularity of the *flat a* during this period has been demonstrated by at least two scholarly studies. Helge Kokeritz, in *Shakespeare's Pronunciation*, reports that the *"southeastern [flat a] was rapidly gaining ground during the 15th century, to become the accepted sound in polite circles by the end of the 16th century"* (p. 162). It is even possible, he says, that *"as an actor Shakespeare may have found it expedient to exchange his native [Italian a] sound for the more fashionable London vowel [flat a]"* (p. 163).

Likewise, E.J. Dobson, in *English Pronunciation, 1500–1700*, writes that in the 16th and 17th centuries there were two pronunciations of the *a* sound in upper class standard English,

> *...a more conservative [Italian a], generally used by careful speakers until 1600 and probably still the more usual pronunciation among such speakers until 1650, which may have continued in occasional use until the end of the century, and a more advanced [flat a], vulgar or popular in the sixteenth century, gradually winning wider acceptance in the first part of the seventeenth century, and generally accepted by careful speakers by about 1670.* (p. 548)

Not all speakers or all dialects switched, however, and a situation developed much like we have in America today, with speakers of one dialect pronouncing a word one way and speakers of another dialect pronouncing it another way.

To take a couple of familiar modern examples, all over America *aunt* may be pronounced with the *flat a* of *apple*, or with the *Boston a* (ah) of *part*. In the New England area of United States, *ask* is often pronounced with a *Boston a* (ahsk), while in the rest of the country it is pronounced with the *flat a*.

In England, during the 18th century, the popularity of the *flat a* apparently went so far as, for a time, to completely oust the *Italian a* from the standard courtly speech. An influential British dictionary published in 1780, *A General Dictionary of the English Language*, written by a popular Irish-English actor, Thomas Sheridan,

omitted the *Italian a* from his list of speech sounds altogether. Words like *car* and *father*, which we now pronounce with the *broad a* vowel, Sheridan pronounced with a the *flat a* of *fat*. And he said that this had been the courtly pronunciation for 60 years or more (p. 3).

Probably Sheridan overstated the situation, but his pronunciation dictionary was enthusiastically accepted and influential, having several reprints over the next seventeen years.

Then, in 1791, John Walker, another actor and friend of the famous actor David Garrick, published *A Critical Pronouncing Dictionary and Expositor of the English Language*, in which he listed the *Italian a* as a proper vowel sound, along with the *flat a*. Walker's dictionary had a tremendous influence on English pronunciation, with over a hundred reprints up to 1904.

Neither Sheridan nor Walker, however listed the *broad a* of *father* as a legitimate vowel in correct pronunciations. They considered the *broad a* to be a rustic and provincial pronunciation used only by uneducated speakers.

The American colonization began just as the *flat a* was being accepted in the polite speech of London and the royal court. Of course the speech mix of the English people coming to America reflected the speech changes going on in the mother country. The middle class, poorer and less educated colonists spoke with a *broad a* and a *flat a*, while the wealthy and educated leaders spoke with a mixture of *flat a* and *Italian a*.

Up to the time of the American Revolution, speech in America followed the same path it took in Great Britain.

H.L. Mencken, in his classic investigation of the evolution of American speech, *The American Language*, 1937, reports that Benjamin Franklin's pronunciation favored the *flat a*. He quotes Franklin's *Scheme for a New Alphabet and a Reformed Mode of Spelling*, published in Philadelphia, in 1768, in which Franklin recommended the *flat a* in words that the majority of Americans outside of the New England region now pronounce with a *broad a*. Words such as *calm*, *far* and *hardly*, Franklin pronounced with the *flat a* of *sack*.

Mencken writes that *"even wh**a**t... was thus made to rhyme with h**a**t."* Franklin's pronunciations, says Mencken, *"were presumably those of the best circles in the London of his time, and it seems likely that they also prevailed in Philadelphia, then the center of American culture"* (*American Language*, p. 335).

However, this complete changeover to *flat a* did not sit well with educated speakers of New England. Noah Webster, in his *Compendious Dictionary of the English Language*, published in 1806, bitterly complained that,

> *Sheridan, the first author whose work engaged public attention, took the liberty to omit, in his scheme, the Italian sound of a, which we hear in ask, demand, father; which letter he has marked in these words as having its short sound in hat.*

Webster indignantly protested its affect on English pronunciation. *"Outrageous as this innovation was,"* he thundered,

> *...extending perhaps to thousands of words, whose pronunciation was thus perverted, it was followed in some parts of this country, producing that mincing, affected pronunciation of dance, psalm, ask, father, &c. which is observed by strangers among the people of the middle States.*

"Sheridan's book," says Webster,

> *...enjoyed unrivalled popularity for ten or fifteen years; and after having corrupted the pronunciation of millions of people, it was succeeded by Walker, who now informs us that Sheridan is not a correct standard; and that he has grossly mistaken the true pronunciation in a great number of particulars — This author has restored the* Italian a, *in most words....* (pp. xii-xiii)

However, influential as Webster was and as much as he disliked the *flat a* in words like *ask* and *dance*, that pronunciation prevailed in America in regions outside New England.

In the New England states, words like *father* and *calm* went back to the *Italian a* sound and words like *marry* and *mat* continued with a *flat a* sound. The New England dialect became distinguished by a typical *Boston a* pronunciation that the rest of American speech does not have.

The popular use of the *broad a*, as in *f**a**ther*, in modern American speech is the result of two influences. One from below and one from above. The common people on the frontier used the *broad a* and they were the ones that pushed west and south with the westward expansion. Their pronunciation travelled with them and eventually covered all of the United States outside the eastern coastal cities.

But, suddenly, stylish pronunciation also changed. For unknown reasons, just after the American Revolution the *broad a* became fashionable in London Standard Speech. Words like *h**a**lf* and *gl**a**ss*, that had been pronounced with a *flat a* were changed to a *broad a* pronunciation, creating some confusion, because in America, the *flat a* remained the correct pronunciation for these words. According to Mencken, the English change affected about 150 words in common use (*American Language*, p. 334). This created an immediate, obvious difference between British Standard Speech and American Standard Speech.

Mencken, says the British switch happened suddenly, around 1780 (*American Language*, p. 335). Another scholar, Albert H. Marckwardt, in *American English* (p. 80), says it happened more gradually, shortly after 1800. The changes in the London Standard pronunciation were reflected in the speech of those groups who retained their associations with London society after the Revolution. The American phonetician, John Samuel Kenyon, in *American Pronunciation* (1950), informs us that,

> *...there is much evidence that the chief colonial centers, Boston, New York, Richmond, and Charleston, continuing closer cultural contact with London than did the rest of the rapidly increasing colonial population, shared more of the advancing changes of Southern British. Hence Eastern and Southern American today are more like present Southern British than is [General American], which preserves more features of the 17th c. standard British.* (p. 14)

The natural result of a growing majority of American speakers using the *broad a* after the American Revolution was that the *broad a*, along with the *flat a*, became acceptable educated pronunciation in all areas outside the New England seaports.

The other speech sound we will look at is the *r*. In the 18th century, in England and America, the *r* was always supposed to be pronounced in educated speech, although there are contemporary references showing it was beginning to be dropped.

Thomas Sheridan wrote in his *General Dictionary* (1780) that *"this letter [r] has always the same sound, and is never silent."* (p. 17)

A few years later, in 1791, John Walker, an actor turned speech teacher and friend of the famous actor David Garrick, wrote in his *Critical Pronouncing Dictionary*, that the *r* is *"never silent."* But, he admitted,

> *In England, and particularly in London, the r in lard, bard, card, regard, &c. is pronounced so much in the throat as to be little more than the middle or* Italian a, *lengthened into baa, baad, caad, regaad; while in Ireland the r, in these words, is pronounced with so strong a jar of the tongue against the forepart of the palate, and accompanied with such an aspiration or strong breathing at the beginning of the letter, as to produce that harshness we call the Irish accent. But if this letter is too forcibly pronounced in Ireland, it is often too feebly sounded in England, and particularly in London, where it is sometimes entirely sunk;...* (p. 50)

As we know, the dropping of the *r* became a distinctive feature of cultured British speech.

In America, Noah Webster noticed this fading of the *r* with disapproval. In his *Dissertations on the English Language* (1789) he said,

> *Some of the southern people, particularly in Virginia, almost omit the sound of r as in* ware, there. *In the best English pronunciation, the sound of r is much softer than in some of the neighboring languages, particularly the Irish and Spanish; and probably much softer than in the ancient Greek. But there seems to be no good reason for omitting the sound altogether; nor can the omission be defended on the ground, either of good practice or of rules. It seems to be a habit contracted by carelessness.* (p. 110).

The revolution of the *r* in polite pronunciation in England happened to coincide with the Revolutionary War in America and the Westward expansion. As a result, some of the colonists picked up the habit of dropping the *r* and others did not.

Shortly after the War for Independence, the American Noah Webster, writing his *Dissertations on the English Language* (1789), condemned these innovations in speech, calling them *"modern corruptions in the English pronunciation."* He blamed them on faddish stage pronunciations popularized by actors such as Garrick, Sheridan and Siddons and picked up by court swells. (p. 148).

However, Webster admitted that, *"In the middle and southern states, there are a few, and those well bred people, who have gone far in attempting to imitate the fashion of the day."* (p. 170). But, he protests, *"the body of the people, even in these states, remain as unfashionable as ever; and the eastern states generally adhere to their ancient custom of speaking, however vulgar it may be thought by their neighbors."* (p. 171).

Despite American attempts to become independent of everything British during and after the Revolution, our current American dialects show that some groups in the United States began dropping their *r*'s along with the British. The reasons are easy to see.

Before and after the Revolution, the wealthy merchant families of New England, especially in Boston, kept in close touch with London social and intellectual circles.

In fact, Krapp says, *"In the mid-nineteenth century, according to many competent observers, the respect for things British in Boston might fairly be called a craze."* (*English Language*, p. 44). But, he cautions, this acceptance was confined to an *"inner and upper circle"* of Boston society and certainly did not apply to the numerous Scotch-Irish immigrants, who remained vigorously anti-British. Nor did it apply to the New Englanders who had already migrated out of the port centers toward the west. Their speech remained the same as it had been before the Revolution.

Despite Webster's efforts, the social elite of the New England cultural centers dropped their *r*'s along with the British. The dropped *r*, along with the *Boston a*, became characteristic of the distinctive "Harvard" dialect spoken by the wealthy, educated and privileged classes of New England.

In the Southern colonies, the aristocratic plantation owners also had strong cultural ties with Great Britain. Krapp quotes J. Fenimore Cooper, writing in *Notions of the Americans* (1828), that *"the gentlemen of the middle and southern states, before the revolution, were very generally educated in England."* (*English Language*, p. 26). There, to fit in and to lose their rustic reputation, these colonial sons quickly learned the latest pronunciations of their British-born schoolmates.

Hans Kurath, in *A Word Geography of the Eastern United States*, describes the situation in the Southern colony seaports as similar to that in New England. Except that the Southern plantation owners had even closer social ties to Britain.

As members of the Church of England, says Kurath, the Southern merchants and planters were *"received as equals in London society, and their sons were admitted as students to the English universities, a privilege that was denied to the dissenters of New England and Pennsylvania."* According to Kurath, if the children didn't go to school in England, they were educated by imported English schoolteachers. *"In this manner,"* he says, *"the speech ways of this social class conformed to those of London to a considerable extent."* (p. 5).

The speech of the Pennsylvania colony had a different history. Philadelphia grew quickly into the center of learning and culture in America and by the mid-1700s had become the largest city in the colonies. However, because of their beliefs, children of the

Quaker settlers were not welcome in England and their sons were not able to attend British universities. Consequently, their speech was not affected by the changes that took place in British speech after they left England.

Kurath reports that *"of all the seaports Philadelphia alone failed to adopt a striking feature of Standard British pronunciation—the loss of r after a vowel, as in hard and corn"* (*Word Geography*, p. 7).

As the westward expansion began, the settlers moving west and south from New England met up with the settlers moving west from Pennsylvania. They had similar speech, a dialect that developed into what became known as **General American**. These settlers continued moving south and west until they met with the settlers in the Southern States who were migrating westward and northward, with the Southern dialect. This created a dialect boundary, separating Southern states, which dropped the *r*, from Northern, which didn't.

As the westward expansion continued, the speakers of General American were much more numerous, taking over the Northern, Middle and Western states. The New England dialect was confined to the New England states and the Southern dialect to the Southern states. These migrations established the three major dialect regions of the United States.

Modern American Dialects

Within these broad regional dialects subdialects have evolved. Speech is a dynamic, continually changing medium. As time passes and people settle into an area, they develop local dialects, reflecting specifically local social and cultural forces. Although the local dialects are not greatly different from the regional dialect, people within the region can tell one local dialect from another, even though people outside the region might not be able to.

Our picture of modern American dialects would be incomplete without noting the presence of **social** and **cultural** dialects both within the geographical dialect regions and also connecting across geographical boundaries. These are not sharply defined speech differences between centuries old social classes, as found in England and Europe, but, nonetheless, they are clearly present. Hans Kurath, in 1949, described them as *"a gradation from cultivated speech through common speech to folk speech"* (*Word Geography*, p. 7).

Cultivated speech, says Kurath, is characteristic of urban areas, **folk speech** is found in more secluded and isolated areas and **common speech** in the in-between areas.

Education plays a great part in establishing social and cultural dialect differences. Students at universities learn new ways of speaking by becoming acquainted with new speech models. They enrich their vocabulary, learn pronunciations favored by educated people and discover the importance of speaking clearly and distinctly. They carry these new speech habits with them when they leave university.

It is not surprising that many Americans habitually use at least two dialects—a cultivated speech in professional situations and more colloquial speech at home.

The American Stage Dialect

Against this panoramic backdrop of American dialects, we can now spotlight our primary interest—the **American Stage Dialect**.

The first American Stage Dialect was British Stage Dialect. Americans have always admired the speech of good British actors. We felt and still feel that their voices are clear, dynamic, emotionally effective and interesting to listen to. These traits were especially looked up to in America during a period when American actors had very little or no speech training available to them. Consequently early American actors copied the British model.

In fact, until relatively recently, the British "received" pronunciation, or "British stage dialect," was advocated and supported for the stage by American speech teachers, who liked the sound of the British speech.

In 1919, H.L. Mencken reported that,

There was a time when all American actors of any pretensions employed a dialect that was a heavy imitation of the dialect of the West End actors of London. It was taught in all the American dramatic schools, and at the beginning of the present century it was so prevalent on the American stage that a flat **a** *had a melodramatic effect almost equal to that of damn.* (*The American Language*, p. 331)

And in 1934, Giles Wilkeson Gray and Claude Merton Wise, in their book, *The Bases of Speech*, stated that on the stage,

American actors have customarily imitated the speech of their English co-workers, and American dramatic schools have taught English speech as correct stage diction. (p. 204.)

In the opinion of Gray and Wise, even though Americans spoke differently offstage—on-stage they should sound British. It was an opinion that by that time was fast losing ground.

We know from old radio recordings and the first talking pictures that a dialect somewhat resembling British speech was popular among some American film and stage stars in the early 1900s.

The two most prominent features of this "actors dialect" were the dropping of the *r*'s and use of the *Boston a*. We can call it an **Eastern Stage Dialect**.

A major force supporting the preference of Eastern Stage Dialect was the teaching of it by speech teachers, like the unusually gifted and charismatic teacher, Edith Skinner, author of *Good Speech for the American Actor*, and Madeleine Marshall, *grande dame* of diction at Juilliard, and author of *The Singer's Manual of English Diction*. They drilled Eastern dialect into many actors and singers who later became well-known on stage and in motion pictures and influential in setting speech style.

It is interesting to note that this Eastern dialect is still preferred and cultivated by many American opera singers today.

The Emergence of Standard American Stage Speech

But if British pronunciation or Eastern dialect was the standard before radio and motion pictures, it didn't last long into the modern era of mass communication.

H. L. Mencken reports that on April 26, 1931, the *Chicago Radio Weekly* claimed that two major American radio chains, Columbia and N.B.C., were requiring their announcers to speak *"English as she is spoke in England."* However, when Mencken inquired about it he was told by Walter M. Stone, of N.B.C., that it was not true. What they were looking for, Stone said, was *"decent American pronunciation, affected as little as possible by localisms"* (*American Language*, p. 332).

Mencken goes on to say that by 1936 the ideal stage dialect on Broadway seemed to be a pronunciation that did not sound British and at the same time did not have any American regional pronunciations.

Copying a British or semi-British dialect never really caught on with the generation of American actors brought up on film and television. Most American actors were not entirely comfortable with dropping their *r*'s and sounding slightly British.

And the majority of American audiences did not accept British or even Eastern Standard dialect as being representative of American speech. They wanted Americans to sound American. Consequently, Eastern speech as a stage standard gradually fell from grace as the preferred dialect for stage, film and television.

However, what did remain from these efforts was a greater awareness of the universal aspects of good speech—clear articulation, vocal strength, a variety of resonance colors and free use of a wide pitch and resonance range. These qualities could be appreciated in any voice, regardless of the dialect used or even of the language spoken.

Gradually, through the influence of the electronic mass media and other social phenomena, such as the increasing mobility of the American population, regional speech barriers in the United States were bridged and a non-regional standard for American speech and diction that was acceptable to all Americans began to emerge.

In 1934, Gray and Wise, in *The Bases of Speech*, had speculated on the possible emergence of a standard American dialect. Even while advocating British speech for the stage, they noted that, *"...many radio announcers use the general American dialect, and... hundreds of actors in sound pictures use the general American dialect without much modification."* (p. 205).

And thirty years later, in 1966, Evangeline Machline, in *Speech for the Stage*, was able to observe,

> *Standard American pronunciation is the speech of most American-born actors and actresses who have reached prominence. It is the speech of the educated American, free from marked regionalisms. It is practiced by leading broadcasters on national radio and television hookups.* (pp. 110–111)

Albert H. Marckwardt notes that during the 1960s,

> *The "neutral" dialect concept of General American was replaced... by that of Network Standard, the speech of television newscasters on the major networks and the kind of English which Americans clearly admired more than any other... This regionally and socially neutral dialect clearly emerged as the ideal, if not the actuality, for most speakers of American English.* (*American English*, pp. 141–142)

In 1969, a study by Tucker and Lambert asked college students to evaluate different types of American speech. They found that *"the most favorable profile of trait ratings was accorded to a style of speech known as 'Network English'."* Which they described as the *"typical mode of speaking used by national newscasters in the United States..."* (Howard Giles and Peter F. Powesland, *Speech Style and Social Evaluation*, 1975, p. 79).

A Standard American Speech had evolved.

Standard American Stage Speech

In general, the terms **Standard American Stage Dialect**, **Standard American Stage Diction**, **Standard American Stage Speech** and **General American Speech** all refer to the same kind of speech. But, if looked at closely, there are some differences in what they describe.

Standard American Stage Dialect specifically refers to a non-regional dialect spoken by an actor or a singer. It is speech that is not identified with a specific locale or region. Yet it is speech that is easily understood in all areas of the United States.

Standard American Stage Diction refers to "diction," that is, "pronunciation," "articulation" and "enunciation." Its meaning includes good pronunciation and good articulation.

Standard American Stage Speech and **General American Stage Speech** have broader definitions. Their meaning expands to include not only diction, but the overall resonant quality of the voice. Its most prominent features are clear diction and a strong, pleasing resonant sound.

Standard American Speech is the speech used in musical theatre and classical singing and variations of it may also be used in pop singing.

We also hear Standard American Speech spoken by national radio and television news announcers, by announcers and hosts on national radio and television programs and by actors when they perform non-dialect roles. And, in many cases, Standard American Speech has also been adopted by national political and business figures as a means of improving their communication and creating an image on a national level.

Although Standard American Speech is independent of any geographical region of the United States, it does not exclude some touches of regional dialect. Frequently a person using Standard American Speech can be identified as coming from a certain region because he or she retains some of the characteristic speech traits of that region. But the retained characteristics serve only to give color and charm to the speech, they do not dominate the speech.

Standard American Speech is neither better nor worse than any other American dialect. It is simply a dialect, on a par with all other dialects. The difference is that it is usually thought of as trained speech, because it is used by professional speakers and singers when they need "non-dialect" diction.

It is important to point out that Standard American Diction is not a standard for censorship. Describing Standard American Speech does not imply that all people in America should speak the same way.

In 1917, Daniel Jones, the preeminent authority on English pronunciation of the 20th century, said,

> *I wish to state that I have no intention of becoming either a reformer of pronunciation or a judge who decides what pronunciations are 'good' and what are 'bad.' My aim is to observe and record accurately, and I do not believe in the feasibility of imposing one particular form of pronunciation on the English-speaking world. I take the view that people should be allowed to speak as they like. And if the public wants a standardized pronunciation, I have no doubt that some appropriate standard will evolve itself.*

(*English Pronouncing Dictionary* [1917], p. xvi)

His statement must stand as the reasonable opinion of all intelligent and practical speech teachers.

Standard American Speech has evolved in response to changing conditions in America. In particular, it satisfies the needs of public performance on stage and in film and television.

In this book and its accompanying CDs you will learn Standard American Diction.

Singing the Words You Speak

Should the words you sing sound like the words you speak?

Of course. How else is your audience going to understand you?

Even though singing is different from speaking in a number of important ways that affect your articulation (which we will note later in this chapter), you must sing words that your audience will recognize. That means the words you sing must sound like the words you speak.

Articulation for Speaking

To say recognizable words, you must

(1) Articulate each sound correctly and

(2) Say the correct sounds for the word.

There is an ideal articulator position, which will be discussed in chapter 2, for each speech sound. When you say *ah*, your articulators are in a different position than when you say *oh*. To form a specific vowel sound, your articulators must be in the ideal position for that sound, or very close to it.

You must also say the correct sounds in the words. If you want your audience to understand that you have said *m**ee**k*, you must say the word with the vowel sound for *m**ee**k*. If, instead, you pronounce it with the vowel found in *m**ay**, your audience will think you have said *m**a**ke*.

Articulation for Singing

It is both desirable and possible to sing so that the audience can understand your words.

All you do is place your articulators in the same positions they take when you speak your words.

Even though you may open your mouth wider for singing than for speaking, your articulators can still take the same relative positions, so that you can say the same sounds.

Modifying the Vowel

There are times in singing when you may need to modify the sound of a vowel slightly. To accommodate a better tone or a more open mouth, you can and should modify the vowel, but within limits.

There is only one instance in which you need to sing a vowel that is different from the one normally said in the word. That is when the vowel is being sung in the high soprano range. (See *Maintaining the Vowel*, p. 20).

But, at all other times, if you've learned your craft well, you should sing words as you speak them, so that your audience will be able to understand you.

Singing With Standard American Diction

Singing words is different from speaking words in four important ways:

(1) **Duration:** The singer sustains the vowel sounds much longer than the speaker.

(2) **Resonating Space:** The singer usually uses a much more open mouth than the speaker.

(3) **Tension:** Singing has a tendency to create more tension in the articulators than does speaking.

(4) **Pitch:** The singer sings words on pitches that the speaker never attempts.

Duration

Sustaining vowels presents an interesting problem. When speaking, we don't sustain vowels, therefore it only takes an instant to say a word and for the word to be recognized by our listeners. But in singing, you sometimes sustain a vowel for several beats or even several measures. During that time your listeners are consciously or unconsciously making guesses as to what the finished word will actually be. In their own mind they finish the word and go even further—they guess at what your finished phrase or thought is going to be.

Imagine their confusion when they guess wrong because of a faulty cue from us.

Your listener is most often led astray when you don't sing and sustain the vowel that is usually heard in the spoken version of the word.

For example, it's not uncommon to hear a singer substitute the vowel in *leave* for the vowel in *live*, so that the amorous plea *Live for me* is sung as *Leave for me*. Or, to use another common substitution, in an unguarded moment *I yearn for you* might become *I yawn for you.*

If you want your listener to understand the words you sing, you must sing and sustain the vowel that your listeners are used to hearing in the word.

Resonating Space

The possibility of changing the vowel is greater when you open your mouth wide for better resonance.

When your jaw is open wider the relative position of your articulators may change. Unless you are aware of this and adjust the positions of your articulators to the larger resonating space, you will change the vowel sound. You must keep the vowel recognizable when you open your mouth wider.

Tension

Sadly, for many singers just the act of singing, even in their easy middle range, seems to generate unnecessary tension.

Even good singers often generate extra tension in the extreme pitches of their high range.

When your articulators are tense, they can't move as quickly and freely as you need them to. Sometimes tension even forces your articulators into positions that are wrong for the vowel you are trying to say.

Fortunately, there is no law that declares a singer must have excessive tension in the articulators. With the exercises in this book, you can learn to keep your articulators relaxed as you sing.

Pitch

Singing extremely high and extremely low pitches requires an open space that, if you are not careful, may distort vowel sounds.

The effort to reach extreme pitches also creates tensions that can affect the sound of the vowel.

You must take care to maintain the correct vowel sound throughout your range, with the one exception of the extreme high range of the soprano. (See the next section.)

Maintaining the Vowel

The respected American teacher, William Vennard, in discussing the "dilemma" singers face in seeking both a beautiful tone and communication through words, said the singer should aim at finding,

...a diction that is as clear as speech, that gives the illusion of being the same, but is really quite otherwise.
(*Singing, the Mechanism and the Technic,* p. 167)

He disagreed with the notion that good diction needs to be sacrificed for tone or pitch. In his view,

...no singer should resort to methods of production in which it is impossible to pronounce his language, merely for the unworthy objective of eking out an extra high or extra low note. (*Singing*, p. 138)

D. Ralph Appelman, author of *The Science of Vocal Pedagogy*, is of the same opinion. While advocating vowel migration (modification) to enhance the quality of the vocal tone, he yet insists that,

When excellent diction is part of a singer's established technique, the listener recognizes instantaneously the word that is directly related to its familiar pronunciation within speech forms. Therefore, it is the singer's duty, throughout all migration in pitch changes, to preserve the integrity of the authentic phoneme and not to select a migration that will cause the phoneme to migrate in a direction that is unnatural and will not enhance the vocalic sound. (p. 204).

Richard Miller, author of The Structure of Singing, and an internationally recognized authority on the teaching of singing, also advocates the singing of understandable words. In an article written for The National

Association of Teachers of Singing (NATS) Journal of Singing, September/October, 1995, What about the "Pure Vowel" and "Vowel Modification"?, he says,

> The task of the singer is to determine the appropriate degree of vowel modification for his or her voice within the rising scale while still retaining language recognition. (p. 39)

Noted teachers of singing, while allowing for slight vowel changes, modifications, or migrations, maintain that singers should pronounce vowels as recognizable speech-vowels, with one exception—the high soprano, who for acoustical reasons finds it impossible to pronounce all the vowels on her highest pitches.

We won't go into detail here, but, basically, above a certain pitch some vowels lose their lower formants, which are an essential part of the vowel's acoustical characteristics. Therefore, it is acoustically impossible to sing some of the vowels in the high soprano range. (For example, *oo*, in m*oo*n and *o*, in s*o*.) (*Singing*, pp. 158–59) (If you want to investigate this subject further, see William Vennard, *Singing, the Mechanism and the Technic*, D. Ralph Appelman, *The Science of Vocal Pedagogy* and Johan Sundberg, *The Science of the Singing Voice*.)

It is possible and sometimes desirable to modify the vowel slightly to improve your vocal quality throughout your whole range, but according to the best authorities, as well as common sense, the vowel modification should not be so drastic that it destroys your diction.

Consonants—Love 'em 'Cause You Can't Live Without 'em

Consonants are natural and essential parts of words. It is impossible to sing words without them. Yet some singers foolishly consider consonants to be necessary evils—rough stone walls separating lush pastures of vowels. *"How much better I'd be able to sing without them!"*

Stop!

That's a completely unrealistic and psychologically self-defeating attitude. It's like thinking how much better you'd be able to sing if you didn't need to breathe!

If you don't like consonants, you're beating your head against a stone wall every time you sing.

Consonants Cannot Be Avoided or Ignored

It's true that consonants break up the flow of the beautiful, resonant sound that you get from your vowels. But singing is not just an uninterrupted flow of vowel sound. When you sing, you sing words, which basically alternate vowels and consonants.

Without clear consonants the audience can't understand what you're saying or singing.

A wrong consonant can change the whole meaning of what you are singing and destroy the emotion in the lines. An inability to handle consonants might change *You **p**lead well* to *You **b**leed well*. Or *I am **c**alling you* to *I am **g**alling you.*

Frequently singers don't pronounce the final consonant of a word. What does *It is dus...* mean to you without the final consonant? (Is it *dus**t*** or *dus**k**?*) Or what is the meaning of *Spe... to me*, without the end of the word? (Is it *spee**d*** or *spea**k**?*)

Obviously, you can't get along without consonants, so as a professional you must learn how to sing them well.

A Positive Approach to Consonants

Instead of disliking consonants and trying to avoid them, it is far more productive to learn how to sing consonant sounds and how to move quickly and smoothly back and forth between vowels and consonants.

To handle consonants without any problems, you need to be able to do two things:

(1) You must be able to move your articulators dexterously from one position to the next.

(2) You must be able to voice a clear vowel following a consonant.

Many singers have difficulty regaining a clear, resonant vowel following a consonant, particularly an unvoiced consonant. When this happens to you, getting upset with the consonant is focusing on the wrong cause. The fault is not with the consonant, it is with your inability to voice a clear vowel immediately following the consonant. The only productive thing to do is to improve your ability to sing a clear vowel after an unvoiced consonant.

Hating consonants and blaming them is not going to make it any easier to sing them. In fact, disliking consonants creates a conflict in your singing and puts you at a psychological disadvantage. On the one hand you don't want to sing consonants and on the other hand you must. Why make yourself unhappy? There's another way.

Conquering Consonants and Singing Better

Your first step to conquering consonants and becoming a better singer is learning how to articulate them.

If you have a clear picture of how to make a consonant, you can have control over it. As a professional singer, you must know exactly where you place your articulators for each consonant sound. Studying the consonant sections in this book will make you an expert. You'll stop feeling helpless around consonants and start feeling in control of them. And you'll start enjoying them.

As you study consonants, you will also learn to keep your resonating spaces (the mouth, nose, sinuses and chest) as open as possible while you are singing the consonant.

Many singers don't seem to realize that most consonants can be articulated with the mouth fairly open. For example, *t* and *d* can be as easily said with your jaw slightly open as with your jaw closed. But most singers close their jaw completely for *t* and *d*, which is unnecessary and detrimental to good resonance. This is true of a number of consonants, as you will see.

Actually, only *s*, as in *see*, *z*, as in *zoo*, **sh**, as in *she* and *z*, as in *azure* require your upper and lower teeth to come almost together. It is possible and desirable to keep your jaw slightly open for the rest of the consonant sounds.

It's much easier to sing when you let your jaw float open most of the time, with your lips and tongue moving independently of your jaw.

The final word is, you know you can't avoid consonants, so you might as well learn to love them. Loving consonants is easy once you find out how easy they are to articulate clearly.

Neuro-Sensory Conditioning™

The Fastest, Easiest Way of Learning Good Articulation

Now that we know how important it is to have good articulation, let's take a look at how to get it.

The easiest, fastest and most effective method of learning good articulation is through a system of natural learning called **neuro-sensory conditioning**™.

Have you ever watched a baby learning how to speak? Daddy and Mommy say the words very slowly and clearly, *da-da* or *ma-ma*. The baby listens carefully to the sound and at the same time intently watches the mouth of its parent.

Then it tries to recreate the movements with its own mouth. It makes a sound. And Mommy or Daddy exclaim, *"That's right!"* or, patiently, say *"No, like this."*

And they redouble their efforts to show the baby how their articulators move.

Eventually the baby makes the right sound. It hears the same sound coming out of its own mouth that it heard from Mommy or Daddy. And it receives support from Mommy and Daddy's excited, *"That's right!"*

Now the baby has to remember what it did with its articulators to get that sound.

Notice the system that the baby uses to learn the basic sounds of speech. The baby:

(1) **Listens** to the sound,

(2) **Sees** the movements of the articulators,

(3) **Feels** itself making the same movements and

(4) **Hears** the sound it makes.

Then it gets:

(5) **Feedback,** from an outside source (Mommy or Daddy) or from critically listening to itself, and it

(6) **Corrects** itself.

This is **neuro-sensory conditioning**™, or natural learning, and it's the easiest, fastest way of acquiring good speaking habits.

Actually, when the baby learns to speak, it probably doesn't intentionally break the word down into its component sounds. It probably tries to learn the word as a whole. The only time the baby may learn individual speech sounds is when the parents repeat a single speech sound to help the baby learn it.

But, as grown-ups, we're smarter and can figure out an easier, faster system.

A System of Natural Learning

Grown-ups learn to articulate new words the same natural way that a baby does. But grown-ups have an advantage.

First, grown-ups can consciously break the word down into individual speech sounds, making the word easier to learn.

Second, grown-ups can recognize a system for learning and consciously use it, so that the process can take place much easier and faster. The baby doesn't consciously understand how it is learning. It doesn't have an awareness of a system for learning and remembering, so it learns much more slowly.

The **neuro-sensory conditioning**™ system for learning good articulation is simple. You concentrate on three things:

(1) **Hearing**

(2) **Seeing**

(3) **Feeling**

Hearing

Why you need hearing is obvious. Listening is really the only way you can know with any certainty what a sound sounds like. (That's the reason we made the *Standard American Diction* CDs to go along with this book.)

Listening carefully to yourself is also the only way you can know if you are saying the sound correctly.

Feeling

Feeling, or your kinesthetic sense, guides your articulators to the right places at the right time. At first it's difficult to tell just what your articulators are doing. But you quickly develop your sense of feel.

Once you are consciously aware of what is happening with your articulation, it's much easier to recreate the correct movements and positions for the sounds.

Seeing

Seeing helps develop your awareness of your articulators. Looking at your articulators in a mirror helps you to place your articulators in the right positions. When you look at your articulators in a specific movement or position and feel what they are doing, you form a mental image of how they make each sound. Then, when you need to recreate that sound, you recall the image and place your articulators in their correct positions.

Forming the right image is important, because your body tries to do what your mind images, especially, on a subconscious level.

After a while, you can dispense with the mirror and see the movements and positions of your articulators through your imagination.

Of course, you must finish the learning cycle with feedback and correction. You do that by listening to the sounds you make and if the sound is not just right you correct the positions or movements of your articulators.

Using three of your senses—hearing, feeling and seeing—you can learn the vowels, diphthongs and consonants much faster than when you concentrate on just the sound.

Make Good Diction a Habit

As a speaker and a singer, you shouldn't have to think about how you are going to make each sound as you are about to say it. In fact, it's very difficult to consciously control your articulation while you're in the act of speaking or singing. It's best to let your articulators automatically form the correct sounds, while you concentrate on the meaning and images in the words.

The way you make good articulation a habit is through your practice. You slow the process down, pay attention to it and teach the articulators how to do what you want them to do. Then you gradually speed up the movements and at the same time keep them accurate. With repetition the movements become automatic and you don't have to think about them any more.

Three Poor Reasons for Poor Articulation

In general, there are three reasons why a singer may habitually sing incorrect vowels and consonants:

(1) **Sloppy singing**, in that the singer is not consciously aware of the vowel or consonant he should be singing.

(2) **Ignorant singing**, in which the singer hasn't learned how to make the sound with the articulators.

(3) **Poor singing**, in which tension in the articulators causes a distortion in the sound.

There is really no excuse for a professional singer to have poor articulation. You should be embarrassed to sing sloppily, ignorantly or poorly.

Pronouncing Words

We learn how to pronounce words by limitation. We hear someone else say the word and then we say it the same way.

Generally, we only use words with which we are familiar and that we have heard other people use. So, usually, we don't have any problem with pronunciation. But we run into difficulties with pronunciation in two situations:

(1) When we need to say a word we have not heard pronounced.

(2) When we are in a situation, such as giving a speech or singing, where we are more conscious of correct pronunciation.

The first situation comes up when we read a word that we have not heard pronounced and we need to say it out loud. We usually try to sound it out from its spelling. But, as you've probably experienced, sounding it out doesn't always work. You can't be sure of what the letters are supposed to sound like.

In the second situation, we feel self-conscious and not sure that our normal pronunciation is good enough for the occasion, so we try to make it better. Usually we try to improve our pronunciation by saying the word the way it is spelled, which, again, doesn't always work.

This brings up the question:

Why can't we pronounce a word the way it is spelled?

Spelling vs. Speaking

When we want to pronounce a new word correctly, why doesn't it work to carefully sound out the syllables and the letters—as we were taught to do in school?

Because, in English, the letters of the spelling alphabet—**A,B,C**...—are not a reliable guide to the way we say our words. We all know this and have been fooled time and time again. Yet many of us continue to expect the spelling to tell us how to pronounce a word.

Don't Let the Spelling Fool You

At one time, centuries ago, words in the English language were spelled phonetically. That is, they were spelled the same way they were spoken. At that time, perhaps it was possible to figure out the pronunciation of a word from the way it was spelled.

But today the spelling of the word often has little to do with its pronunciation. The reason is that our spelling has stayed the same through the centuries, but the way we pronounce our words has changed.

Some of the changes are easy to see. For example, in the word *knife*, the *k* is no longer pronounced and neither is the *e*. And in a word like *rough*, we no longer say the sound that *gh* originally represented. These inconsistencies are easy to spot.

But with some words the mismatch between spelling and pronunciation is not so obvious.

For example, what is the first vowel sound in the word *about*? If you were asked what sound to say or sing there, the first thing you would probably think of is *A*, as in A,B,C. But if you say it in the word, it doesn't sound right.

Then you might be tempted to say *a*, as in c*a*n, or *a*, as in c*a*r, neither of which are right.

The first vowel in the word *about* sounds like the vowel in *up*. But you don't get a clue about that from the spelling.

Particularly when you're trying to be correct or formal in your speech or singing, you run into the danger of mispronunciation.

Take the word *delight*, for example. What is the first vowel sound? Say the word out loud and listen carefully—*delight*.

If you pronounced it with the same vowel as in *it*, you were correct. That's the way *delight* is normally said. But, if, in trying to be correct, you pronounced it with the same vowel as in *seat*, you let the spelling fool you.

On the other hand, if you pronounced it with the vowel in *up*, you're not using Standard American pronunciation.

If all this sounds hopeless, it's not.

There is a better system than the spelling alphabet for learning **pronunciation**. It is a system based on **speech sounds** rather than spelling letters. And you'll be amazed at how well it works. Let's look at this system next.

The International Phonetic Alphabet (IPA)

All dictionaries use some system of symbols to describe the pronunciation of words, just as they use a system of symbols for the spelling of words. Symbols in this context are simply letters, like the letters of the alphabet, A,B,C,D, and so on.

What is a Phonetic Alphabet?

A phonetic alphabet is a set of symbols that represent the **sounds** of speech.

The Phonetic Alphabet is Easy to Learn

Many people, when they first hear about the phonetic alphabet, think it's some kind of complicated and strange new way of spelling and writing—and they think it is going to be hard to learn. But they quickly change their mind as soon as they start working with it.

The phonetic alphabet is easy to learn.

In fact, after a person first learns the phonetic alphabet, a frequently heard comment is, *"Why don't they teach this in school? It makes learning speech so much easier."*

The International Phonetic Alphabet

The **International Phonetic Alphabet (IPA)** is one of a number of systems that identify each speech sound. We have chosen to use the **IPA** because it is international and because it is an easy method of teaching pronunciation and articulation in all languages.

The phonetic alphabet is a list of the sounds of speech. These speech sounds are not new to you. They are the vowels, diphthongs and consonants that you say every time you talk.

The wonderful, helpful thing about the phonetic alphabet is that there is **only one sound for each symbol** and **each symbol has only one sound**. This makes it possible to precisely identify each speech sound. And, once the sounds are identified, learning how to say them clearly and correctly presents few difficulties.

Use Your CDs

To make learning the sounds of speech even easier, we have recorded two CDs for you to practice with, called **Standard American Diction**.

Hearing the sounds is the only way that you can be sure you are pronouncing them correctly. And having the CDs with you to practice makes your learning faster and more fun.

Pronunciation Dictionaries

If you're in doubt about the pronunciation of a word you're speaking or singing, there are three things you might do:

(1) Pronounce the word as you usually pronounce it and listen to the sounds you say. Of course, you may not be sure that the sounds you say are correct.

(2)   Ask someone to pronounce it for you and copy them. However, that may not be convenient. Also, the person you ask may not be any better informed than you are.

(3)   Look the word up in an American pronunciation dictionary.

If you have any doubt at all—look up the word and make sure.

Having your own good pronunciation dictionary is a necessity when you are working on diction. Certain Standard American pronunciations, which educated American speakers generally use, have evolved over the years. These have been recorded in various pronunciation dictionaries.

Looking up the word takes only a few seconds and it can save your ego from many moments of embarrassment. Two good pronunciation dictionaries are:

(1)   *A Pronouncing Dictionary of American English*, by John S. Kenyon and Thomas A. Knott.

(2)   *NBC Handbook of Pronunciation*, revised and updated by Eugene Ehrlich and Raymond Hand, Jr..

A Pronouncing Dictionary of American English can usually be found in bookstores. It is described by the authors as a guide to the pronunciation of words in *"the conversational and familiar utterance of cultivated speakers when speaking in the normal contacts of life and concerned with what they are saying, not how they are saying it"* (p. xvi).

The *NBC Handbook of Pronunciation* also tells us how to pronounce words in normal, everyday American English. The *NBC Handbook* does not use IPA, which is not necessarily a defect, although, if you know IPA, it is certainly easier to use. But one shortcoming of this dictionary is that it doesn't list some of the more common words, like *and* and *table*. On the other hand, it lists many foreign words frequently used in American English, that are not listed in *A Pronouncing Dictionary of American English*.

The respected broadcaster, Edwin Newman, in his informative and entertaining introduction to the *NBC Handbook*, recommends an approach to pronunciation that we should all embrace. First of all, he says, *"Pronouncing words correctly can be fun."* Then he expresses the opinion that people who speak in public have *"an obligation... to speak correctly, not only in matters of grammar and usage, but in pronunciation, as well."*

Of course, speech is a living, changing thing. The pronunciation of a word may change over a period of years and printed descriptions of it may go out of date. Pronunciation dictionaries, while they are a great help, are not infallible.

The best guide to Standard American Speech is the way respected speakers actually pronounce their words today.

How can you study that?

By listening to others as part of your continuing education in diction. Take the time to listen to the pronunciations of singers and speakers you respect on stage, film and television.

Using This Book

This study begins with the series of general articulation exercises in Chapter Two. You should practice them once a day for a week before you start on the phonetic sounds.

These general articulation exercises are designed to make you more aware of your articulators and to give you more control over their movements. They have been carefully worked out and tested in the classroom and in private teaching, to make them the most effective articulation exercises possible.

If you do the general articulation exercises the way they are explained, a week is enough preparation.

At the end of Chapter Two is a short *Articulation Warm-up*, which you should include in your daily practice.

The Natural Learning system we ask you to follow in practicing each speech sound is specially designed to show you how to make the sounds in the most efficient, relaxed and clear way possible.

The system is incorporated into the directions for the articulation of each of the sounds. All you have to do is follow the directions.

You may find it helpful to study the sounds in the order in which they are presented—there is a logic in their arrangement—but it is not essential. You can start with any of the vowels, diphthongs or consonants.

The best way of learning the phonetic sounds is to first of all concentrate on only one new sound a day. At the same time, keep a list of all the sounds you learn and repeat them all at least once each day, along with their practice words and sentences.

Your practice sessions do not need to be long. Fifteen to thirty minutes a day will do the job. (Of course, you should be aware of your diction as you practice your singing and as you speak during the day.)

In a very short time you will have learned all of the speech sounds of Standard American Speech and you will have acquired good diction habits.

Linking is the finishing work on articulation. The chapter on *Pronunciation* describes the various combinations of linking that are possible. Here you learn to smoothly connect the individual sounds together to form words and phrases. This chapter also explains and gives exercises for syllable stress, which is another aspect of correct pronunciation and is especially important in expressive singing. Read this chapter soon after you begin your study and practice its precepts while you are working on the rest of your diction.

The chapter on *Pop Diction* is very important. Elisabeth Howard has generously contributed this chapter on diction for all styles of popular music (in addition to her invaluable advice on the rest of this book). Ms. Howard is particularly qualified in this area. She has a B.S. and M.S. in Voice from Juilliard, where she studied with the great diction coach, Madeleine Marshall. She is also coauthor of the popular video, audiocassette and book series on singing, *Sing Like a Pro* and *Born To Sing*. She has had exceptional success as a singing teacher and coach of professional singers in New York and Los Angeles, in rock, country/western, pop, musical theatre, blues, jazz and other nonclassical styles. You will find her insights revealing, practical and useful for all styles of music.

In the chapter on *Inflections and Intonations* we introduce you to pitch/resonance changes that affect meaning and emotion in the speaking voice. Though inflections and intonations relate primarily to speech, we have included them because of the relationship between expression and pitch/resonance changes. Understanding how inflections and intonations affect meaning and emotion helps you to interpret your music and sing your words with their full expression.

As a singer you also speak, so remember to practice with your speaking voice as well as with your singing voice.

The chapter on *Expressive Singing* is an acting lesson with emphasis on the words. In performance you're not only a singer, you are also an actor. You must sing your words with emotion and expression, as if they were your own. In this chapter we show you how to find the images and emotions locked in the words. Here you bring together all of the elements of diction—articulation, pronunciation, meaning and emotion.

Two Unbreakable Rules

The words you sing have great beauty, with power to move emotions. But for this magic to happen, you must follow two unbreakable rules of communication:

(1) You must be **HEARD**.

(2) You must be **UNDERSTOOD**.

If either of these two rules is broken the word loses its power—and you lose half of your impact on your audience. Hearing a beautiful voice resounding through the theatre is one of the glorious experiences of life. How much more deeply felt it is, when, at the same time, we understand the words and the thoughts being expressed.

We'll finish this introduction with one of the most important thoughts we can leave with you.

Love the words along with the music and the sound of your voice.

Love the feel of words. The sound of them. Revel in their sensuality.

Loving everything about singing is part of the charisma of a great performer.

You can have that.

Notes:

vowel #2 oɪ "aɪ"
vowel #7 ə "uh"
consonant #8 ʃ "sh"
consonant #21 t "t"

Beginning Exercises

(1) Record yourself reading a short poem or paragraph, about one minute long.

(2) Record yourself singing a short song.

(3) Keep the recording in a safe place, so that you can find it and listen to it later.

(4) Do not listen to the recording until we ask you to, at the end of Chapter Nineteen, *Expressive Singing*.

(5) At that time, we will ask you to rerecord the same material and compare your pronunciation in the two recordings.

(6) You will be surprised at your improvement.

2 Exercises for the Articulators

What Are Your Articulators?

Your articulators are:

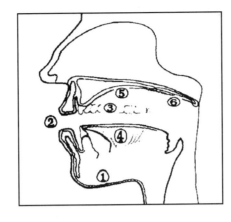

(1) jaw
(2) lips
(3) teeth
(4) tongue
(5) hard palate
(6) soft palate

What Do Your Articulators Do?

You make the sounds of speech with your articulators.

How Do Your Articulators Work?

When you speak, your articulators don't move by themselves, by accident or randomly. If it seems like your articulators move by themselves, it's only because you're not aware of the very precise control you have over them.

When you were a child, just learning how to talk, your articulators didn't start creating speech sounds by themselves. You taught them.

When you wanted to say *b*, you watched other speakers carefully and learned how to bring your lips together to make the *b* sound. That was fairly easy. And, almost immediately, it became automatic. Now, any time you want to say *b*, as part of a word, your lips just do it, without you having to think about it.

But when you wanted to say *a*, as in *am*, you couldn't see how other speakers made that sound. You had to experiment with various positions of your articulators until you made the right sound. By accident, you moved your tongue to the right position. But you didn't know how you did it.

As a child, you experimented with making speech sounds without any idea of what you were doing, as we all did. You controlled the movements of your articulators. But you didn't

realize it. As a result, it took a long time to learn some speech sounds and it was sometimes frustrating.

How much easier it will be to control the movements of your articulators when you're aware of what you're doing. You'll learn much faster and handle words with much greater confidence.

To make you more aware of the control you have over your articulators, let's take a quick look at how your articulators move.

Jaw

You close your jaw by contracting your jaw muscles and lifting your jaw up.

When you open your jaw, you relax your jaw muscles to let your jaw drop down. You don't have to pull your jaw open. All you do is release your jaw muscles and let gravity do the work for you.

Lips

Your upper and lower lips are muscles that you can move up or down, into a smile, or into a pucker (the position they take when you whistle). They can move together or independently of each other.

Teeth

Your teeth are connected to your jaw and are brought closer together or further apart by opening or closing your jaw.

Tongue

Your tongue is a very flexible muscle that you can move into a variety of positions. You can lift up the front, to touch your upper gum ridge or your teeth. You can lift up the middle, to bring it closer to your hard palate. And you can lift up the back to bring it closer to your soft palate.

You can also move your tongue toward the front of your mouth and draw it back towards the back of your mouth.

Hard Palate

Your hard palate (roof of your mouth) cannot be moved. Whatever shape it is, that's how it stays.

Soft Palate

Your soft palate is a muscle. With it you can open up or close the passage from your throat into the nasal space.

Purpose of Articulation Exercises

The articulation exercises in this chapter make you more aware of your articulators and their movements. Practicing them gives you better control over your articulators and improves your coordination of their movements.

Articulation exercises should do more than just stretch your articulators. They should:

(1) Make you more aware of the state of relaxation or tension in your articulators.

(2) Help you to release any unnecessary tension that is inhibiting their free movement.

(3) Teach you how to freely move your lips and tongue to all the articulation positions, while your jaw is open wide enough to give you good sound.

To keep your articulators flexible and free of tension, do your articulation exercises at least once a day through your whole singing career.

Overcoming Inhibitions

Some people have an aversion to thinking about, seeing or feeling their lips, tongue or the inside of their mouth. They think it is impolite or repulsive in some way. Or they get embarrassed about doing exercises with their lips or tongue. But to acquire good diction control, you need to feel your articulators. You need to imagine how they are moving and the positions they are taking.

Do the exercises and concentrate on your reason for doing them—that is, to have better diction. In a short time you'll lose your embarrassment.

Dynamic Relaxation

Before starting the articulation exercises, you should understand the relationship between tension and relaxation when you move your articulators.

How a Muscle Works

A muscle works by contracting, in which it gets shorter, and then relaxing, in which it returns to its original length. Its work is done in its contraction. The release is simply letting go of the contraction.

You Are In Control

You have control over whether a muscle is contracted or relaxed. But you may not be consciously aware of it. You may only be aware of the movement of some part of your body from one position to another.

For example, move your hand up to touch your cheek. When you lift your hand to your face, you contract your biceps, or shorten it. Your biceps is connected to your shoulder on one end and to your forearm on the other end. When you shorten it, it lifts your forearm up. When you want to drop your forearm, you release the contraction in your biceps—and your arm drops down.

When you moved your arm you were probably not aware that you contracted your biceps muscle, you were only aware that your hand touched your face. You were not aware of the muscle activity itself because your arm is light and your muscle did not have to work very hard to move it. But if it is difficult to move your arm, you become aware of the extra tension in the muscle. For example:

Tighten up all the muscles in your arm and lift your hand to your face.

Feel how difficult it is to move your arm? Now release the extra tension and lift your hand to your face.

Feel how easy that is?

You can also control how quickly your muscles tense or relax. You can contract your biceps quickly and move your hand quickly to your face or you can contract your biceps slowly and move your hand slowly to your face.

If you release the contraction quickly, your forearm falls quickly. If you release the contraction slowly, your forearm drops slowly.

The point of these obvious statements is to show you that you can be aware of the state of tension or relaxation in your muscles, if you pay attention to it.

Tension vs. Relaxation

When a muscle is completely relaxed, it is totally limp and non-functioning—which is not a bad state to be in, if you're not doing anything.

But if you want to perform some activity, like singing or walking, you need a certain amount of energy in the singing and walking muscles.

On the other hand, too much tension gets in the way of the efficient operation of your muscles.

Having the right balance of tension and relaxation in your muscles is the desirable state. This balance we term **dynamic relaxation**.

How Does Dynamic Relaxation Help Your Diction and Singing?

When your articulators are too tense, they are hard to move. Tension is one of the causes of poor diction.

But when your articulators are in a state of dynamic relaxation, they move quickly, deftly and easily. Dynamic relaxation helps you to have good diction.

Getting to Know Your Articulators

Look in a mirror to see what your articulators look like. Pay close attention to their movements. If you can't look in a mirror, do the exercise anyway and imagine what they look like.

Exercise

Open and close your jaw.

See and feel how it moves.

Move your lips around.

See them and feel them.

Look inside your mouth at your tongue.

Move it around.

See it and feel it.

Feel your teeth with your tongue, both the upper and the lower, front and back.

Look at your hard palate.

Feel it with your tongue.

Look in the back of your mouth at your soft palate.

Yawn and see your soft palate lift and stretch up in a dome shape.

Feel it stretching.

Do the above exercise two or three times, taking your time.

Jaw Exercises

Look in a mirror as you do these exercises. See and feel what your jaw does as it opens and closes.

When you open your jaw properly, it naturally swings down and slightly back, as it does when you laugh or smile.

Don't thrust your jaw forward as you open it.

Let your jaw muscles relax and allow your jaw to drop open, without pulling it—let gravity do the work.

At first, it may feel like you have to make an effort to open your jaw wide. But, as you release unnecessary tension, your jaw will learn to drop open easily by just letting go of the muscles that hold the jaw closed.

Two Finger Widths

Your jaw should easily relax open about two finger widths. Two finger widths is just a convenient measurement. Put your first two fingers together, as if you are pointing at something. Now place the ends of those fingers between your upper and lower front teeth. Your jaw will be open about as wide as it needs to be for the articulation exercises. Of course, if you have large fingers and a small mouth, don't open your jaw quite that wide. But, generally, two finger widths is about right for practice.

However, when you are actually speaking, your jaw floats open about one finger width. Don't think that you have to open your jaw two finger widths when you are speaking normally.

You may notice some resistance or stiffness when you open your jaw wide. Although it may feel strange or uncomfortable at first, it's not harmful.

None of these exercises are dangerous. They are all natural movements. But, if you feel actual pain as you do any of these exercises, don't do it. See your doctor for advice.

Tongue Position for the Jaw Exercises

For all the jaw exercises, feel and see your tongue relaxed on the floor of your mouth, lightly touching the backs of your lower teeth all the way around. When you open your jaw wide, the back of your tongue should be relaxed down low enough for you to see all the way to the back of your throat.

(1) Jaw Stretch

Gently open your jaw wide. And close.
Feel the movement and see your jaw opening.
Open. And close.
Open. And close.

(2) Jaw Muscle Massage #1

This exercise will make your jaw more flexible and relaxed.
Place your hands on your jaw, just in front of your ears.
Clench your teeth together, see and feel the bulge of your jaw muscles under your hands. (These are the muscles that close your jaw.)
Relax your jaw open slightly and give those muscles a brisk massage.
Feel the muscles relaxing.
As you massage, feel and see your jaw drop open wider, until it is about two finger widths open.

(3) Jaw Muscle Massage #2

Place your fingertips on your temples at the sides of your head.
Clench your teeth and see and feel the muscles tighten at your temples. (These muscles also affect jaw tension.)
Feel and see your jaw relax open slightly.
Massage the muscles at your temples with a firm, rhythmic movement.
Feel the muscles relaxing.
Take your time and continue massaging downward to the big muscle at your jaw.
As you massage down, see and feel your jaw drop open wider, until it is about two finger widths open.
Do the exercise again.

(4) Moving Your Jaw

As you do this exercise, keep the muscles in the back of your neck relaxed.
Grasp the front of your jaw firmly with your fingers.
With your fingers, gently swing your jaw open about two finger widths.
Feel your jaw muscles relaxed, so that your fingers move your jaw. (Tell your jaw muscles to let go and let your fingers do the moving.)
Take a full breath without tensing your jaw muscles.
With your fingers, gently lift your jaw closed. Again.
Gently open. (Feel your jaw muscles relaxed.) Breathe.
Gently close. (Feel your jaw muscles relaxed.) Repeat this exercise daily until you don't feel any resistance in your jaw muscles as your hands do the moving.

(5) Shaking Your Jaw

Begin by carefully opening and closing your jaw with your hands.
Feel your jaw completely relaxed.
Go a little faster. (Be careful that you don't bite your tongue or crack your teeth together.)
Feel the physical release of your jaw as you go faster.

Feel the back of your neck relaxed.

Breath deeply five or six times as you are shaking your jaw.

Don't tighten your jaw muscles as you take a breath.

Stop the shaking after you have breathed in and out five or six times.

Repeat the exercise five times.

As your jaw loosens up, for fun, go faster and faster.

(6) Shaking Your Jaw With an A*h*

Begin by carefully shaking your jaw up and down.

Feel your jaw completely relaxed.

Breathe fully and easily.

Say a clear, strong *aaah*, as you are shaking your jaw.

Don't tighten your jaw muscles as you add the sound, feel them relaxed.

Don't tighten the back of your neck as you add the sound, feel them relaxed.

Repeat the exercise five times.

Lip Exercises

The following exercises will help you become aware of how your lips move. They will also give your lips greater strength, flexibility and dexterity.

Watch yourself in a mirror as you do these exercises and concentrate on feeling what your lips feel like.

Tongue Position for the Lip Exercises

For all the lip exercises, feel and see your tongue relaxed on the floor of your mouth, lightly touching the backs of your lower teeth all the way around. When you open your jaw, the back of your tongue should be relaxed down low enough for you to see all the way to the back of your throat.

(1) Smile and Pucker

The most important part of this exercise is the pucker. This is the rounded and pushed out position of your lips in the sound oo, as in moon, or the position your lips take when you whistle. Feel it full, but relaxed.

See and feel your jaw relax open a little more than one finger width.

See and feel your lips smile a wide, but relaxed smile.

See and feel your lips move forward into a full, but relaxed, pucker.

Smile (see and feel it).

Pucker (see and feel it).

Keep going, faster and faster.

(Don't let your jaw close. Keep it relaxed open.)

Continue the exercise for ten seconds.

Relax.

Lightly massage your lips with your fingertips to help release any tension left in them.

(2) Press and Release

Feel and see your jaw relax open approximately one finger width.

Press your lips firmly together. (Don't close your teeth together.)

Feel the press.

Relax your lips (feel the relaxation).

Press them together (feel it).

Release (feel it).

Repeat five times.

Press one more time very hard and release.

Feel the tingling sensation and the warmth in the muscles of your lips.

Feel how far out into your cheeks you can feel the sensations.

Relax.

(3) Move Your Upper Lip

Touch your lower lip and jaw with your fingers to help stop them from moving as you do this exercise.

See and feel your jaw open approximately two finger widths. (See p. 39.)

Stretch your upper lip down, without closing your jaw or moving your lower lip.

Feel and see your lip moving down and covering your upper teeth.

Relax your lip and feel and see it return naturally to its normal position.

Repeat ten times.

(4) Move Your Lower Lip

See and feel your jaw open approximately two finger widths.

Stretch your lower lip up, without closing your jaw or moving your upper lip.

Feel and see your lip moving and covering your lower teeth.

Relax your lip and see and feel it return naturally to its normal position.

Repeat ten times.

You may find that you have much more control over the movements of your lower lip than you have over the movements of your upper lip. Eventually, you will be able to move your upper lip just as easily as your lower lip.

(5) Touch Your Lips Together

Touch your lips lightly together and open your jaw as far you can without opening your lips.

Feel the stretch in your lips.

Don't let your jaw close. Touch your jaw with your fingers to help keep it relaxed and open.

Relax your lips and feel them return to their normal positions. (Don't let your jaw close.)

Touch your lips together again, without closing your jaw.

Now open and close your lips ten times, without moving your jaw.

(6) Blowing Your Lips

This exercise helps release any excess tension left in your lips.

Touch your lips together and blow through them, making them flap in the breeze.

Feel your lips relaxed and free.

Tongue Exercises

The three parts are:

(1) front (blade)

(2) middle

(3) back

Normal Resting Place for the Tongue

The home position for your tongue is on the floor of your mouth, lightly touching the backs of your lower teeth. Feel it and see it in that position.

Your tongue should always feel flat, thin and wide. When you open your mouth and look inside, your tongue should be lying flat down on the floor of your mouth, so that you can see all the way to the back of your throat. It should not be bunched up in the middle of your mouth.

Sometimes, the tongue has a habit of bunching up and filling up the mouth, even when your mouth is open wide. This is caused by excessive, unnecessary tension in your tongue.

If your tongue doesn't relax and drop low, use something, like a popsicle stick, to press your tongue down so that you can see all the way to the back of your throat. Try to relax your tongue so that it lies flat and low in your mouth. Gradually, your tongue will learn to relax its tension and lie flat.

The following exercises give your tongue flexibility and give you control over its movements. They are also awareness exercises to help you feel the movements and positions of your tongue.

(1) Yawn

Look in a mirror and yawn a big, open yawn.

See and feel the front of your tongue lightly touching the backs of your lower teeth. (If your tongue pulls to the back, move it to the front.) The middle of your tongue should be very low as you yawn.

You should be able to see all the way to the back of your throat.

If your tongue is bunched up high in your mouth, lower it.

Feel and see what it feels like to have your tongue low in your mouth.

Repeat the exercise three times.

(2) Tongue Stretch

Stretch your tongue straight out of your mouth. (Try to touch the opposite wall, across the room.)

Feel the stretch.

Try to touch your nose with the front of your tongue.

Feel the stretch.

Try to touch your chin.

Feel the stretch.

Try to touch your ear.

Feel the stretch.

And your other ear.

Feel the stretch.

Again.

Straight out (feel it).

To your nose (feel it).

Chin (feel it).

Ear (feel it).

Other ear (feel it).

Relax your tongue and feel how flexible it feels.

(3) Point and Widen

Watch yourself in a mirror.

Feel and see your mouth relax open about a finger width.

Place the front of your tongue between your lips.

Tense your tongue into a point.

Feel and see what that feels like.

Relax your tongue and stretch it wide and flat, so that its sides touch the corners of your mouth.

See and feel what that feels like. Repeat five times.

(4) Tongue Roll

Open your jaw approximately two finger widths.

Feel the edge of the blade of your tongue lightly touching the backs of your lower front teeth.

Keep the blade of your tongue behind your lower teeth. Roll the middle of your tongue as far out of your mouth as you can.

Feel the stretch in the back of your tongue.

Release the stretch and let your tongue roll back inside, flat on the floor of your mouth.

Feel what it feels like.

Repeat ten times.

Now, for fun, do the exercise faster.

Roll your tongue quickly out and in for about ten seconds.

When you do the rolling exercise, don't tense your tongue and bunch it up. Keep it flat, wide and relaxed.

(5) Tongue Roll and Sound

Roll your tongue quickly in and out of your mouth.

Feel that your tongue is relaxed and free.

Add vocal sound as you are rolling your tongue out and in. (It won't be any specific speech sound, just a kind of *uuuh*.)

Feel that your tongue continues to roll relaxed and free when you add sound. If feel your tongue tightens up, go back to rolling without sound. Then add sound again, while keeping your tongue relaxed.

(6) Tongue Edge to Gum Ridge

When you do this exercise, keep your tongue relaxed and wide.

Feel as though the back of your tongue stays low in your mouth.

See and feel your jaw relax open approximately two finger widths.

Touch your jaw with your fingers to help keep it open.

Raise the edge of the blade of your tongue to lightly touch your upper gum ridge. (That's where your teeth go into your gums.)

Feel your tongue wide, flat and relaxed.

Don't put any pressure on your tongue or try to push it to the front.

Touch with just the edge of your tongue, not the whole top surface. (Feel like the middle of your tongue is still relaxed down toward the floor of your mouth.)

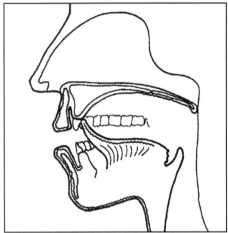

This way .

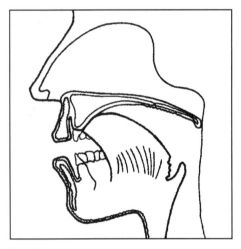

Not this way.

Move your tongue back and forth over the gum ridge area.

Explore it and feel what it feels like.

Lower your tongue back down to the floor of your mouth, with the edge of the blade of your tongue lightly touching the backs of your lower teeth.

Feel and see it in that position.

Again.

Open your jaw.

Touch your upper gum ridge.

Relax your tongue back down.

Repeat the exercise five times.

(7) Back of Tongue to Soft Palate

See and feel your jaw relax open approximately two finger widths.

Touch your jaw with your fingers to help keep it open.

Feel the front edge of your tongue lightly touching the backs of your lower teeth.

Raise the back of your tongue to touch your soft palate (the back part of the roof of your mouth), as though you were going to say *k*. (Don't say it, just touch.)

Feel what that feels like.

Keep the front edge of your tongue lightly touching the backs of your lower teeth.

Feel as though the front and middle of your tongue are still flat on the floor of your mouth.

Relax the back of your tongue down flat.

Again.

Open your jaw approximately two finger widths.

Raise the back of your tongue to touch your soft palate.

Feel it touch.

Relax your tongue down.

Repeat the exercise five times.

How Often to Practice

Practice the exercises in this chapter five to fifteen minutes at least once a day for a week. If you have time, do them two or three times a day. Space your practice sessions several hours apart. It is better to practice in short, frequent sessions than one long session.

Always practice your articulation exercises before you practice the sounds of speech.

Daily Articulation Exercises

Jaw

(1) Jaw Stretch
Open and close your jaw.
10 times.

(2) Jaw Muscle Massage
Massage from your temples to your jaw.
Let your jaw drop open two finger
widths.

(3) Shaking Your Jaw (no sound)
Shake your jaw with your fingers.

(4) Shaking Your Jaw (with Ah)
Shake your jaw with your fingers.
Say *aaah*.

Lips

(1) Smile and Pucker
10 times.

(2) Press and Release
Press your upper and lower lips together
and release.
10 times.

(3) Move Your Upper Lip
Cover your upper teeth with your upper
lip and release.
10 times.

(4) Move Your Lower Lip
Cover your lower teeth with your lower
lip and release.
10 times.

(5) Touch Your Lips Together
With your jaw open, touch your lips
together.
10 times.

(6) Blowing Your Lips

Tongue

(1) Yawn
3 times.

(2) Tongue Stretch
Out. Nose. Chin. Ear. Other ear. In.
3 times.

(3) Point and Widen
10 times.

(4) Tongue Roll (no sound)
Out and in.
10 times.

(5) Tongue Roll (with Ah)
Out and in. Add sound.
10 times.

(6) Tongue Edge to Gum Ridge
5 times.

(7) Back of Tongue to Soft Palate
5 times.

Notes:

vowel #a ɔˤ "ai"

vowel #y ə "uh"

consonant #8 ʃ "sh"

consonant #21 l "l"

3 Speech Sounds

Vowels, Diphthongs, Consonants

What are Speech Sounds?

Speech sounds are the **vowels, diphthongs** and **consonants** that make up the **syllables** and **words** of speech.

You can't help but use speech sounds. There is no other way to say words.

Speech is made up of words.

Words are made up of syllables.

Syllables are made up of speech sounds.

When you sing you use exactly the same speech sounds as you do when you speak. That's only common sense. If you don't, people can't understand the words you're singing.

It's true that in singing you may need to modify the vowel sounds slightly to maintain your quality of tone, but the modification should not be so drastic that it changes the vowel in the word to a different vowel altogether. (See p. 20.)

You probably don't think much about the individual sounds of speech. Not many people do. Most people, when they speak, think a little bit about the words they are going to say, if they need to. And, if they have some trouble pronouncing the words, they try to sound out the syllables. But that's about as far as they go.

You may be aware that words and syllables are made up of separate sounds, but, like most people, you have probably become so used to saying them in combinations that you can't remember what the individual speech sounds sound like by themselves.

Why We Forgot About Speech Sounds

We've all been using speech sounds since we first began to talk. We studied them when we were babies, trying to figure out how all those big people around us made the sounds that made the words that we wanted to say. Each of us did figure it out and we began to talk.

However, when we started school we received a big shock. We started to learn how to spell words for reading and writing. And, to our dismay, we found out that in many ways spelling is different from the way we speak. We discovered that there are a lot of words that we don't spell the way we say them or say the way we spell them.

And we began the process of learning how to read and to spell words for writing. We learned the spelling alphabet—A,B,C... This was great because we learned how to read and write.

But we found out that sounding out words according to the spelling alphabet didn't always work. In spelling we couldn't be sure of what alphabet letter to write for the sound we were saying. And in reading we couldn't be sure of how the letter we were looking at should be pronounced when we said the word out loud. Sometimes it was embarrassing. Remember all those misspelled and mispronounced words?

We had to learn a whole new approach to words—a reading and writing approach— that at times seemed to have little to do with speaking. Reading and writing became so important in our learning lives that it took up most of our time.

We lost our early fascination with speech sounds and how to say them clearly and distinctly—and our speech today suffers because of it.

Of course, schools cannot be blamed for teaching an essential skill—but an unfortunate side effect of this concentration on the written word was that our early awareness of how we speak faded out of memory. Most people today are far more conscious of their spelling, than of their speaking.

But now all of that is over. You're reading this book. You're once again fascinated with speech sounds. And here you're going to remember some of the things you've forgotten about speech and learn a lot more that you never knew. And for those of you who speak English as a second language, you're going to learn how to say some English speech sounds that you didn't have an opportunity to learn when you were a child.

Spelling vs. Speaking

What Vowel Should We Say?

When we look at the alphabet letter representing a vowel in a word, it is possible for that letter to have a number of different pronunciations.

Let's take a look at the letter A,a, for example. As the first letter of the spelling alphabet, **A**, is pronounced like the vowel in c*a*ke. But in some words **A** may be pronounced differently—as in the words c*a*n, c*a*r, c*a*re or f*a*ll.

Unless you have already memorized how to say these words, it is impossible to know from the spelling which spoken vowel to say.

Exercise

Say the vowel sounds in each of the following words out loud and hear the difference between them. First say the whole word slowly, as you would normally pronounce it, and listen carefully to the vowel in the word, then say the same vowel sound by itself.

> c*a*ke... c*a*ke... a... a...
> c*a*n... c*a*n... a... a...
> c*a*r... c*a*r... a... a...
> f*a*ll... f*a*ll... a... a...

These are four distinct, different speech sounds—all symbolized by the letter **a** of the spelling alphabet. The other vowels of the spelling alphabet also have more than one sound. (Don't worry, you already know all or most of them.)

It's no wonder that when we see the written letter in a word, we're not quite sure of how it's supposed to be sounded out.

What Consonant Do We Say?

Now let's look at the consonants.

The spelling alphabet consonants present two problems for pronunciation:

(1) We don't pronounce consonants in the spelling alphabet the same way we pronounce them when we speak.

(2) The spelling alphabet symbols for some of the consonants represent more than one speech sound.

All of the consonants in the spelling alphabet are pronounced differently from the way we actually say them in speech.

For example, **B**, in the alphabet, **ABC...**, is pronounced as *bee*.

Say, *A,B,C,* out loud and listen to the way you pronounce *B.*

Ready

A... B... C...

Again.

A... B... C...

Hear that you are actually saying two sounds *b*, as in *back*, and *ee*, as in *see*.

But in some words with **B** as a consonant there is no *ee* sound. Obviously, in *back*, there is no *ee* sound pronounced.

Say *back*, out loud.

back...

There is no *ee* sound after the *b*.

Now let's look at the second problem. Some of the spelling alphabet consonants stand for more than one sound. For example:

The alphabet letter **C** has two possible pronunciations: *cease* (which sounds like *s* in *see*) and *come* (which sounds like *k* in *keep*).

Say *cent* out loud and listen to the sound of *c*.

cent... cent... c... c...

cent... cent... c... c...

Now say *come* out loud and listen to the sound of *c*.

come... come... c... c...

come... come... c... c...

When we spell a word out loud, we use the spelling alphabet pronunciations normal for the letters of the alphabet, **A,B,C**... But when we say the word in speech, we don't pronounce it with the sounds of the spelling alphabet letters.

The Difference Between Speaking and Spelling

Let's compare the way we spell a word out loud and the way we actually say the word in speech.

Take the word *love*, for example. We spell *love* with the alphabet letters **l**, **o**, **v**, **e**. Spell *love* out loud and listen carefully to the sounds of the letters you say.

Ready,

l, o, v, e

Again. Listen carefully.

l, o, v, e

*N*otice that what you are saying and hearing sounds something like *el, oh, vee, ee*. But you don't pronounce *love* as *elohveeee*.

Now say the word *love* out loud slowly and listen to the sounds you say.

Ready,

Love (l, uh, v)

Again. Listen carefully.

Love (l, uh, v)

When you say the word as it is normally spoken you say only three distinct, single, speech sounds. (As opposed to four spelling letters.) We'll go over the actual sounds in the section, *A Fast Way of Learning Good Diction*, on the next page.

This is a wonderful revelation! It puts the whole concept of sounding out a word in a new light!

We should sound out a word with the sounds of speech, not the sounds of the spelling alphabet.

Try the sounding out exercise with a few of your favorite words, just to familiarize yourself with the concept. Spell the word and listen to the sounds you make. Then say the word normally and listen to the sounds you make.

From now on, when you're working on diction, think in terms of how you say words rather than how you spell them. You'll have far fewer problems with pronunciation.

The Phonetic Alphabet

Now that we know about the **sounds of speech**, we need some way of identifying them.

The easiest way is using the **phonetic alphabet**.

The word **"phonetic"** refers to **speech sounds**.

Phonetic: of or relating to spoken language or speech sounds. (*Webster's Seventh New Collegiate Dictionary*)

The phonetic alphabet uses **phonetic symbols** that represent the sounds of speech.

The most universally accepted phonetic alphabet is the **International Phonetic Alphabet (IPA)**, which is the one we use in this book.

The Advantages of Using the Phonetic Alphabet

The wonderful thing about the phonetic alphabet is that it has only **one symbol** for each **speech sound** and only **one speech sound** for each **symbol**. This makes it very easy to identify the sound you want to say.

Many of the symbols in the phonetic alphabet are the same as the symbols in the regular spelling alphabet, so you're not getting into totally unfamiliar territory. There are some new symbols, but they are not difficult to learn.

Learning the exact sounds and symbols of the phonetic alphabet is easy. If you speak English, you already say the speech sounds with some degree of accuracy every time you speak or sing. You just need to become aware of how you create the sound.

And learning the symbol for the sound is easy. You learn it as you learn how to make the sound.

If you speak English as a second language, some of the speech sounds may be unfamiliar to you. But if you follow the directions and listen carefully to the **Standard American Diction** CDs, you will learn them easily and quickly.

When we intend to use a symbol as part of the phonetic alphabet, we enclose it in square brackets, like this, [   ].

A whole word written in the phonetic alphabet is likewise enclosed in square brackets, [   ].

A Fast Way of Learning Good Diction: Neuro-sensory Conditioning™

The speech sounds that make up syllables and words are exactly the same for both speaking and singing.

You make the speech sounds with your articulators—your **jaw, lips, tongue, teeth, hard palate** (roof of your mouth) and **soft palate**. You create the sounds of speech by moving and placing your articulators in different positions.

The movement and placement of the articulators is called articulation.

The fastest and easiest way of learning speech sounds is through **Neuro-sensory Conditioning™**, a sensuous approach based on natural learning. You learn through:

> **Hearing**
> **Feeling**
> **Seeing**

You hear the sound, feel the movement of your articulators as you make the sound and see the movement and position of your articulators. You can see the movement either by looking in a mirror or by imagining how the articulators move.

Let's practice this:

Hearing

Say the speech sounds in the word *love* out loud and listen closely to them.

[l]   Do not pronounce it as *el*.

[ʌ]   This is the phonetic symbol for the vowel in *love*.

[v]   Do not pronounce it as *vee*.

Again,

[l] [ʌ] [v]

Feeling

Now say the sounds again. Feel how your tongue and lips move and where they touch as they make the sounds.

[l]   Feel the front edge of the blade of your tongue rising and touching your upper gum ridge.

[ʌ]   Feel your tongue lower to the floor of your mouth, touching the backs of your lower teeth.

[v]   Feel your lower lip touching your front upper teeth.

Seeing

Say the sounds again. This time look in a mirror to see how you move your tongue and lips and where you touch them. If you can't look in the mirror right now, imagine what your tongue and lips look like as they move and make the sounds.

Ready.

[l] [ʌ] [v]

Again.

[l] [ʌ] [v]

Now say the whole word again. Hear the separate sounds, feel the movement of your tongue and lips and see, or imagine, the movement of your tongue and lips.

Ready.

[lʌv]

Again

[lʌv]

Now sing the word love on a comfortable pitch. Feel your tongue drop quickly from the [l] position to [ʌ]. Feel and hear yourself holding [ʌ] with your articulators relaxed and unmoving. And feel your articulators move to the position for [v] at the end.

Ready, sing.

[lʌv]

Feel how much more control you have and how easy it is to sing the word when you're aware of how you articulate the speech sounds.

You can learn to recognize and say the speech sounds of Standard American Speech in a very short time. If you learn one sound a day, you can learn them all in forty-five days. If you take a couple of days a week off and learn only five a week, you can learn them all in only nine weeks.

That's fast!

And it's easy!

And your diction improves immediately!

Learn the sounds one at a time and immediately start applying what you've learned to your speaking and singing. Your diction begins improving as soon as you learn the first sound.

The Speech Vowels and Diphthongs

Listed at the end of this chapter are the **fifteen vowels, five diphthongs** and **twenty-five consonants** of Standard American Speech. We have numbered them in sequence, so that you can identify them quickly and easily.

Tongue Vowels

The first six vowels are made primarily by the position of your tongue. Your lips remain relaxed and unmoving.

Your tongue is in its highest position for Vowel #1 and it lowers slightly for each vowel through Vowel #7.

For Vowel #7 both your lips and your tongue are in their "at rest" positions, with your jaw open.

Lip Vowels

Vowels #8 through #12 are made primarily by the position of your lips. Your tongue should remain fairly low in your mouth.

Your lips are most open for Vowel #8 and they round slightly more for each vowel through Vowel #12.

Other Vowels

Vowels #13, #14 and #15 are placed at the end because they don't quite fit smoothly into the tongue or lip sequence—but they are not difficult to learn.

Diphthongs

Four of the five diphthongs are combinations of vowel sounds. Diphthong #4 is a combination of a consonant and a vowel.

Consonants

The twenty-five consonants are arranged in subgroups having similar characteristics.

We have included example words to help you identify the consonant sounds.

Don't let any new symbols confuse you. **Remember you're working on speech, not spelling.** In the following chapters we will show you in detail how to make each sound.

How to Practice

(1) Practice for fifteen minutes to half an hour every day. Only work on one sound a day—make it easy on yourself.

(2) Sing a short passage each day concentrating on the correct pronunciation of your sound for the day.

(3) As you talk during the day, listen to yourself and make sure you're saying your new sound correctly. If you hear yourself say it wrong, either stop and correct yourself right then or make a note to practice that word later.

(4) Listen carefully to the articulation and diction of radio and television personalities. Copy the way they say their words.

Record Yourself Saying the Sounds of Speech

(1) Record yourself speaking the following list of speech sounds and example words.

(2) Then record yourself singing the following list of speech sounds and example words. Sing them on an easy middle pitch.

(3) Keep the recording without listening to it until we ask you to record the sounds again, so that you can hear your improvement.

Vowels

Tongue Vowels

(1) [i] *eel... even... need... easy...* [i]

(2) [ɪ] *in... big... fit... give...* [ɪ]

(3) [eɪ] *aim... able... tail... bake...* [eɪ]
    (diphthong)

(4) [ɛ] *edge... every... beg... enter...* [ɛ]

(5) [æ] *am... annual... bag... add...* [æ]

(6) [a] *I... tie ... ice ... buy...* [a]

(7) [ɑ] *art... father... option... car...* [ɑ]

Lip Vowels

(8) [ɒ] *on... honest... bomb... cross...* [ɒ]

(9) [ɔ] *or... warm... hawk... before...* [ɔ]

(10) [oʊ] *old... oak... moan... solo...* [oʊ]
     (diphthong)

(11) [ʊ] *wool... book... put... could...* [ʊ]

(12) [u] *moon... ooze... loop... soon...* [u]

Other Vowels

(13) [ʌ] *up... above... custom... some...* [ʌ]
     (stressed symbol)
     [ə] (non-stressed symbol)

(14) [ɝ] *earn... germ... stir... firm...* [ɝ]
     (stressed symbol)
     [ɚ] (non-stressed symbol)

(15) [ɜ] *earn... world... furry... pearl...* [ɜ]

Diphthongs

(1) [aɪ] *I... nine... light... try...* [aɪ]

(2) [aʊ] *out... loud... gown... cow...* [aʊ]

(3) [ɔɪ] *oil... boy... noise... joint...* [ɔɪ]

(4) [ju] *you... cue... beauty... music...* [ju]

(5) [ɪu] *new... few... juice... June...* [ɪu]

Consonants

Fricatives

(1) [v] *van... veil... live...* [v]

(2) [f] *fun... far... if...* [f]

(3) [ð] *the... that... other...* [ð]

(4) [θ] *thank... thing... booth...* [θ]

(5) [z] *zoom... zip... buzz...* [z]

(6) [s] *song... sail... voice...* [s]

(7) [ʒ] *Asia... rouge... garage...* [ʒ]

(8) [ʃ] *she... shore... dash...* [ʃ]

(9) [h] *has... help... who...* [h]

Plosives

(10) [b] *ball... about... web...* [b]

(11) [p] *pull... apple... pop...* [p]

(12) [d] *dean... door... lad...* [d]

(13) [t] *tall... tend... lot...* [t]

(14) [g] *got... give... dog...* [g]

(15) [k] *can... call... look...* [k]

Affricatives

(16) [dʒ] *jar... joke... fudge...* [dʒ]

(17) [tʃ] *chair... chum... church...* [tʃ]

Glides

(18) [w] *will... were... awake...* [w]

(19) [ʍ] *while... when... what...* [ʍ]

(20) [j] *yes... yacht... loyal...* [j]

Semi-Vowels

(21) [l] *lake... laugh... all...* [l]

(22) [r] *rule... rain... are...* [r]

Nasals

(23) [m] *me... man... came...* [m]

(24) [n] *no... name... bin...* [n]

(25) [ŋ] *young... king... angle...* [ŋ]

Notes:

vowel #3 eɪ "ai"

vowel #7 ə "uh"

consonant #8 ʃ "sh"

consonant #21 l "l"

4 Vowels

A spoken vowel is a voiced sound, said or sung with an open mouth, and with no fricative, breathy noise.

Daniel Jones, in *The Pronunciation of English*, gives the following description of a spoken vowel:

> In the production of vowels the tongue is held at such a distance from the roof of the mouth that there is no perceptible frictional noise. (p. 12.)

And Peter Ladefoged, in *A Course in Phonetics*, says,

> In the production of vowel sounds none of the articulators come very close together, and the passage of the airstream is relatively unobstructed. (p. 11.)

A vowel is also a sound that does not change as you say it.

How Do You Speak or Sing a Vowel?

For both singing and speaking, you make the vowels by placing your articulators in the correct position for the sound and maintaining that position until you have finished saying the vowel.

If you change the position of your articulators, you also change the sound of the vowel.

Of course, in speaking, you say the vowels very quickly, so you can't tell that your articulators are stopping briefly for each sound—it feels like they are in continuous motion.

But in singing, you often sustain a vowel for several beats or even several measures, during which time it is particularly important to keep your articulators in the correct position for the vowel so that you maintain its true sound.

Problem Terminology

If you have read any voice and diction books, you are probably familiar with descriptions of the vowels labeling them *front, middle* and *back*; *high, middle* and *low*; *close* and *open*; or *tense* and *lax*.

This terminology uses the tongue as the point of reference and identifies the vowels in terms of *"the part of the tongue most actively involved in the production of the sound."* (Jon Eisenson, *The Improvement of Voice and Diction*, p. 142)

Using these descriptions, front vowels are made with the front or blade of the tongue, middle (mid) vowels with the middle of the tongue and back vowels with the back of the tongue. A high, front vowel means the front or blade of the tongue is lifted high. A high, back vowel means the back of the tongue is high.

Close and open also refer to how high or low the tongue is in your mouth. In the formation of a close vowel, the tongue is close to the roof of your mouth. In an open vowel, the tongue lies low in your mouth.

In forming a tense vowel the tongue has more tension in it than in forming a lax vowel. The tense vowel is also associated with the close vowel because it takes more tension to lift the tongue high in the mouth.

Generally, along with these descriptions, you also see a diagram visually presenting the high vowels at the top of the diagram and the low vowels at the bottom.

The problem with this approach is that it describes the back of the tongue as being raised fairly high for the high, back vowels. But having a vowel described to you as high, back gives you the wrong image of its articulation. Thinking high, back makes you think you should lift your tongue up high in the back, which, if you do, strangles your sound.

It is not necessary to raise the back of your tongue high to make any of the vowels.

And it is harmful to good sound and diction to think of raising the back of your tongue high as you say a vowel.

This is not a new or radical approach to diction. The respected phonetics expert, Peter Ladefoged, warns us that *"the labels high-low and front-back should not be taken as descriptions of tongue positions"* (*A Course in Phonetics*, p. 74).

And John Glenn Paton, in his revision of Van A. Kristy's book, *Foundations In Singing*, advises against *"tensing and lifting the back of the tongue."* He says, *"You will have a much more beautiful and comfortable sound if you learn to sing* [the 'oo'] *with rounded lips and relaxed tongue"* (p. 46). (*oo,* as in *soon,* is often called a *"high, back"* vowel.)

The terminology tense and lax also presents the wrong image. The terms tense and lax give the impression that on some vowels you tighten up your tongue and on other vowels you loosen it. But that is not true.

Though the middle of your tongue raises higher and toward the front of your hard palate for some vowels, it should never actually become tense. And you should never think of it as being tense. Instead, you should pronounce all of your vowels with your tongue in a state of dynamic relaxation. You should think of your tongue as being as relaxed as possible in all of its movements and positions.

For good voice production and articulation, you should always think of all of your articulators as being relaxed and free.

Any terminology that creates psychological and physical obstacles to good resonance and good diction should be avoided.

Tongue Vowels and Lip Vowels

In our system, we will refer to the vowels in terms of their primary articulator, that is *Tongue Vowels* and *Lip Vowels*.

Tongue Vowels are made primarily by movements and positions of your tongue.

Lip Vowels are made primarily by movements and positions of your lips.

The terminology *Tongue Vowel* and *Lip Vowel* has the advantage of avoiding imagery that gives the sense of blocking the vocal passages or creating tension in the articulators.

Categorizing the vowels as tongue or lip vowels also makes it easier to learn them. It clearly identifies the vowel with the articulator that forms it. You can then form an image of your lips or tongue taking a series of positions, each position creating a related, but different, vowel sound.

Basic Jaw Position

All vowels, whether you are speaking or singing, are made with your mouth relaxed open and your front teeth apart.

For speech, your jaw floats open approximately one finger width.

For singing, you may sometimes open your jaw wider, up to approximately two finger widths.

To find that space, hold your first and middle fingers together, as if you are pointing at something. Place the ends of those two fingers between your upper and lower front teeth. If your fingers are large and your mouth small, that may make you open your mouth too wide for comfort—so you can close slightly—Your jaw should not open past what feels like a little dislocation movement in the jaw joint. This measurement is a quick and easy reference when you are practicing with an open jaw.

At first, if your jaw is stiff and not used to opening wide, it may feel uncomfortable to open approximately two finger widths. But as you practice, your jaw will loosen up and it will become easier and more natural to articulate with a wide jaw.

Whenever you think of saying a vowel, you should have an image of a relaxed, open jaw.

Neuro-sensory Conditioning™

Neuro-sensory Conditioning™ is a natural method of learning speech sounds. It utilizes your hearing, feeling and seeing senses to learn the sound quickly, easily and permanently (see p. 30).

Neuro-sensory Conditioning™ is the natural way we learn to speak as a child. But as a child we don't know there is a system. So it is all hit and miss and takes a long time. As an adult, you can take advantage of the system and learn very quickly.

Imaging a Good Vowel

The legendary singing teacher, Giovanni Battista Lamperti, carrying on the traditions of the Golden Age of Song, declared that *"to know the result before we act is the 'golden rule' of singing"* (*Maxims of Vocal Wisdom*, transcribed by William Earl Brown, p. 28).

He taught that,

> *To anticipate the 'feel' of resonance (vowels) before singing, and to keep the sensation during pauses and after singing, is the lost art of the Golden Age of Song.* (*Vocal Wisdom*, p. 54)

In her lectures on voice, Elisabeth Howard, coauthor of *Born to Sing*, voices the same thought. *"A clear concept of the pure vowel sound is absolutely necessary for maintaining the quality of the vocal tone,"* she says. And, *"The vowel sound must be in the singer's mind just prior to vocalization and maintained from beginning to end."* (Conversations with the author.)

Both of these inspired teachers advocate the same principle—correct mental imagery.

How Do You Get Good Mental Imagery?

The muscles of your body do, or try to do, whatever your mind tells them to do. They respond to your mental picture of what their movements should be.

When you first learn to do things involving muscular coordination, such as walking and speaking, your imagery is conscious. You are aware that you must make your muscles move in certain ways to achieve certain results.

After a while, the movements that you work on consciously, become habits. That is, they become automatic and unconscious. You are no longer aware of controlling your movements. Your imagery is still in control, but you are no longer aware of your control.

In speaking and singing, you form habits of articulation in three steps:

(1) You **hear** the correct sound in your mind.

(2) You create a **mental image** of the movements and positions of your articulators as they make the sound.

(3) Then you consciously **practice** the correct movements of your articulators, repeating them over and over, until they become automatic.

Your imagery must match the correct movement and position of your articulators for each speech sound. If your imagery is different, you create tension and conflict in your articulators. You force them to fight between going to the position you image and the position they must take to make the correct vowel sound. The result may be an incorrect vowel sound or stiff articulators, or both.

The exercises in this book are designed to help you to develop a correct mental image of each vowel that includes:

(1) The concept of its **sound**.

(2) The **feel** of your articulators in the correct positions.

(3) A **mental picture** of the positions of the articulators.

(4) A sense of the sound's resonance **feel**.

This is the same as the **Natural Learning** —hearing, feeling, seeing—that you practiced in the last chapter, with the addition of feeling the specific resonance of each sound.

After you have learned the speech sounds you don't have to think about each sound every time you say it. Your articulators automatically take the right positions, because that is what you have trained them to do.

You are left free to focus on singing with emotion and beauty.

5   Tongue Vowels

Vowel #7 [ɑ]   "a̲h̲"

(We are starting with Vowel #7 because it is easier to learn the vowels from this point.)

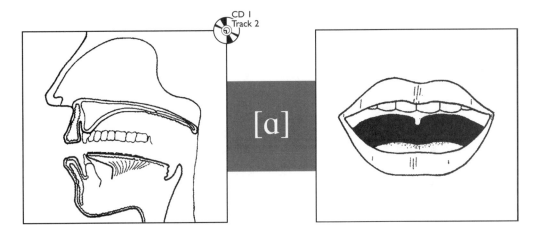

CD 1
Track 2

[ɑ]

Hearing

Listen carefully to this sound on the Standard American Diction CDs.

Jaw

Open your jaw about two finger widths or to a comfortable position almost two finger widths wide. (For speech and much of your singing, your jaw floats open about one finger width. But sometimes you need to open your jaw wider. So it's best to practice with a wide jaw.)

Lips

Leave your lips relaxed. Do not pull them back or round them.

Tongue

Feel the sides of your tongue lightly touching the backs of your lower teeth all the way around as you say the sound.

Feel the whole of your tongue relaxed down flat on the floor of your mouth.

Say the sound out loud. Sustain it for two counts.

[ɑ]... [ɑ]...

[ɑ]... [ɑ]...

Now sing the sound at a medium volume, on a comfortable pitch.

[ɑ]... [ɑ]...

[ɑ]... [ɑ]...

Mirror Exercise

Now watch yourself in a mirror as you say [ɑ].

For a clear [ɑ] sound, your jaw should stay open with your teeth about a finger width to two finger widths apart. Your lips should be relaxed, not pulled back, or rounded.

Say the sound out loud.

[ɑ]... [ɑ]...

[ɑ]... [ɑ]...

Now sing the sound at a medium volume, on a
comfortable pitch.

[ɑ]... [ɑ]...

[ɑ]... [ɑ]...

Possible Problems

The problem some people have with this sound is bunching the tongue up and raising it too high in the back of the mouth. Your tongue should lie low and relaxed, as it does in a yawn. However, when you say [ɑ] don't pull your tongue down excessively. It should be relaxed and level along the floor of your mouth.

If you are having difficulty with keeping your tongue low, practice the yawn exercise on p. 42.

Practice Words

Speak these practice words out loud, then sing them on a
comfortable pitch.

_a_re... _a_re...	h_ea_rt... h_ea_rt...
_o_n... _o_n...	c_a_lm... c_a_lm...
_o_live... _o_live...	d_o_ll... d_o_ll...
_o_ften... _o_ften...	w_a_nt... w_a_nt...
_o_ption... _o_ption...	l_o_gic... l_o_gic...

Practice Sentences

Say these practice sentences slowly at first, then faster. In the beginning, accuracy is more important than speed.

Speak them out loud, then sing them on a comfortable pitch.

_F_a_ther w_a_s c_a_lm at the f_a_rm._

_H_o_nesty and h_o_nor come fr_o_m the h_ea_rt._

_T_o_m w_a_nts l_a_rge _o_lives._

_It's c_o_mmonly h_o_t _o_n the g_o_lf course._

Daily Exercises—Vowel #7 [ɑ]

(1) Practice saying this sound and the other speech sounds you have learned with the Standard American Diction CDs.

(2) Read aloud from a newspaper, magazine or book until you feel and hear yourself say the [ɑ] sound five times. Underline the words.

(3) Speak the following reading out loud, slowly at first, then faster. Right now accuracy is more important than speed. Underline the words with [ɑ].

> *O never say that I was false of heart,*
> *Though absence seemed my flame to qualify.*
> *As easy might I from myself depart,*
> *As from my soul, which in thy breast doth lie.*
> *That is my home of love; if I have ranged,*
> *Like him that travels I return again,*
> *Just to the time, not with the time exchanged,*
> *So that myself bring water for my stain.*
> *Never believe, though in my nature reigned*
> *All frailties that besiege all kinds of blood,*
> *That it could so preposterously be stained*
> *To leave for nothing all thy sum of good:*
> > *For nothing this wide universe I call,*
> > *Save thou, my rose; in it thou art my all.*
> > SHAKESPEARE, *Sonnet 109.*

(4) Sing a short passage from one of your songs or arias that has [ɑ] in it. Repeat it several times, concentrating on singing [ɑ] correctly.

(5) Repeat the entire section for [ɑ] three times today.

(6) And make sure you're saying [ɑ] correctly as you speak during the day.

Vowel #6 [a] "<u>a</u>sk" (Northeastern States dialect)

This vowel is not used by itself in Standard American Speech, although it is heard by itself in some East Coast dialects. However, in Standard American Speech the [a] vowel is heard as the first part of the diphthongs [aᴵ] and [aᵁ]. (Diphthongs #1 & #2.)

If you have a little trouble hearing this vowel, go on to Vowel #5, then practice the comparison exercise included with Vowel #5.

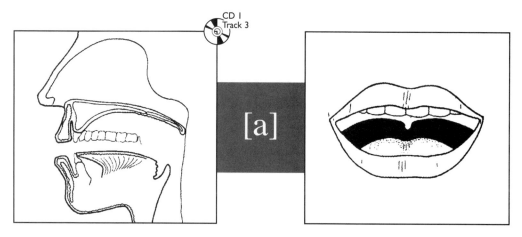

CD I
Track 3

[a]

Hearing

Listen carefully to this sound on the Standard American Diction CDs.

Jaw

Open your jaw about two finger widths or to a comfortable position almost two finger widths wide. (For speech and much of your singing, your jaw floats open about one finger width. But sometimes you need to open your jaw wider. So it's best to practice with a wide jaw.)

Lips

Leave your lips relaxed. Do not pull them back or round them.

Tongue

Feel the blade of your tongue lightly touching the backs of your lower teeth and keep it there as you say the sound.

Feel the sides of your tongue lightly touching your lower molars.

Feel the middle of your tongue raising up slightly and moving a little forward.

Your tongue should move in a relaxed way, with no pressure against your teeth.

Keep your tongue in place as you say the sound.

After you say the sound relax your tongue back down to the floor of your mouth.

Say the sound out loud. Sustain it for two counts.

[a]... tongue down. [a]... tongue down.
[a]... tongue down. [a]... tongue down.

Now sing the sound at a medium volume, on a comfortable pitch.

[a]... tongue down. [a]... tongue down.
[a]... tongue down. [a]... tongue down.

Mirror Exercise

Now watch yourself in a mirror as you say this sound. For a clear [a] sound, your jaw should stay open with your teeth approximately a finger width to two finger widths apart. Your lips should be relaxed, not pulled back, or rounded.

Say the sound out loud.
[a]... [a]...
[a]... [a]...

Now sing the sound at a medium volume, on a comfortable pitch.

[a]... [a]...

[a]... [a]...

Possible Problems

Listen to yourself carefully as you say [a]. If you hear the vowel change at the end, with a little [ə] (the vowel sound in *uh*), [aə], it means you're lowering your tongue before you finish saying the sound. Keep the sound pure, that is, a single sound. Notice that when your tongue stays in place the sound doesn't change.

Speak or sing the sound out loud.

[a]... [a]...

[a]... [a]...

If you're having trouble hearing and saying the [a] vowel, think of it as the beginning of the diphthong [aɪ] (as in *I*). Start to say [aɪ] but don't slide to [ɪ]. Say the first part and hold it longer.

It is also helpful to think of the tongue position of [a] as being between Vowel #7 and Vowel #5. (See the *Comparison Exercise* on p. 65.)

Flexibility Exercise

Here is a flexibility exercise to practice the movement of your tongue from [ɑ] to [a]. Make sure your jaw remains two finger widths open. Let your tongue do the moving.

Speak, then sing the sounds at a medium volume.

[ɑ,a,ɑ,a]... [ɑ,a,ɑ,a]...

[ɑ,a,ɑ,a]... [ɑ,a,ɑ,a]...

Practice Words

These are not the Standard American pronunciations for these words. The [a] vowel will give them an Eastern States sound and perhaps a slight British or Irish accent. The words are used here only to give you practice in the [a] sound.

Speak these practice words out loud, then sing them on a comfortable pitch.

<u>a</u>sk... <u>a</u>sk..	*f<u>a</u>ther... f<u>a</u>ther...*
<u>au</u>nt... <u>au</u>nt...	*n<u>o</u>t... n<u>o</u>t...*
<u>a</u>nswer... <u>a</u>nswer...	*c<u>a</u>n't... c<u>a</u>n't...*
<u>a</u>fter... <u>a</u>fter...	*l<u>au</u>gh... l<u>au</u>gh...*
	p<u>a</u>ss... p<u>a</u>ss...

Daily Exercises—Vowel #6 [a]

Because the [a] sound is used in Standard American Speech only as part of the diphthongs [aɪ] and [aʊ], there are no specific exercises for this sound by itself. (See exercises under the diphthongs [aɪ] and [aʊ] sections.)

(1) Practice saying this sound and the other speech sounds you have learned with the Standard American Diction CDs.

(2) Repeat the entire section for [a] three times today.

Vowel #5 [æ] "am"

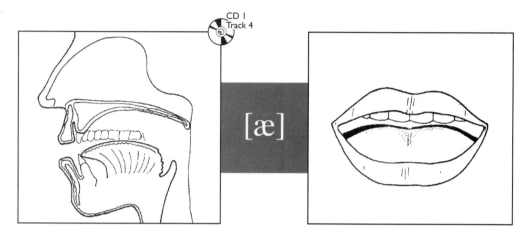

CD 1
Track 4

Hearing

Listen carefully to this sound on the Standard American Diction CDs.

Jaw

Open your jaw about two finger widths or to a comfortable position almost two finger widths wide. (For speech and much of your singing, your jaw floats open about one finger width. But sometimes you need to open your jaw wider. So it's best to practice with a wide jaw.)

Lips

Leave your lips relaxed. Do not pull them back or round them.

Tongue

Feel the blade of your tongue lightly touching the backs of your lower teeth and keep it there as you say the sound.

Feel the sides of your tongue lightly touching your lower molars.

Feel the middle of your tongue raising up and moving slightly forward. It'll be a little higher than for Vowel #6.

Your tongue should move in a relaxed way, with no pressure against your teeth.

Keep your tongue in place as you say the sound.

After you say the sound relax your tongue back down to the floor of your mouth.

Say the sound out loud. Sustain it for two counts.

[æ]... tongue down. [æ]... tongue down.

[æ]... tongue down. [æ]... tongue down.

Now sing the sound at a medium volume, on a comfortable pitch.

[æ]... tongue down. [æ]... tongue down.

[æ]... tongue down. [æ]... tongue down.

Mirror Exercise

Now watch yourself in a mirror as you say this sound. For a clear [æ] sound, your jaw should stay open with your teeth approximately a finger width to two finger widths apart. Your lips should be relaxed, not pulled back, or rounded.

Say the sound out loud.

[æ]... [æ]...

[æ]... [æ]...

Now sing the sound at a medium volume, on a comfortable pitch.

[æ]... [æ]...

[æ]... [æ]...

Possible Problems

Listen to yourself carefully as you say [æ]. If you hear the vowel change right at the end, with a little [ə] (the vowel sound in *uh*), [æᵊ], it means you're lowering your tongue before you finish saying the sound. Keep the sound pure, that is, a single sound. Notice that when your tongue stays in place the sound doesn't change.

Speak, then sing the sound at a medium volume.

[æ]... [æ]...

[æ]... [æ]...

Some people make this vowel too tight and nasal sounding. It should have a full, open resonance, more like an [ɑ]. The tight nasality comes from tensing your tongue and pushing it too high in your mouth. Relax your tongue and jaw and say the sound through a free, open throat.

Flexibility Exercise

Here is a flexibility exercise to practice the movement of your tongue from [ɑ] to [æ]. Make sure your jaw remains two finger widths open. Let your tongue do the moving.

Speak, then sing the sounds at a medium volume.

[ɑ,æ,ɑ,æ]... [ɑ,æ,ɑ,æ]...

[ɑ,æ,ɑ,æ]... [ɑ,æ,ɑ,æ]...

Comparison Exercise

If you're having trouble hearing the difference between Vowels #7, #6 and #5, [ɑ], [a], [æ], here is a comparison exercise.

Repeat the sounds one after the other. Hear the difference between their sounds and feel the difference between their tongue positions.

Speak, then sing the sounds at a medium volume.

[ɑ,a,æ]... [ɑ,a,æ]...

[ɑ,a,æ]... [ɑ,a,æ]...

Now let's reverse the order.

Speak, then sing the sounds at a medium volume.

[æ,a,ɑ]... [æ,a,ɑ]...

[æ,a,ɑ]... [æ,a,ɑ]...

Practice Words

Speak these practice words out loud, then sing them on a comfortable pitch.

at... at...	*can... can...*
and... and...	*rap... rap...*
ask... ask...	*van... van...*
am... am...	*back... back...*
after... after...	*began... began...*

Practice Sentences

Say these practice sentences slowly at first, then faster.
Right now accuracy is more important than speed.
Underline the words with [æ].
Say them out loud, then sing them on a comfortable pitch.

The tragical actor made a magical Hamlet.
Dancing in France is enchanting.
The sad lass wore a black cat mask.
Can Lance catch the fast rabbit?

Daily Exercises—Vowel #5 [æ]

(1) Practice saying this sound and the other speech sounds you have learned with the Standard American Diction CDs.

(2) Read aloud from a newspaper, magazine or book until you feel and hear yourself say the [æ] sound five times. Underline the words.

(3) Speak the following reading out loud, slowly at first, then faster. Right now accuracy is more important than speed. Underline the words with [æ].

Since brass, nor stone, nor earth, nor boundless sea,
But sad mortality o'ersways their power,
How with this rage shall beauty hold a plea,
Whose action is no stronger than a flower?
O how shall summer's honey breath hold out
Against the wrackful siege of batt'ring days,
When rocks impregnable are not so stout,
Nor gates of steel so strong but time decays?
O fearful meditation; where, alack,
Shall time's best jewel from time's chest lie hid?
Or what strong hand can hold his swift foot back?
Or who his spoil or beauty can forbid?
  O none, unless this miracle have might
  That in black ink my love may still shine bright.
    SHAKESPEARE, Sonnet 65.

(4) Sing a short passage from one of your songs or arias that has [æ] in it. Repeat it several times, concentrating on singing [æ] correctly.

(5) Repeat the entire section for [æ] three times today.

(6) And make sure you're saying [æ] correctly as you speak during the day.

Vowel #4 [ɛ] "<u>e</u>nd"

CD I
Track 5

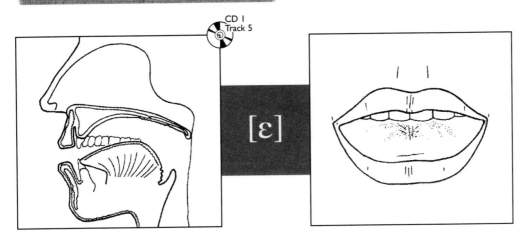

[ɛ]

Hearing

Listen carefully to this sound on the Standard American Diction CDs.

Jaw

Open your jaw about two finger widths or to a comfortable position almost two finger widths wide. (For speech and much of your singing, your jaw floats open about one finger width. But sometimes you need to open your jaw wider. So it's best to practice with a wide jaw.)

Lips

Leave your lips relaxed. Do not pull them back or round them.

Tongue

Feel the blade of your tongue lightly touching the backs of your lower teeth and keep it there as you say the sound.

Feel the middle of your tongue raising up and moving slightly forward.

You'll feel the sides of your tongue just lightly touching your upper molars.

Your tongue should move in a relaxed way, with no pressure against your teeth.

Keep your tongue in place as you say the sound.

After you say the sound relax your tongue back down to the floor of your mouth.

Say the sound out loud. Sustain it for two counts.

[ɛ]... tongue down. [ɛ]... tongue down.

[ɛ]... tongue down. [ɛ]... tongue down.

Now sing the sound at a medium volume, on a comfortable pitch.

[ɛ]... [ɛ]...

[ɛ]... [ɛ]...

Notice that when you say [ɛ] the middle of your tongue feels a little higher and further forward than when you say [æ]

Alternate between [ɛ] and [æ] and feel the difference in the position of your tongue. Don't let your jaw move.

Say the sounds out loud.

[æ,ɛ,æ,ɛ,æ,ɛ]... [æ,ɛ,æ,ɛ,æ,ɛ]...

[æ,ɛ,æ,ɛ,æ,ɛ]... [æ,ɛ,æ,ɛ,æ,ɛ]...

Mirror Exercise

Now watch yourself in a mirror as you say [ɛ]. For a clear [ɛ] sound, your jaw should stay open with your teeth approximately a finger width to two finger widths apart. Touch your jaw to keep it open. Your lips should be relaxed, not pulled back, or rounded.

Say the sound out loud.

[ɛ]... [ɛ]...

[ɛ]... [ɛ]...

Now sing the sound at a medium volume, on a
comfortable pitch.

[ɛ]... [ɛ]...

[ɛ]... [ɛ]...

Possible Problems

Listen to yourself carefully as you say [ɛ]. If you hear the vowel change right
at the end, with a slight [ə] (the vowel sound in *uh*), [ɛə], it means you're lowering your tongue
before you finish saying the sound. Keep the sound pure, that is, a single sound. Notice that
when your tongue stays in place the sound doesn't change.

Speak, then sing the sound at a medium volume.

[ɛ]... [ɛ]...

[ɛ]... [ɛ]...

Flexibility Exercise

Here is a flexibility exercise to practice the movement of your tongue from [ɑ] to [ɛ].
Make sure your jaw remains two finger widths open. Let your tongue do the moving.

Speak, then sing the sounds at a medium volume.

[ɑ,ɛ,ɑ,ɛ,ɑ,ɛ]... [ɑ,ɛ,ɑ,ɛ,ɑ,ɛ]...

[ɑ,ɛ,ɑ,ɛ,ɑ,ɛ]... [ɑ,ɛ,ɑ,ɛ,ɑ,ɛ]...

Practice Words

Speak these practice words out loud, then sing them on a
comfortable pitch.

egg... egg...	*bed... bed...*
else... else...	*sell... sell...*
end... end...	*pen... pen...*
edge... edge...	*get... get...*
effort... effort...	*empty... empty...*

Practice Sentences

Say these practice sentences slowly at first, then faster. Right now accuracy is
more important than speed.

Speak them out loud, then sing them on a comfortable pitch.

Every elbow bends.

Dennis likes tennis better than fencing.

Let Fred get the pen he left on the desk.

A leather belt gets stretched when it's wet.

Daily Exercises—Vowel #4 [ɛ]

(1) Practice saying this sound and the other speech sounds you have learned with the Standard American Diction CDs.

(2) Read aloud from a newspaper, magazine or book until you feel and hear yourself say the [ɛ] sound five times. Underline the words.

(3) Speak the following reading out loud, slowly at first, then faster. Right now accuracy is more important than speed. Underline the words with [ɛ].

> *So am I as the rich whose blessed key*
> *Can bring him to his sweet up-locked treasure,*
> *The which he will not every hour survey,*
> *For blunting the fine point of seldom pleasure.*
> *Therefore are feasts so solemn and so rare,*
> *Since seldom coming in the long year set,*
> *Like stones of worth they thinly placed are,*
> *Or captain jewels in the carcanet.*
> *So is the time that keeps you as my chest,*
> *Or as the wardrobe which the robe doth hide*
> *To make some special instant special blest,*
> *By new unfolding his imprisoned pride.*
> > *Blessed are you whose worthiness gives scope,*
> > *Being had to triumph, being lacked to hope.*
> > *SHAKESPEARE, Sonnet 52*

(4) Read aloud for five minutes, concentrating on saying [ɛ] correctly.

(5) Sing a short passage several times, concentrating on saying [ɛ] correctly.

(6) Repeat the entire section for [ɛ] three times today.

(7) And make sure you're saying [ɛ] correctly as you speak during the day.

Vowel #3 [eᴵ] "<u>ai</u>m" (diphthong)

The International Phonetic Alphabet has a pure, or single, vowel sound, [e], but in Standard American Speech this vowel is always said as a diphthong. Sometimes you may hear [ə] as the first sound in this diphthong, however, the difference is minimal and either is acceptable.

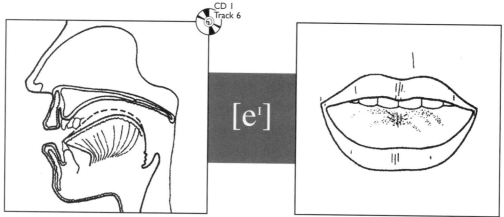

CD I
Track 6

[eᴵ]

Hearing

Listen carefully to this sound on the Standard American Diction CDs.

Jaw

Open your jaw about two finger widths or to a comfortable position almost two finger widths wide. (For speech and much of your singing, your jaw floats open about one finger width. But sometimes you need to open your jaw wider. So it's best to practice with a wide jaw.)

Lips

Leave your lips relaxed. Do not pull them back or round them.

Tongue

Feel the blade of your tongue lightly touching the back of your lower teeth and keep it there as you say the sound.

Feel the middle of your tongue raising up and moving slightly forward until it's close to your hard palate, that's the roof of your mouth.

You'll feel the sides of your tongue lightly touching your upper molars.

Your tongue will move slightly upward and toward the front as you say the sound.

Your tongue should move in a relaxed way, with no pressure against your teeth.

It's important that you keep your jaw open about a finger width to two finger widths as you say this sound, the movement should be with your tongue only.

After you say the sound relax your tongue back down to the floor of your mouth.

The first sound of the diphthong is more strongly stressed than the second sound. The diphthong ends just as you say the second sound.

Say the sound out loud. Sustain it for two counts.

[eᴵ]... tongue down [eᴵ]... tongue down
[eᴵ]... tongue down [eᴵ]... tongue down

Now sing the sound at a medium volume, on a comfortable pitch.

[eᴵ]... tongue down [eᴵ]... tongue down
[eᴵ]... tongue down [eᴵ]... tongue down

Mirror Exercise

Now watch yourself in a mirror as you say [eᴵ]. For a clear [eᴵ] sound, your jaw should stay open with your teeth approximately a finger width to two finger widths apart. Only your tongue should move to make the sound. Touch your jaw to help it stay open. Your lips should be relaxed, not pulled back, or rounded.

Say the sound out loud.

[eɪ]... [eɪ]...

[eɪ]... [eɪ]...

Now sing the sound at a medium volume, on a comfortable pitch.

[eɪ]... [eɪ]...

[eɪ]... [eɪ]...

Possible Problems

Listen to yourself carefully as you say [eɪ]. If you hear the vowel change right at the end, with a slight [ə] (the vowel sound in *uh*), [eɪə], it means you're lowering your tongue before you finish saying the sound. Keep the sound pure, that is, a single sound.

Speak, then sing the sound at a medium volume.

[eɪ]... [eɪ]...

[eɪ]... [eɪ]...

Flexibility Exercise

Here is a flexibility exercise to practice the movement of your tongue from [ɑ] to [eɪ]. Make sure your jaw remains two finger widths open. Let your tongue do the moving.

Speak, then sing the sounds at a medium volume.

[ɑ, eɪ, ɑ, eɪ, ɑ, eɪ]... [ɑ, eɪ, ɑ, eɪ, ɑ, eɪ]...

[ɑ, eɪ, ɑ, eɪ, ɑ, eɪ]... [ɑ, eɪ, ɑ, eɪ, ɑ, eɪ]...

Practice Words

Speak these practice words out loud, then sing them on a comfortable pitch.

*ai*m... *ai*m...	*fa*te... *fa*te...	*day*... *day*...
*a*ble... *a*ble...	*mai*n... *mai*n...	*may*... *may*...
*a*ce... *a*ce...	*la*ke... *la*ke...	*say*... *say*...
*ei*ght... *ei*ght...	*mai*l... *mai*l...	*they*... *they*...
*a*pron... *a*pron...	*rai*sin... *rai*sin...	*okay*... *okay*...

Practice Sentences

Say these practice sentences slowly at first, then faster. Right now accuracy is more important than speed.

Speak them out loud, then sing them on a comfortable pitch.

__Ai__m the fl__a__me aw__ay__ from the h__ay__.

St__a__le c__a__ke and __a__le were pl__a__ced on the t__a__ble.

__Ei__ght l__a__zy, cr__a__zy d__ay__s in M__ay__.

Sh__a__pely J__a__ne compl__ai__ns of __a__ches and p__ai__ns.

Daily Exercises—Vowel #3 [eᴵ]

(1) Practice saying this sound and the other speech sounds you have learned with the Standard American Diction CDs.

(2) Read aloud from a newspaper, magazine or book until you feel and hear yourself say the [eᴵ] sound five times. Underline the words.

(3) Speak the following reading out loud, slowly at first, then faster. Right now accuracy is more important than speed. Underline the words with [eᴵ].

> Like as the waves make towards the pebbled shore,
> So do our minutes hasten to their end,
> Each changing place with that which goes before,
> In sequent toil all forwards do contend.
> Nativity, once in the main of light,
> Crawls to maturity, wherewith being crowned,
> Crooked eclipses 'gainst his glory fight,
> And time that gave, doth now his gift confound.
> Time doth transfix the flourish set on youth,
> And delves the parallels in beauty's brow,
> Feeds on the rarities of nature's truth,
> And nothing stands but for his scythe to mow.
>   And yet to times in hope, my verse shall stand,
>   Praising thy worth, despite his cruel hand.
>   *SHAKESPEARE, Sonnet 60.*

(4) Sing a short passage from one of your songs or arias that has [eᴵ] in it. Repeat it several times, concentrating on singing [eᴵ] correctly.

(5) Repeat the entire section for [eᴵ] three times today.

(6) And make sure you're saying [eᴵ] correctly as you speak during the day.

Vowel #2   [ɪ]   "it"

Many singers, especially those who speak English as a second language, pronounce this sound as Vowel #1, [i], which is a serious diction fault.

If you're having trouble with the [ɪ] sound, practice the *Comparison Exercises* included with Vowel #1, until you can clearly hear and feel the difference.

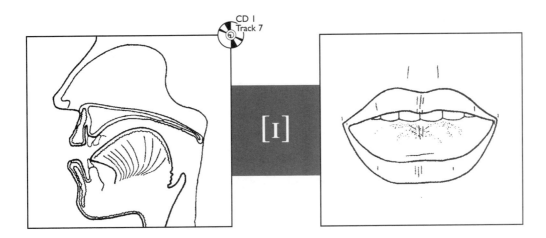

CD I
Track 7

[ɪ]

Hearing

Listen carefully to this sound on the Standard American Diction CDs.

Jaw

Open your jaw about two finger widths or to a comfortable position almost two finger widths wide. (For speech and much of your singing, your jaw floats open about one finger width. But sometimes you need to open your jaw wider. So it's best to practice with a wide jaw.)

Lips

Leave your lips relaxed. Do not pull them back or round them.

Tongue

Feel the blade of your tongue lightly touching the backs of your lower teeth and keep it there as you say the sound.

Feel the middle of your tongue raising up and moving slightly forward until it's close to your hard palate, that's the roof of your mouth.

You'll feel the sides of your tongue lightly touching your upper molars.

Your tongue should move in a relaxed way, with no pressure against your teeth.

Keep your tongue in place as you say the sound.

After you say the sound relax your tongue back down to the floor of your mouth.

Say the sound out loud. Sustain it for two counts.

[ɪ]... tongue down [ɪ]... tongue down

[ɪ]... tongue down [ɪ]... tongue down

Now sing the sound at a medium volume, on a comfortable pitch.

[ɪ]... tongue down [ɪ]... tongue down

[ɪ]... tongue down [ɪ]... tongue down

Notice that when you say [ɪ] the middle of your tongue feels higher than when you say [ɛ].

Alternate between [ɛ] and [ɪ] and feel the difference in the position of your tongue. Don't let your jaw move.

Say the sounds out loud.

[ɛ,ɪ,ɛ,ɪ,ɛ,ɪ]... [ɛ,ɪ,ɛ,ɪ,ɛ,ɪ]

[ɛ,ɪ,ɛ,ɪ,ɛ,ɪ]... [ɛ,ɪ,ɛ,ɪ,ɛ,ɪ]

Mirror Exercise

Now watch yourself in a mirror as you say [ɪ].

For a clear [ɪ] sound, your jaw should stay open with your teeth approximately a finger width to two finger widths apart. Touch your jaw to help keep it open. Your lips should be relaxed, not pulled back, or rounded.

Say the sound out loud.

[ɪ]... [ɪ]...

[ɪ]... [ɪ]...

Now sing the sound at a medium volume, on a comfortable pitch.

[ɪ]... [ɪ]...

[ɪ]... [ɪ]...

Possible Problems

Listen to yourself carefully as you say [ɪ]. If you hear the vowel change right at the end, with a slight [ə] (the vowel sound in *uh*), [ɪə], it means you're lowering your tongue before you finish saying the sound. Keep the sound pure, that is, a single sound. Notice that when your tongue stays in place the sound doesn't change.

Speak, then sing the sound at a medium volume.

[ɪ]... [ɪ]...

[ɪ]... [ɪ]...

Flexibility Exercise

Here is a flexibility exercise to practice the movement of your tongue from [ɑ] to [ɪ]. Make sure your jaw remains two finger widths open. Let your tongue do the moving.

Speak, then sing the sounds at a medium volume.

[ɑ,ɪ,ɑ,ɪ,ɑ,ɪ]... [ɑ,ɪ,ɑ,ɪ,ɑ,ɪ]...

[ɑ,ɪ,ɑ,ɪ,ɑ,ɪ]... [ɑ,ɪ,ɑ,ɪ,ɑ,ɪ]...

Practice Words

Speak these practice words out loud, then sing them on a comfortable pitch.

in... in...	*bid... bid...*
is... is...	*sit... sit...*
it... it...	*give... give...*
ink... ink...	*him... him...*
image... image...	*thing... thing...*

Practice Sentences

Say these practice sentences slowly at first, then faster. Right now accuracy is more important than speed.

Speak them out loud, then sing them on a comfortable pitch.

I think this is England.

Chicago is a windy city in the winter.

Dick stuck his finger with a pin.

If it is, it is; if it isn't, it isn't.

Daily Exercises—Vowel #2 [ɪ]

(1) Practice saying this sound and the other speech sounds you have learned with the Standard American Diction CDs.

(2) Read aloud from a newspaper, magazine or book until you feel and hear yourself say the [ɪ] sound five times. Underline the words.

(3) Speak the following reading out loud, slowly at first, then faster. Right now accuracy is more important than speed. Underline the words with [ɪ].

> *Sin of self-love possesseth all mine eye,*
> *And all my soul, and all my every part;*
> *And for this sin there is no remedy,*
> *It is so grounded inward in my heart.*
> *Methinks no face so gracious is as mine,*
> *No shape so true, no truth of such account,*
> *And for myself mine own worth do define,*
> *As I all other in all worths surmount.*
> *But when my glass shows me myself indeed*
> *Beated and chopped with tanned antiquity,*
> *Mine own self-love quite contrary I read;*
> *Self so self-loving were iniquity.*
> > *'Tis thee, myself, that for myself I praise,*
> > *Painting my age with beauty of thy days.*
> > > *SHAKESPEARE, Sonnet 62.*

(4) Sing a short passage from one of your songs or arias that has [ɪ] in it. Repeat it several times, concentrating on singing [ɪ] correctly.

(5) Repeat the entire section for [ɪ] three times today.

(6) And make sure you're saying [ɪ] correctly as you speak during the day.

Vowel #1 [i] "eel"

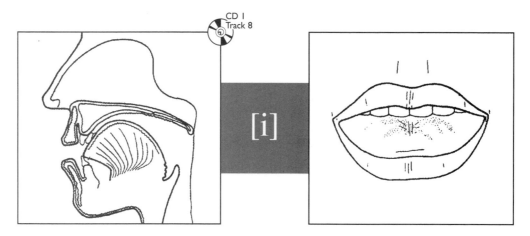

CD 1
Track 8

Hearing

Listen carefully to this sound on the Standard American Diction CDs.

Jaw

Open your jaw about two finger widths or to a comfortable position almost two finger widths wide. (For speech and much of your singing, your jaw floats open about one finger width. But sometimes you need to open your jaw wider. So it's best to practice with a wide jaw.)

Lips

Leave your lips relaxed. Do not pull them back or round them.

Tongue

Feel the blade of your tongue lightly touching the backs of your lower teeth and keep it there as you say [i].

Feel the middle of your tongue raising up and moving slightly forward until it's close to your hard palate, that's the roof of your mouth.

You'll feel the sides of your tongue lightly touching your upper molars.

This position will feel slightly higher than the [ɪ] position

Your tongue should move in a relaxed way, with no pressure against your teeth.

Keep your tongue in place as you say the sound.

After you say the sound relax your tongue back down to the floor of your mouth.

Say the sound out loud. Sustain it for two counts.

[i]... tongue down [i]... tongue down

[i]... tongue down [i]... tongue down

Now sing the sound at a medium volume, on a comfortable pitch.

[i]... tongue down [i]... tongue down

[i]... tongue down [i]... tongue down

Mirror Exercise

Now watch yourself in a mirror as you say [i].

For a clear [i] sound, your jaw should stay open with your teeth approximately a finger width to two finger widths apart. Your lips should be relaxed, not pulled back, or rounded.

Say the sound out loud.

[i]... [i]...

[i]... [i]...

Now sing the sound at a medium volume, on a comfortable pitch.

[i]... [i]...

[i]... [i]...

Possible Problems

Listen to yourself carefully as you say [i]. If you hear the vowel change right at the end, with a slight [ə] (the vowel sound in *uh*), [iə], it means you're lowering your tongue before you finish saying the sound. Keep the sound pure, that is, a single sound. Notice that when your tongue stays in place the sound doesn't change.

Speak, then sing, the sound at a medium volume.

[i]... [i]...

[i]... [i]...

Another problem people have with [i] is closing your jaw so that your teeth are almost touching as they say the sound. Be sure you keep your jaw open, with your teeth approximately one finger width apart.

Flexibility Exercises

Here is a flexibility exercise to practice the movement of your tongue from [ɑ] to [i]. Make sure your jaw remains two finger widths open. Let your tongue do the moving.

Speak, then sing, the sounds at a medium volume.

[ɑ,i,ɑ,i,ɑ,i]... [ɑ,i,ɑ,i,ɑ,i]...

[ɑ,i,ɑ,i,ɑ,i]... [ɑ,i,ɑ,i,ɑ,i]...

Comparison Exercise

Here are some comparison exercises for Vowels #1, #2 and #4.

Repeat the sounds one after the other. Hear the difference between their sounds and feel the difference between their tongue positions.

Speak, then sing, the sounds at a medium volume.

[i,ɪ,ɛ]... [i,ɪ,ɛ]...

[i,ɪ,ɛ]... [i,ɪ,ɛ]...

And repeat the following words.

Speak, then sing, them at a medium volume.

s*ea*t, s*i*t, s*e*t... s*ea*t, s*i*t, s*e*t...

s*ea*t, s*i*t, s*e*t... s*ea*t, s*i*t, s*e*t...

Now let's reverse the order.

Speak, then sing, the sounds at a medium volume.

[ɛ,ɪ,i]... [ɛ,ɪ,i]...

[ɛ,ɪ,i]... [ɛ,ɪ,i]...

And repeat the following words.

Speak, then sing, them at a medium volume.

s*e*t, s*i*t, s*ea*t... s*e*t, s*i*t, s*ea*t...

s*e*t, s*i*t, s*ea*t... s*e*t, s*i*t, s*ea*t...

Here is a comparison exercise for vowels #1 and #2.

Speak, then sing, the sounds at a medium volume.

[i,ɪ,i,ɪ,i,ɪ]... [i,ɪ,i,ɪ,i,ɪ]...

[i,ɪ,i,ɪ,i,ɪ]... [i,ɪ,i,ɪ,i,ɪ]...

And repeat the following words.

Speak, then sing, them at a medium volume.

eat, it, eat, it... eat, it, eat, it...

eat, it, eat, it... eat, it, eat, it...

Repeat the above comparison exercises, until you can clearly hear and feel the difference between the sounds.

Practice Words

Speak these practice words out loud, then sing them on a comfortable pitch.

even... even...	*feet... feet...*	*see... see...*
each... each...	*please... please...*	*me... me...*
eel... eel...	*keep... keep...*	*key... key...*
east... east...	*kneel... kneel..*	*tea... tea...*
equal... equal...	*tease... tease...*	*agree... agree...*

Practice Sentences

Say these practice sentences slowly at first, then faster. Right now accuracy is more important than speed.

Speak them out loud, then sing them on a comfortable pitch.

Green peas pleased Keith.

Neat teeth make eating easy.

Deep sleep is frequently easy to achieve by reading.

He sheared the sheep with the green feet.

Daily Exercises—Vowel #1   [i]

(1) Practice saying this sound and the other speech sounds you have learned with the Standard American Diction CDs.

(2) Read aloud from a newspaper, magazine or book until you feel and hear yourself say the [i] sound five times. Underline the words.

(3) Speak the following reading out loud, slowly at first, then faster. Right now accuracy is more important than speed. Underline the words with [i].

> *How like a winter hath my absence been*
> *From thee, the pleasure of the fleeting year!*
> *What freezings have I felt, what dark days seen!*
> *What old December's bareness everywhere!*
> *And yet this time removed was summer's time,*
> *The teeming autumn big with rich increase,*
> *Bearing the wanton burthen of the prime,*
> *Like widowed wombs after their lord's decease.*
> *Yet this abundant issue seemed to me*
> *But hope of orphans, and unfathered fruit;*
> *For summer and his pleasures wait on thee,*
> *And thou away, the very birds are mute.*
>> *Or if they sing, 'tis with so dull a cheer,*
>> *That leaves look pale, dreading the winter's near.*
>> *SHAKESPEARE, Sonnet 97.*

(4) Sing a short passage from one of your songs or arias that has [i] in it. Repeat it several times, concentrating on singing [i] correctly.

(5) Repeat the entire section for [i] three times today.

(6) And make sure you're saying [i] correctly as you speak during the day.

The Lowered [i̯] "city"

In Standard American Speech there is a sound, called a Lowered [i̯]. This sound is between Vowel #1, [i], and Vowel #2, [ɪ]. (The symbol, [̯], means "lowered.") Your tongue position is a little lower than Vowel #1, [i], and a little higher than Vowel #2, [ɪ].

It is used for the *y* ending of words like *pity, copy, city*.

This sound is so close to the sound of [ɪ] that it is often referred to as [ɪ]. Because it is simpler to think of the Lowered [i̯] as [ɪ], that is what we will do.

If the *y* ending is sustained, as it is in some Pop music, it is sung as [ɪ] or [i].

Hearing

Listen carefully to this sound on the Standard American Diction CDs.

CD 1
Track 9

Practice Words

Speak, then sing, these practice words. Listen to how you are saying the final y.

pity... pity...
very... very...
city... city...
carry... carry...
only... only...
beauty... beauty...

Congratulations! You've learned to recognize and say all the **Tongue Vowels** of **Standard American Speech**.

Review of Tongue Vowels

Let's do a quick review of Vowels #1 through #7. All these vowels are made by movements and positions of the tongue. We'll start with Vowel #1.

Hear the sounds and picture the positions of your articulators. Feel your tongue lowering slightly for each sound and feel the resonance for each sound.

Speak, then sing, the sounds at a medium volume.

[i, ɪ, eᴵ, ɛ, æ, a, ɑ]

Again.

[i, ɪ, eᴵ, ɛ, æ, a, ɑ]

Now let's go the other way, from #7 to #1. Feel your tongue raising slightly for each sound and feel the resonance for each sound.

Speak, then sing, the sounds at a medium volume.

[ɑ, a, æ, ɛ, eᴵ, ɪ, i]

Again.

[ɑ, a, æ, ɛ, eᴵ, ɪ, i]

Notice how much more clearly and easily you can say each vowel sound now that you've practiced them.

Exercise

(1) Record yourself saying the Tongue Vowels and their example words on p. 52.

(2) Compare this recording with your first recording.

(3) Notice the improvement in your diction.

Notes:

vowel #2 eɪ "ai"

vowel #7 ɑ "uh"

consonant #6 ʃ "sh"

consonant #21 l "l"

6 Lip Vowels

Vowel #8   [ɒ] "all"

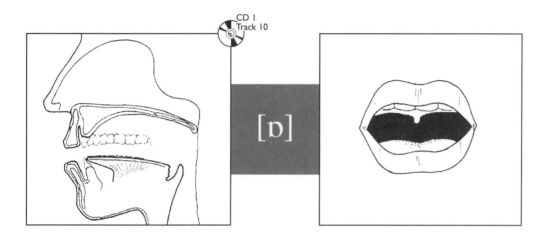

CD 1
Track 10

[ɒ]

Hearing

Listen carefully to this sound on the Standard American Diction CDs.

In Standard American Speech, this sound is used in such words as *law*, *caught*, and *autumn*. Your lips do not round as much for this sound as for the more British sounding Vowel #9, [ɔ].

Jaw

Open your jaw about two finger widths or to a comfortable position almost two finger widths wide. (For speech and much of your singing, your jaw floats open about one finger width. But sometimes you need to open your jaw wider, so it's best to practice with a wide jaw.)

Tongue

Feel the whole of your tongue relaxed down flat on the floor of your mouth, lightly touching your lower teeth.

Lips

Feel the corners of your lips move forward a little bit to slightly round your lips.

Feel the whole of your tongue relaxed down flat on the floor of your mouth.

After you say the sound release your lips.

Say the sound out loud. Sustain it for two counts.

[ɒ]... release lips [ɒ]... release lips

[ɒ]... release lips [ɒ]... release lips

Now sing the sound at a medium volume on a comfortable pitch.

[ɒ]... release lips [ɒ]... release lips

[ɒ]... release lips [ɒ]... release lips

Mirror Exercise

Now watch yourself in a mirror as you say [ɒ].

For a clear [ɒ] sound, your jaw should stay open with your teeth about a finger width to two finger widths apart. Your lips should round in a relaxed way, not tensed.

Say the sound out loud. Sustain it for two counts.

[ɒ]... [ɒ]...

[ɒ]... [ɒ]...

Now sing the sound at a medium volume on a comfortable pitch.

[ɒ]... [ɒ]...

[ɒ]... [ɒ]...

Possible Problems

Listen to yourself carefully as you say [ɒ]. If you hear the vowel change right at the end, with a little [ə] (the vowel sound in *uh*), [ɒə], it means you're releasing your lips before you finish the sound. Keep the vowel pure, that is, a single sound. Notice that when your lips stay in place the vowel doesn't change.

Speak, then sing the sound at a medium volume.

[ɒ]... [ɒ]... [ɒ]... [ɒ]...

Comparison Exercise

Here is a comparison exercise between Vowels #7 and #8. Repeat them one after the other. Hear the difference between their sounds and feel the difference between their lip positions.

Speak, then sing, the sounds at a medium volume.

[ɑ,ɒ,ɑ,ɒ,ɑ,ɒ]... [ɑ,ɒ,ɑ,ɒ,ɑ,ɒ]...

[ɑ,ɒ,ɑ,ɒ,ɑ,ɒ]... [ɑ,ɒ,ɑ,ɒ,ɑ,ɒ]...

Practice Words

Speak these practice words out loud, then sing them on a comfortable pitch.

all... all...	*dawn... dawn...*	*caw... caw...*
auto... auto...	*lawn... lawn...*	*jaw... jaw...*
on... on...	*caught... caught...*	*law... law...*
awful... awful...	*saw... saw...*	*draw... draw...*
almost... almost...	*auction... auction...*	*thaw... thaw...*

Practice Sentences

Say these practice sentences slowly at first, then faster. In the beginning, accuracy is more important than speed.

Speak them out loud, then sing them on a comfortable pitch.

A rock cannot walk or talk.

A sunny autumn makes thought wander.

The author tossed the awful coffee out.

The office boss walked to the auction.

Daily Exercises—Vowel #8 [ɒ]

(1) Practice saying this sound and the other speech sounds you have learned with the Standard American Diction CDs.

(2) Read aloud from a newspaper, magazine or book until you feel and hear yourself say the [ɒ] sound five times. Underline the words.

(3) Speak the following reading out loud, slowly at first, then faster. Right now accuracy is more important than speed. Underline the words with [ɒ].

> That thou hast her it is not all my grief,
> And yet it may be said I loved her dearly;
> That she hath thee is of my wailing chief,
> A loss in love that touches me more nearly.
> Loving offenders, thus I will excuse ye:
> Thou dost love her, because thou know'st I love her,
> And for my sake ev'n so doth she abuse me,
> Suff'ring my friend for my sake to approve her.
> If I lose thee, my loss is my love's gain,
> And losing her, my friend hath found that loss;
> Both find each other, and I lose both twain,
> And both for my sake lay on me this cross.
> > But here's the joy, my friend and I are one;
> > Sweet flatt'ry, then she loves but me alone.
> > SHAKESPEARE, Sonnet 42.

(4) Sing a short passage from one of your songs or arias that has the [ɒ] in it. Repeat it several times, concentrating on singing [ɒ] correctly.

(5) Repeat the entire section for [ɒ] three times today.

(6) And make sure you're saying [ɒ] correctly as you speak during the day.

Vowel #9 [ɔ] "or"

This sound is most often heard in Standard American Speech in the *o, r* spelling combination of words like *or* and *organ*. Words that used to be pronounced with the [ɔ] sound, like *law*, are now more often pronounced with Vowel #8, [ɒ].

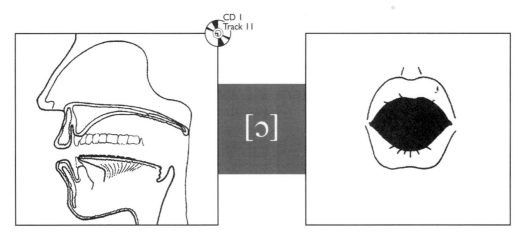

CD I
Track I I

[ɔ]

Hearing

Listen carefully to this sound on the Standard American Diction CDs.

Jaw

Open your jaw about two finger widths or to a comfortable position almost two finger widths wide. (For speech and much of your singing, your jaw floats open about one finger width. But sometimes you need to open your jaw wider, so it's best to practice with a wide jaw.)

Tongue

Feel the whole of your tongue relaxed down flat on the floor of your mouth, lightly touching your lower teeth.

Lips

Feel the corners of your lips move forward to round your lips in a circle, as if you were going to say *or*, without the *r*.

Your lips are more rounded for this sound than for Vowel #8, [ɒ].

After you say the sound release your lips.

Say the sound out loud. Sustain it for two counts.

[ɔ]... release lips [ɔ]... release lips

[ɔ]... release lips [ɔ]... release lips

Now sing the sound at a medium volume on a comfortable pitch.

[ɔ]... release lips [ɔ]... release lips

[ɔ]... release lips [ɔ]... release lips

Mirror Exercise

Now watch yourself in a mirror as you say [ɔ].

For a clear [ɔ] sound, your jaw should stay open with your teeth about a finger width to two finger widths apart. Your lips should round in a relaxed way, not tensed.

Say the sound out loud. Sustain it for two counts.

[ɔ]... [ɔ]...

[ɔ]... [ɔ]...

Now sing the sound at a medium volume on a comfortable pitch.

[ɔ]... [ɔ]...

[ɔ]... [ɔ]...

Possible Problems

Listen to yourself carefully as you say [ɔ]. If you hear the vowel change right at the end, with a little [ə] (the vowel sound in *uh*), [ɔᵊ], it means you're releasing your lips before you finish the sound. Keep the vowel pure, that is, a single sound. Notice that when your lips stay in place the vowel doesn't change.

Speak, then sing the sound at a medium volume.

[ɔ]... [ɔ]...

[ɔ]... [ɔ]...

Flexibility Exercise

Here is a flexibility exercise to practice the movement of your lips from [ɑ] to [ɔ]. Make sure your jaw remains one finger width to two finger widths open. Let your lips do the moving.

Say the sounds out loud.

[ɑ,ɔ,ɑ,ɔ,ɑ,ɔ]... [ɑ,ɔ,ɑ,ɔ,ɑ,ɔ]...

[ɑ,ɔ,ɑ,ɔ,ɑ,ɔ]... [ɑ,ɔ,ɑ,ɔ,ɑ,ɔ]...

Comparison Exercises

Here is a comparison exercise between Vowels #7, #8 and #9. Repeat them one after the other. Hear the difference between their sounds and feel the difference between their lip positions.

Speak, then sing, the sounds at a medium volume.

[ɑ,ɒ,ɔ]... [ɑ,ɒ,ɔ]...

[ɑ,ɒ,ɔ]... [ɑ,ɒ,ɔ]...

And repeat these words.

Speak, then sing, the words at a medium volume.

*c**a**r, c**a**ll, c**o**re... c**a**r, c**a**ll, c**o**re...*

*c**a**r, c**a**ll, c**o**re... c**a**r, c**a**ll, c**o**re...*

Now let's reverse the order.

Speak, then sing, the sounds at a medium volume.

[ɔ,ɒ,ɑ]... [ɔ,ɒ,ɑ]...

[ɔ,ɒ,ɑ]... [ɔ,ɒ,ɑ]...

Speak, then sing, the words at a medium volume.

*c**o**re, c**a**ll, c**a**r... c**o**re, c**a**ll, c**a**r...*

*c**o**re, c**a**ll, c**a**r... c**o**re, c**a**ll, c**a**r...*

Practice Words

Here are the practice words for [ɔ]. In Standard American Speech some of these words would be pronounced with Vowel #8, [ɒ], but for practice say them with Vowel #9, [ɔ].

Speak these practice words out loud, then sing them on a comfortable pitch.

<u>o</u>r... <u>o</u>r...	*w<u>a</u>rm... w<u>a</u>rm...*	*p<u>aw</u>... p<u>aw</u>...*
<u>o</u>rder... <u>o</u>rder...	*n<u>o</u>rth... n<u>o</u>rth...*	*l<u>aw</u>... l<u>aw</u>...*
<u>o</u>rgan... <u>o</u>rgan...	*c<u>au</u>ght... c<u>au</u>ght...*	*j<u>aw</u>... j<u>aw</u>...*
<u>au</u>thor... <u>au</u>thor...	*l<u>a</u>wyer... l<u>a</u>wyer...*	*th<u>aw</u>... th<u>aw</u>...*
<u>o</u>range... <u>o</u>range...	*n<u>o</u>rmal... n<u>o</u>rmal...*	*cl<u>aw</u>... cl<u>aw</u>...*

Practice Sentences

In Standard American Speech some of these words would be pronounced with Vowel #8, [ɒ], but for practice say them with Vowel #9, [ɔ].

Say these practice sentences slowly at first, then faster. In the beginning, accuracy is more important than speed.

Speak them out loud, then sing them on a comfortable pitch.

*Either the fl**oo**r **o**r the d**oo**r.*

*The **o**rchard is **o**range in **au**tumn.*

*The h**aw**k c**au**ght the b**a**ll with its cl**aw**.*

*The h**o**rse was t**a**ll and **aw**kward.*

Daily Exercises—Vowel #9 [ɔ]

(1) Practice saying this sound and the other speech sounds you have learned with the Standard American Diction CDs.

(2) Read aloud from a newspaper, magazine or book until you feel and hear yourself say the [ɔ] sound five times. Underline the words.

(3) Speak the following reading out loud, slowly at first, then faster. Right now accuracy is more important than speed. Underline the words with [ɔ].

Or I shall live your epitaph to make,
Or you survive when I in earth am rotten,
From hence your memory death cannot take,
Although in me each part will be forgotten.
Your name from hence immortal life shall have,
Though I, once gone, to all the world must die.
The earth can yield me but a common grave,
When you entombed in men's eyes shall lie.
Your monument shall be my gentle verse,
Which eyes not yet created shall o'er-read,
And tongues to be your being shall rehearse,
When all the breathers of this world are dead,
   You still shall live (such virtue hath my pen)
   Where breath most breathes, ev'n in the mouths of men.
               SHAKESPEARE, Sonnet 81.

(4) Sing a short passage from one of your songs or arias that has the [ɔ] in it. Repeat it several times, concentrating on singing [ɔ] correctly.

(5) Repeat the entire section for [ɔ] three times today.

(6) And make sure you're saying [ɔ] correctly as you speak during the day.

Vowel #10 $[o^U]$ "<u>oh</u>" (diphthong)

This sound is a combination of Vowel #10, [o], and Vowel #11, [ʊ].

In the International Phonetic Alphabet there is a pure, or single, vowel sound, [o], but in Standard American Speech this vowel is always said as a diphthong, $[o^U]$. (We follow *A Pronouncing Dictionary of American English* in including this sound in this position under vowels.)

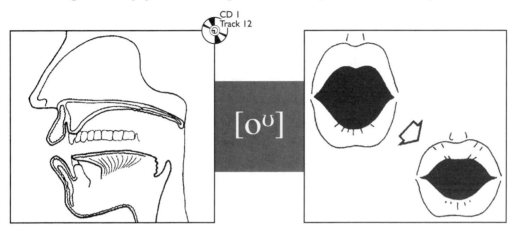

CD 1
Track 12

$[o^U]$

Hearing

Listen carefully to this sound on the Standard American Diction CDs. Hear it change as it is spoken.

Jaw

Open your jaw about two finger widths or to a comfortable position almost two finger widths wide. (For speech and much of your singing, your jaw floats open about one finger width. But sometimes you need to open your jaw wider, so it's best to practice with a wide jaw.)

Tongue

Feel your tongue relaxed on the floor of your mouth, lightly touching your lower teeth.

Lips

Feel the corners of your lips move forward to round your lips into a circle. This circle is a little smaller than for Vowel #9.

Feel your lips make the circle a little smaller as you slide to Vowel #11, [ʊ]. The sound does not slide all the way to Vowel #12, [u], but only to Vowel #11, [ʊ].

After you say the sound release your lips.

Say the sound out loud. Sustain it for two counts.

$[o^U]$... release $[o^U]$... release
$[o^U]$... release $[o^U]$... release

Now sing the sound at a medium volume on a comfortable pitch.

$[o^U]$... release $[o^U]$... release
$[o^U]$... release $[o^U]$... release

Mirror Exercise

Now watch yourself in a mirror as you say $[o^U]$.

For a clear $[o^U]$ sound, your jaw should stay open with your teeth about a finger width to two finger widths apart. Your lips should move in a relaxed way.

Say the sound out loud. Sustain it for two counts.

$[o^U]$... $[o^U]$...
$[o^U]$... $[o^U]$...

Now sing the sound at a medium volume on a comfortable pitch.

$[o^U]$... $[o^U]$...
$[o^U]$... $[o^U]$...

Notice that the first sound of the diphthong, [o], is more strongly stressed than the second sound, [ʊ]. The diphthong ends just as you say the second sound.

Possible Problems

Listen to yourself carefully as you say the sound. If it slides to [u] at the end, you're rounding your lips too much and holding on to the last part of the sound too long. Only slide to [ʊ].

Speak, then sing, the sound at a medium volume.

[oʊ]... [oʊ]...

[oʊ]... [oʊ]...

Listen to yourself carefully as you say [oʊ]. If you hear the vowel change right at the end, with a little [ə] (the vowel sound in *uh*), [oʊə], it means you're releasing your lips before you finish the sound. Keep the vowel pure, that is, a single sound. Notice that when your lips stay in place the vowel doesn't change.

Speak, then sing the sound at a medium volume.

[oʊ]... [oʊ]...

[oʊ]... [oʊ]...

Flexibility Exercise

Here is a flexibility exercise to practice the movement of your lips from [ɑ] to [oʊ]. Make sure your jaw remains one finger width to two finger widths open. Let your lips do the moving.

Speak, then sing, the sounds at a medium volume.

[ɑ,oʊ,ɑ,oʊ,ɑ,oʊ]... [ɑ,oʊ,ɑ,oʊ,ɑ,oʊ]...

[ɑ,oʊ,ɑ,oʊ,ɑ,oʊ]... [ɑ,oʊ,ɑ,oʊ,ɑ,oʊ]...

Practice Words

Speak these practice words out loud, then sing them on a comfortable pitch.

oak... oak...	*gold... gold..*	*no... no...*
old... old...	*tone... tone...*	*crow... crow...*
own... own...	*soap... soap...*	*tow... tow...*
oat... oat...	*boat... boat...*	*though... though...*
only... only...	*frozen... frozen...*	*hello... hello...*

Practice Sentences

Say these practice sentences slowly at first, then faster. In the beginning, accuracy is more important than speed.

Speak them out loud, then sing them on a comfortable pitch.

His old boat froze in the moat.

You won't find an oak tree growing in the ocean.

Joe opened the oval window and looked out over the snow.

The stove is cold moaned the soldier.

Daily Exercises—Vowel #10 [o^U]

(1) Practice saying this sound and the other speech sounds you have learned with the Standard American Diction CDs.

(2) Read aloud from a newspaper, magazine or book until you feel and hear yourself say the [o^U] sound five times. Underline the words.

(3) Speak the following reading out loud, slowly at first, then faster. Right now accuracy is more important than speed. Underline the words with [o^U].

> *O how much more doth beauty beauteous seem,*
> *By that sweet ornament which truth doth give.*
> *The rose looks fair, but fairer we it deem*
> *For that sweet odor which doth in it live.*
> *The canker blooms have full as deep a dye*
> *As the perfumed tincture of the roses,*
> *Hang on such thorns, and play as wantonly,*
> *When summer's breath their masked buds discloses;*
> *But for their virtue only is their show,*
> *They live unwooed, and unrespected fade,*
> *Die to themselves. Sweet roses do not so;*
> *Of their sweet deaths are sweetest odors made.*
> > *And so of you, beauteous and lovely youth,*
> > *When that shall vade, my verse distils your truth.*
> > > *SHAKESPEARE, Sonnet 54.*

(4) Sing a short passage from one of your songs or arias that has the [o^U] in it. Repeat it several times, concentrating on singing [o^U] correctly.

(5) Repeat the entire section for [o^U] three times today.

(6) And make sure you're saying [o^U] correctly as you speak during the day.

Vowel #11 [ʊ] "w<u>ou</u>ld"

CD 1
Track 13

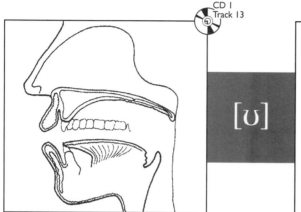

[ʊ]

Hearing

Listen carefully to this sound on the Standard American Diction CDs.

Jaw

Open your jaw about two finger widths or to a comfortable position almost two finger widths wide. (For speech and much of your singing, your jaw floats open about one finger width. But sometimes you need to open your jaw wider, so it's best to practice with a wide jaw.)

Tongue

Feel your tongue relaxed and touching the backs of your lower teeth.

Lips

Feel the corners of your lips move forward to round your lips into a circle. A little more rounded and further forward than for [o].

After you say the sound release your lips. Say the sound out loud. Sustain it for two counts.

[ʊ]... release lips [ʊ]... release lips

[ʊ]... release lips [ʊ]... release lips

Now sing the sound at a medium volume on a comfortable pitch.

[ʊ]... release lips [ʊ]... release lips

[ʊ]... release lips [ʊ]... release lips

Mirror Exercise

Now watch yourself in a mirror as you say [ʊ].

For a clear [ʊ] sound, your jaw should stay open with your teeth about a finger width to two finger widths apart. Your lips should round in a relaxed way, not tensed. Your tongue should not be raised high in your mouth.

Say the sound out loud. Sustain it for two counts.

[ʊ]... [ʊ]...

[ʊ]... [ʊ]...

Now sing the sound at a medium volume on a comfortable pitch.

[ʊ]... [ʊ]...

[ʊ]... [ʊ]...

Possible Problems

Listen to yourself carefully as you say [ʊ]. If you hear the vowel change right at the end, with a little [ə] (the vowel sound in *uh*), [ʊᵊ], it means you're releasing your lips before you finish the sound. Keep the vowel pure, that is, a single sound. Notice that when your lips stay in place the vowel doesn't change.

Speak, then sing the sound at a medium volume.

[ʊ]... [ʊ]...

[ʊ]... [ʊ]...

Flexibility Exercise

Here is a flexibility exercise to practice the movement of your lips from [ɑ] to [ʊ]. Make sure your jaw remains one finger width to two finger widths open. Let your lips do the moving.

Speak, then sing, the sounds at a medium volume.

[ɑ,ʊ,ɑ,ʊ,ɑ,ʊ]... [ɑ,ʊ,ɑ,ʊ,ɑ,ʊ]...

[ɑ,ʊ,ɑ,ʊ,ɑ,ʊ]... [ɑ,ʊ,ɑ,ʊ,ɑ,ʊ]...

Practice Words

Speak these practice words out loud, then sing them on a comfortable pitch.

book... book...	*put... put...*
could... could...	*good... good...*
wood... wood...	*crook... crook...*
pull... pull...	*wolf... wolf...*
look... look...	*sugar... sugar...*

Practice Sentences

Say these practice sentences slowly at first, then faster. In the beginning, accuracy is more important than speed.

Speak them out loud, then sing them on a comfortable pitch.

He took a good look at the book.

Would you put the bush by the brook.

The cook put too much sugar in the cookies.

The wolf stood under the bushes in the woods.

Daily Exercises—Vowel #11 [ʊ]

(1) Practice saying this sound and the other speech sounds you have learned with the Standard American Diction CDs.

(2) Read aloud from a newspaper, magazine or book until you feel and hear yourself say the [ʊ] sound five times. Underline the words.

(3) Speak the following reading out loud, slowly at first, then faster. Right now accuracy is more important than speed. Underline the words with [ʊ].

> *Betwixt mine eye and heart a league is took,*
> *And each doth good turns now unto the other.*
> *When that mine eye is famished for a look,*
> *Or heart in love with sighs himself doth smother,*
> *With my love's picture then my eye doth feast,*
> *And to the painted banquet bids my heart.*
> *Another time mine eye is my heart's guest,*
> *And in his thoughts of love doth share a part.*
> *So either by thy picture or my love,*
> *Thyself away are present still with me;*
> *For thou no farther than my thoughts canst move,*
> *And I am still with them, and they with thee;*
> > *Or, if they sleep, thy picture in my sight*
> > *Awakes my heart to heart's and eye's delight.*
> > SHAKESPEARE, *Sonnet 47.*

(4) Sing a short passage from one of your songs or arias that has the [ʊ] in it. Repeat it several times, concentrating on singing [ʊ] correctly.

(5) Repeat the entire section for [ʊ] three times today.

(6) And make sure you're saying [ʊ] correctly as you speak during the day.

Vowel #12 [u] "oops"

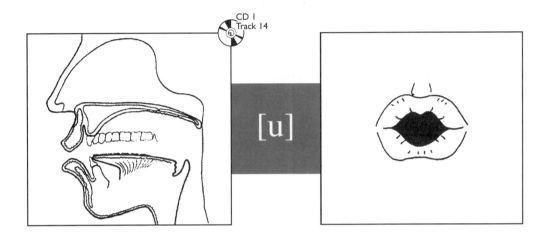

CD 1
Track 14

[u]

Hearing

Listen carefully to this sound on the Standard American Diction CDs.

Jaw

Open your jaw about two finger widths or to a comfortable position almost two finger widths wide. (For speech and much of your singing, your jaw floats open about one finger width. But sometimes you need to open your jaw wider, so it's best to practice with a wide jaw.)

Tongue

Feel your tongue relaxed and touching the backs of your lower teeth. The back of your tongue should not be high in your mouth.

Lips

Feel the corners of your lips move forward to round your lips into a circle that is a little smaller than for [ʊ].

After you say the sound release your lips. Say the sound out loud. Sustain it for two counts.

[u]... release lips [u]... release lips
[u]... release lips [u]... release lips

Now sing the sound at a medium volume on a comfortable pitch.

[u]... release lips [u]... release lips
[u]... release lips [u]... release lips

Mirror Exercise

Now watch yourself in a mirror as you say [u].

For a clear [u] sound, your jaw should stay open with your teeth about a finger width to two finger widths apart. Your lips should round in a relaxed way, not tensed.

Say the sound out loud. Sustain it for two counts.
[u]... [u]...
[u]... [u]...

Now sing the sound at a medium volume on a comfortable pitch.
[u]... [u]...
[u]... [u]...

Possible Problems

Listen to yourself carefully as you say [u]. If you hear the vowel change right at the end, with a little [ə] (the vowel sound in *uh*), [uᵊ], it means you're releasing your lips before you finish the sound. Keep the vowel pure, that is, a single sound. Notice that when your lips stay in place the vowel doesn't change.

Speak, then sing the sound at a medium volume.

[u]... [u]...

[u]... [u]...

Flexibility Exercise

Here is a flexibility exercise to practice the movement of your lips from [ɑ] to [u]. Make sure your jaw remains one finger width to two finger widths open. Let your lips do the moving.

Speak, then sing, the sounds at a medium volume.

[ɑ,u,ɑ,u,ɑ,u]... [ɑ,u,ɑ,u,ɑ,u]...

[ɑ,u,ɑ,u,ɑ,u]... [ɑ,u,ɑ,u,ɑ,u]...

Practice Words

Speak these practice words out loud, then sing them on a comfortable pitch.

oops... oops...	m*oon*... m*oon*...	*to... to...*
ooze... ooze...	c*ool*... c*ool*...	wh*o*... wh*o*...
oodles... oodles...	s*oup*... s*oup*...	bl*ue*... bl*ue*...
	tooth... *tooth*...	m*o*ve... m*o*ve...
	true... *true*...	bamb*oo*... bamb*oo*...

Practice Sentences

Say these practice sentences slowly at first, then faster. In the beginning, accuracy is more important than speed.

Speak them out loud, then sing them on a comfortable pitch.

*The s*oup* will c*ool* s*oon*.*

*Wh*o* has a bl*ue* bamb*oo* tatt*oo*.*

*The f*ool* thr*ew* his sh*oe* at the m*oon*.*

*The t*oo*thless buff*oo*n used a sp*oo*n to sh*oo*t p*oo*l.*

Daily Exercises—Vowel #12 [u]

(1) Practice saying this sound and the other speech sounds you have learned with the Standard American Diction CDs.

(2) Read aloud from a newspaper, magazine or book until you feel and hear yourself say the [u] sound five times. Underline the words.

(3) Speak the following reading out loud, slowly at first, then faster. Right now accuracy is more important than speed. Underline the words with [u].

> *Look in thy glass and tell the face thou viewest,*
> *Now is the time that face should form another,*
> *Whose fresh repair if now thou not renewest,*
> *Thou dost beguile the world, unbless some mother.*
> *For where is she so fair whose uneared womb*
> *Disdains the tillage of thy husbandry?*
> *Or who is he so fond will be the tomb*
> *Of his self-love to stop posterity?*
> *Thou art thy mother's glass, and she in thee*
> *Calls back the lovely April of her prime;*
> *So thou through windows of thine age shalt see,*
> *Despite of wrinkles, this thy golden time.*
> > *But if thou live rememb'red not to be,*
> > *Die single and thine image dies with thee.*
> > > *SHAKESPEARE, Sonnet 3.*

(4) Sing a short passage from one of your songs or arias that has the [u] in it. Repeat it several times, concentrating on singing [u] correctly.

(5) Repeat the entire section for [u] three times today.

(6) And make sure you're saying [u] correctly as you speak during the day.

Congratulations! You've learned to recognize and say all the **Lip Vowels** of **Standard American Speech**.

Review of Vowels #7–#12

Now let's do a quick review of Vowels #7 through #12. These vowels are made primarily by movements and positions of your lips.

Hear the sounds and feel your lips rounding slightly more for each sound.

Speak, then sing, the sounds at a medium volume.

[ɑ,ɒ,ɔ,oᵁ,ʊ,u]

[ɑ,ɒ,ɔ,oᵁ,ʊ,u]

Now let's go the other way, from #12 to #7.

Hear the sounds and feel your lips opening slightly for each sound.

Speak, then sing, the sounds at a medium volume.

[u,ʊ,oᵁ,ɔ,ɒ,ɑ]

[u,ʊ,oᵁ,ɔ,ɒ,ɑ]

Notice how much more clearly and easily you can say each vowel.

Exercise
(1) Record yourself saying the Lip Vowels and their example words on p. 52.
(2) Compare this recording with your first recording.
(3) Notice the improvement in your diction.

Notes:

vowel #x eɪ "ai"
vowel #y ɔ "uh"
consonant #8 ʃ "sh"
consonant #22 l "l"

7 Other Vowels

Vowels #13 through #15 are placed at the end of the vowel section partly because they don't fit conveniently into the tongue/lips vowel sequence and partly to conform somewhat to the sequence Kenyon and Knott established in *A Pronouncing Dictionary of American English*. (Note, however, that we do have a different sequence for Vowels #13, [ʌ], #14, [ɝ], and #15, [ɜ]. In Kenyon and Knott [ʌ] is the last vowel listed.

Vowel #13   [ʌ] "**u**p" or [ə] "**a**bout"

[ʌ] is the symbol used to represent this sound in a stressed syllable.

[ə] is the symbol used to represent this sound in a nonstressed syllable.

However, your articulators are in the same positions and the sound is the same for both the stressed and the nonstressed symbol.

We are showing you both phonetic symbols for this vowel, not because they sound different—they sound exactly alike—but because dic-tionaries and books on phonetics use the stressed and nonstressed symbols and you should know the difference.

You don't need to be concerned with whether you are stressing or not stressing the sound. Just practice the correct positions of the articulators. [ʌ] will automatically be stressed as you say a stressed syllable. (We explain stressed and nonstressed syllables in the chapter on *Pronunciation*.)

CD 1
Track 15

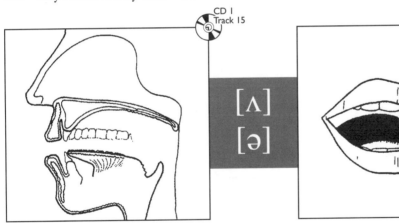

[ʌ]
[ə]

Hearing
Listen carefully to this sound on the Standard American Diction CDs.

Jaw
Open your jaw about two finger widths or to a comfortable position almost two finger widths wide. (For speech and much of your singing, your jaw floats open about one finger width. But sometimes you need to open your jaw wider, so it's best to practice with a wide jaw.)

Lips
Leave your lips relaxed. Do not pull them back or round them.

Tongue
Feel the sides of your tongue lightly touching the backs of your lower teeth all the way around as you say the sound.

Feel the whole of your tongue relaxed down flat on the floor of your mouth.

Say the sound out loud. Sustain it for two counts.

[ʌ]... [ʌ]...
[ʌ]... [ʌ]...

Now sing the sound at a medium volume, on a comfortable pitch.

[ʌ]... [ʌ]...
[ʌ]... [ʌ]...

Mirror Exercise

Now watch yourself in a mirror as you say [ʌ].

For a clear [ʌ] sound, your jaw should stay open with your teeth about a finger width to two finger widths apart. Your lips should be relaxed, not pulled back, or rounded.

Say the sound out loud.

[ʌ]... [ʌ]...
[ʌ]... [ʌ]...

Now sing the sound at a medium volume, on a comfortable pitch.

[ʌ]... [ʌ]...
[ʌ]... [ʌ]...

Comparison Exercise

It is difficult to see or feel any difference between the placement of the articulators for this vowel and for Vowel #7, [ɑ]. (Actually, your tongue is a little further forward for [ʌ] than for [ɑ].)

But you can easily hear the difference in the sound. (The sound difference is demonstrated on the Standard American Diction CDs.)

Listen carefully to the vowel sounds in the following words, as you say them.

Say the words out loud.

up... are... up... are

Here's a comparison exercise between this vowel and Vowel #7, [ɑ]. Listen carefully to yourself as you say the sounds.

Speak, then sing, the sounds at a medium volume.

[ɑ,ʌ,ɑ,ʌ,ɑ,ʌ]... [ɑ,ʌ,ɑ,ʌ,ɑ,ʌ]...
[ɑ,ʌ,ɑ,ʌ,ɑ,ʌ]... [ɑ,ʌ,ɑ,ʌ,ɑ,ʌ]...

Practice Words

Say these practice words out loud, then sing them on a comfortable pitch.

up... up...	*fun... fun...*
us... us...	*some... some...*
uncle... uncle...	*luck... luck...*
oven... oven...	*jump... jump...*
other... other...	*come... come...*
soda... soda...	*above... above...*
arena... arena...	*undone... undone...*
sofa... sofa...	*custom... custom...*
tuba... tuba...	*affront... affront...*
vanilla... vanilla...	*fulcrum... fulcrum...*

Practice Sentences

Say these practice sentences slowly at first, then faster. In the beginning, accuracy is more important than speed.

Speak them out loud, then sing them on a comfortable pitch.

A month of Mondays and Sundays.

Sometimes the pup runs after the duck.

The monkey's uncle sat under the umbrella.

Hungry bear cubs love honey for lunch.

Daily Exercises—Vowel #13 [ʌ]

(1) Practice saying this sound and the other speech sounds you have learned with the Standard American Diction CDs.

(2) Read aloud from a newspaper, magazine or book until you feel and hear yourself say the [ʌ] sound five times. Underline the words.

(3) Speak the following reading out loud, slowly at first, then faster. Right now accuracy is more important than speed. Underline the words with [ʌ].

> *Sweet love, renew thy force, be it not said*
> *Thy edge should blunter be than appetite,*
> *Which but today by feeding is allayed,*
> *Tomorrow sharp'ned in his former might.*
> *So love be thou, although today thou fill*
> *Thy hungry eyes, ev'n till they wink with fullness,*
> *Tomorrow see again, and do not kill*
> *The spirit of love with a perpetual dullness.*
> *Let this sad int'rim like the ocean be*
> *Which parts the shore, where two contracted new*
> *Come daily to the banks, that when they see*
> *Return of love, more blest may be the view;*
> > *As call it winter, which being full of care,*
> > *Makes summer's welcome, thrice more wished, more rare.*
> > > *SHAKESPEARE, Sonnet 56.*

(4) Sing a short passage from one of your songs or arias that has the [ʌ] in it. Repeat it several times, concentrating on singing [ʌ] correctly.

(5) Repeat the entire section for [ʌ] three times today.

(6) And make sure you're saying [ʌ] correctly as you speak during the day.

Vowel #14   [ɝ] "f<u>ur</u>" or [ɚ] "lev<u>er</u>"

[ɝ] is the symbol for this sound in a stressed syllable.

[ɚ] is the symbol for this sound in a non-stressed syllable.

The articulators are in the same positions for both the stressed and the nonstressed symbol and the sound is exactly the same.

You don't need to be concerned with whether you are stressing or not stressing the sound. [ɝ] will automatically be stressed as you say a stressed syllable. (We explain stressed and nonstressed syllables in the chapter on *Pronunciation*.)

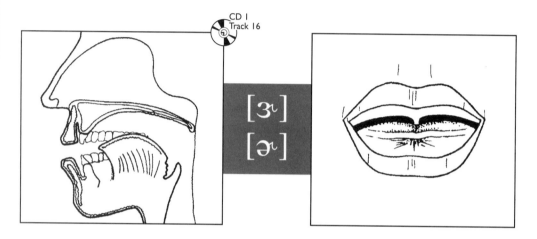

CD 1
Track 16

[ɝ]
[ɚ]

Hearing
Listen carefully to this sound on the Standard American Diction CDs.

Jaw
Open your mouth about two fingers. (For speech and much of your singing, your jaw floats open about one width. But sometimes you need to open your jaw wider, so it's best to practice with a wide jaw.)

Lips
Leave your lips relaxed. Do not pull them back or round them.

Tongue
Feel the sides of your tongue rise up to lightly touch your upper molars. This feels approximately like the position for [ə], but slightly farther back.

Feel the blade of your tongue lift up to about midway between the roof and the floor of your mouth and move back slightly.

Keep your tongue relaxed.

This is the position for [ɝ/ɚ].

(When you actually say the sound the blade of your tongue moves into position at the same time the sides of your tongue lift up, so that the movement is one easy motion.)

Release your tongue back down to the floor of your mouth after you say the sound.

(You never sustain [ɝ] in speech or singing (except in some pop styles), but sustaining [ɝ] in practice helps you to learn the sound.)

Say the sound out loud. Sustain it for two counts.

[ɝ]... release [ɝ]... release

[ɝ]... release [ɝ]... release

Now sing the sound at a medium volume, on a comfortable pitch.

[ɝ]... release [ɝ]... release

[ɝ]... release [ɝ]... release

Mirror Exercise

Now watch yourself in a mirror as you say [ɝ].

For a clear [ɝ] sound, your jaw should stay open with your teeth approximately a finger width to two finger widths apart. Only your jaw should move to make the sound. Touch your jaw to help it stay open.

If it looks like you are pointing the tip of your tongue to the roof of your mouth or curling it backwards, you are pulling your tongue too far back and tensing it too much. Say the sound with your tongue more relaxed and the blade more toward the front of your mouth.

Your lips may round a little bit for the [ɝ] sound, but for clear speech they should not round too much.

Practice saying [ɝ] without rounding your lips.

> Say the sound out loud.
>
> [ɝ]... [ɝ]...
>
> [ɝ]... [ɝ]...
>
> Now sing the sound at a medium volume, on a comfortable pitch.
>
> [ɝ]... [ɝ]...
>
> [ɝ]... [ɝ]...

Possible Problems

Listen to yourself carefully as you say [ɝ]. If you hear the vowel change right at the end, with a little [ə] (the vowel sound in *uh*), [ɝə], it means you're releasing your tongue before you finish the sound. Keep the vowel pure, that is, a single sound. Notice that when your tongue stays in place the vowel doesn't change.

Speak, then sing the sound at a medium volume.

> [ɝ]... [ɝ]...
>
> [ɝ]... [ɝ]...

You may have three problems in saying this sound:

> (1) Lifting the blade of your tongue too high and too far to the back
>
> (2) Tensing your tongue too much.
>
> (3) Rounding your lips too much.

Two Good Exercises to Find the [ɝ] Position

> To teach your tongue the correct position for [ɝ], practice sliding from [ɛ] to [ɝ].
>
> Feel your tongue relaxed in the [ɛ] position.
>
> Move your tongue slightly back and lift the blade of your tongue up off your lower front teeth.
>
> Feel the sides of your tongue slide lightly along your upper molars as you move it slightly back.
>
> See the flat blade of your tongue pointing toward the front and midway between the roof and the floor of your mouth.

Say the sounds out loud.

[ɛ,ɝ,ɛ,ɝ]... [ɛ,ɝ,ɛ,ɝ]...

[ɛ,ɝ,ɛ,ɝ]... [ɛ,ɝ,ɛ,ɝ]...

Here is another good way of learning the correct position of your tongue for [ɝ]

Say [ʒ] (see p. 143), then open your jaw without changing the position of your tongue.

Make sure you open your jaw without tensing your tongue.

(This method is described by Daniel Jones, in *The Pronunciation of English*, p. 109.)

Say the sounds out loud.

[ʒ,ɝ,ʒ,ɝ,ʒ]... [ʒ,ɝ,ʒ,ɝ,ʒ]...

[ʒ,ɝ,ʒ,ɝ,ʒ]... [ʒ,ɝ,ʒ,ɝ,ʒ]...

Flexibility Exercise

Here is a flexibility exercise to practice the movement of your tongue from [ɑ] to [ɝ].

Make sure your jaw remains relaxed one finger width to two finger widths open.

Let your tongue do the moving.

Speak, then sing, the sounds at a medium volume, on a comfortable pitch.

[ɑ,ɝ,ɑ,ɝ,ɑ,ɝ]... [ɑ,ɝ,ɑ,ɝ,ɑ,ɝ]...

[ɑ,ɝ,ɑ,ɝ,ɑ,ɝ]... [ɑ,ɝ,ɑ,ɝ,ɑ,ɝ]...

Practice Words

Say the practice words out loud, then sing them on a comfortable pitch.

earn... earn...	*curb... curb...*
urge... urge...	*turn... turn...*
earth... earth...	*heard... heard...*
early... early...	*dirt... dirt...*
urchin... urchin...	*person... person...*
were... were...	*further... further...*
sir... sir...	*pervert... pervert...*
burr... burr...	*murder... murder...*
under... under...	*learner... learner...*
weather... weather...	*server... server...*

Practice Sentences

Say the practice sentences slowly at first, then faster. In the beginning, accuracy is more important than speed.

Speak them out loud, then sing them on a comfortable pitch.

The early bird catches the worm.

The girl heard the word and turned.

The colonel tersely ordered the shirking soldier to work.

Herb earnestly urged the actor to rehearse.

Daily Exercises—Vowel #14 [ɝ]

(1) Practice saying this sound and the other speech sounds you have learned with the Standard American Diction CDs.

(2) Read aloud from a newspaper, magazine or book until you feel and hear yourself say the [ɝ] sound five times. Underline the words.

(3) Speak the following reading out loud, slowly at first, then faster. Right now accuracy is more important than speed. Underline the words with [ɝ].

> *The other two, slight air and purging fire,*
> *Are both with thee, wherever I abide;*
> *The first my thought, the other my desire,*
> *These present-absent with swift motion slide.*
> *For when these quicker elements are gone*
> *In tender embassy of love to thee,*
> *My life, being made of four, with two alone*
> *Sinks down to death, oppressed with melancholy;*
> *Until life's composition be recured*
> *By those swift messengers returned from thee,*
> *Who ev'n but now come back again, assured*
> *Of thy fair health, recounting it to me.*
> > *This told, I joy, but then no longer glad,*
> > *I send them back again, and straight grow sad.*
> > > *SHAKESPEARE, Sonnet 45.*

(4) Sing a short passage from one of your songs or arias that has the [ɝ] in it. Repeat it several times, concentrating on singing [ɝ] correctly.

(5) Repeat the entire section for [ɝ] three times today.

(6) And make sure you're saying [ɝ] correctly as you speak during the day.

The Spelling Letter r:—Vowel or Consonant?

In spelling, the letter **r** is always a classified as a consonant.

But, in speech, the sound of *r* is sometimes classified as consonant and sometimes as a vowel.

In speech, the three speech sounds [ɝ], [ɚ] and [r] are all pronounced alike. The different phonetic symbols identify the sound as belonging to a particular category (vowel or consonant) or function (stressed or nonstressed).

[r] is classified as a consonant when a vowel is pronounced in the syllable along with the [r].

For example, in the word *hard* there are four speech sounds, [h,ɑ,r,d]. Both the vowel, [ɑ], and the consonant, [r], are sounded and [r] functions as a consonant.

[ɝ] and [ɚ] are classified as vowels when the spelling letter **r** combines with the vowel in the syllable to form a single spoken vowel sound.

For example, in the word *herd* there are only three speech sounds, [h,ɝ,d]. The spelling letters, **e**, and **r** combine to form a single sound, [ɝ].

It is helpful to keep these distinctions in mind when you are trying to figure out what sounds you are actually saying in a word.

Singing r

None of the *r* sounds are sustained in singing with Standard American Diction.

If the music calls for a sustained note on [ɝ] or [ɚ], as in *further*, change the vowel to Vowel #15, [ɜ], and follow it with the spoken consonant *r*, as you would any other vowel.

Or, if you are dropping the r's, use [ɜ] in the stressed syllable and [ə] in the nonstressed syllable. (See p. 221, *Dropping the r* and Kenyon & Knott, *A Pronouncing Dictionary of American English*, p. xvii.)

Vowel #15 [ɜ] "<u>ea</u>rly"

In Standard American Speech [ɜ] is sometimes heard as a separate vowel before the [r] sound, where it can help soften the "hard American *r*."

When [ɜ˞] or [ə˞] falls on a sustained note, substitute this sound and follow it with the [r], as you would with any other vowel.

The [ɜ] sound is frequently heard in Eastern and Southern dialects that drop the *r*'s. (See p. 221, *Dropping the r* and Kenyon & Knott, *A Pronouncing Dictionary of American English*, p. xvii.)

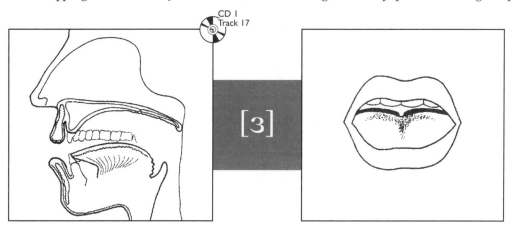

CD 1
Track 17

[ɜ]

Hearing

Listen carefully to this sound on the Standard American Diction CDs.

Jaw

Open your mouth about two finger widths or to a comfortable position almost two finger widths wide. (For speech and much of your singing, your jaw floats open about one finger width. But sometimes you need to open your jaw wider, so it's best to practice with a wide jaw.)

Tongue

Feel the middle of your tongue relaxed on the floor of your mouth, touching the backs of your lower teeth on the sides.

Leave the blade of your tongue touching the backs of your front lower teeth.

Feel your tongue slightly higher than it is for [ɑ].

Lips

Feel the corners of your lips move slightly forward.

Keep your lips in place as you say the sound.

Release your lips and tongue back to their normal positions after you say the sound.

Say the sound out loud. Sustain it for two counts.

[ɜ]... release lips [ɜ]... release lips
[ɜ]... release lips [ɜ]... release lips

Now sing the sound at a medium volume, on a comfortable pitch.

[ɜ]... release lips [ɜ]... release lips
[ɜ]... release lips [ɜ]... release lips

Mirror Exercise

Now watch yourself in a mirror as you say [ɜ].

For a clear [ɜ] sound, your jaw should stay open with your teeth approximately a finger width to two finger widths apart. Touch your jaw to help it stay open.

Your lips will round a little bit for the [ɜ] sound.

Say the sound with your tongue relaxed and the blade touching the backs of your lower front teeth.

Say the sound out loud.

[ɜ]... release lips [ɜ]... release lips

[ɜ]... release lips [ɜ]... release lips

Now sing the sound at a medium volume, on a comfortable pitch.

[ɜ]... release lips [ɜ]… release lips

[ɜ]... release lips [ɜ]... release lips

Possible Problems

Listen to yourself carefully as you say [ɜ]. If you hear the vowel change right at the end, with a little [ə] (the vowel sound in *uh*), [ɜə], it means you're releasing your lips before you finish the sound. Keep the vowel pure, that is, a single sound. Notice that when your lips stay in place the vowel doesn't change.

Speak, then sing the sound at a medium volume.

[ɜ]... [ɜ]... [ɜ]... [ɜ]...

Flexibility Exercise

Here is a flexibility exercise to practice the movement of your tongue and lips from [ɑ] to [ɜ]. Make sure your jaw remains one finger width to two finger widths open. Let your tongue and lips do the moving.

Speak, then sing, the sounds at a medium volume.

[ɑ,ɜ,ɑ,ɜ,ɑ,ɜ]... [ɑ,ɜ,ɑ,ɜ,ɑ,ɜ]....

[ɑ,ɜ,ɑ,ɜ,ɑ,ɜ]... [ɑ,ɜ,ɑ,ɜ,ɑ,ɜ]....

Practice Words

These words are not always said with [ɜ] before the [r], but they are good for practice.

Say them out loud, then sing them on a comfortable pitch.

*ea*rly... *ea*rly...	*wo*rry... *wo*rry...
*ea*rn... *ea*rn...	*wo*rd... *wo*rd...
*wo*rld... *wo*rld...	*wo*rst... *wo*rst...
*tu*rn... *tu*rn...	*bu*rn... *bu*rn...
*fu*rry... *fu*rry...	*fe*rn... *fe*rn...
*me*rge... *me*rge...	*colo*nel... *colo*nel...

Practice Sentences

Say the practice sentences slowly at first, then faster. In the beginning, accuracy is more important than speed.

Speak them out loud, then sing them on a comfortable pitch.

The fu̱rry bunny didn't hu̱rry or wo̱rry.

The colo̱nel preferred a flu̱rry of wo̱rds.

Daily Exercises—Vowel #15 [ɜ]

(1) Practice saying this sound and the other speech sounds you have learned with the Standard American Diction CDs.

(2) Read aloud from a newspaper, magazine or book until you feel and hear yourself say the [ɜ] sound five times. Underline the words.

(3) Sing a short passage from one of your songs or arias that has the [ɜ] in it. Repeat it several times, concentrating on saying [ɜ] correctly.

(4) Repeat the entire section for [ɜ] three times today.

(5) And make sure you're saying [ɜ] correctly as you speak during the day.

Congratulations! You've learned to recognize and say all the **Vowel** sounds of **Standard American Speech**.

Review of Vowels #1–#15

Now let's do a quick review of vowels #1 through #15.

Speak, then sing, the sounds at a medium volume.

[i] [ɪ] [eɪ] [ɛ] [æ] [a] [ɑ]
[ɒ] [ɔ] [oᵁ] [ʊ] [u]
[ʌ] [ɝ] [ɜ]

Again.

[i] [ɪ] [eɪ] [ɛ] [æ] [a] [ɑ]
[ɒ] [ɔ] [oᵁ] [ʊ] [u]
[ʌ] [ɝ] [ɜ]

Now let's go the other way, from #15 to #1.

[ɜ] [ɝ] [ʌ]
[u] [ʊ] [oᵁ] [ɔ] [ɒ]
[ɑ] [a] [æ] [ɛ] [eɪ] [ɪ] [i]

Again.

[ɜ] [ɝ] [ʌ]
[u] [ʊ] [oᵁ] [ɔ] [ɒ]
[ɑ] [a] [æ] [ɛ] [eɪ] [ɪ] [i]

Notice how much more clearly and easily you can say each vowel.

Exercise
(1) Record yourself saying Vowels #1–#15, with their example words on p. 52.
(2) Compare this recording with your first recording.
(3) Notice the improvement in your diction.

Notes:

vowel #3 eɪ "ai"

vowel #7 ɔ "ah"

consonant #8 ʃ "sh"

consonant #21 l "l"

8 Diphthongs

A diphthong is a single speech sound in which your articulators start in the position for one sound and immediately slide to another sound.

A diphthong is often described as a combination of two vowel sounds. But that is not exactly true. You can't just connect the two sounds. The two sounds used to define the diphthong are the beginning and ending points, but the diphthong is actually the sound made as you slide from the first sound to the second sound.

Except for Diphthong #4, the beginning and ending sounds are vowels, but Diphthong #4 begins with the Consonant glide [j] (see p. 195).

Speaking a Diphthong

When you say a diphthong in normal speech, as soon as you begin the first sound, you immediately start to slide toward the second sound, and as soon as you reach the second sound, you end the diphthong.

Singing a Diphthong

When you sing a diphthong on a note that is sustained, one of the vowel sounds, either the beginning or ending vowel, is sustained as a pure vowel for as long as the note requires, then you quickly slide to the second sound.

(We tell you whether the beginning or ending vowel sound is sustained in each diphthong description.)

Diphthong #1 [aɪ] "ɪ"

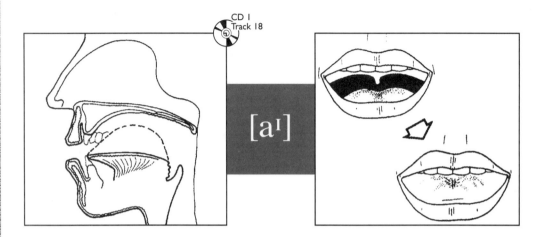

CD 1
Track 18

Beginning/Ending
Slide from Vowel #6, [a], to Vowel #2, [ɪ].

Hearing
Listen carefully to this sound on the Standard American Diction CDs.

Jaw
Open your jaw about two finger widths or to a comfortable position almost two finger widths wide. (For speech and much of your singing, your jaw floats open about one finger width. But sometimes you need to open your jaw wider, so it's best to practice with a wide jaw.)

Lips
Leave your lips relaxed. Do not pull them back or round them.

Tongue
Feel the blade of your tongue lightly touching the backs of your lower teeth and keep it there as you say the sound.

Feel the middle of your tongue rising up slightly to the [a] position, before you begin the sound.

Begin the sound and simultaneously feel your tongue gliding up to the [ɪ] position.

Your tongue should move in a relaxed way, with no pressure against the teeth.

After you say the sound relax your tongue back down to the floor of your mouth.

Say the sound out loud.

[aɪ]... tongue down [aɪ]... tongue down
[aɪ]... tongue down [aɪ]... tongue down

Now sing the sound at a medium volume, on a comfortable pitch.

[aɪ]... tongue down [aɪ]... tongue down
[aɪ]... tongue down [aɪ]... tongue down

Sustaining the Sound
When you sustain [aɪ], the first sound of the diphthong, [a], is pronounced fully and is more strongly stressed than the second sound, [ɪ]. The diphthong ends just as you say [ɪ]. Say the sound out loud. Sustain it for two counts. (Hold the [a] for two counts and glide quickly to [ɪ] at the end.)

[aɪ]... [aɪ]...
[aɪ]... [aɪ]...

Now sing the sound at a medium volume, on a comfortable pitch. Sustain it for two counts. (Hold the [a] for two counts and glide quickly to [ɪ] at the end.)

[aɪ]... [aɪ]...

[aɪ]... [aɪ]...

Mirror Exercise

Now watch yourself in a mirror. Your jaw should stay open with your teeth approximately a finger width to two finger widths apart.

Touch your jaw to help it stay open.

Say the sound out loud. Sustain it for two counts. (Hold the [a] for two counts and glide quickly to [ɪ] at the end.)

[aɪ]... [aɪ]...

[aɪ]... [aɪ]...

Now sing the sound at a medium volume, on a comfortable pitch. Sustain it for two counts. (Hold the [a] for two counts and glide quickly to [ɪ] at the end.)

[aɪ]... [aɪ]...

[aɪ]... [aɪ]...

Possible Problems

The problem most people have with this sound is closing their jaw as they glide toward the [ɪ]. This gives the [aɪ] a tight, closed sound and moves the final [ɪ] to [i].

Practice the mirror exercise to teach your tongue to move instead of your jaw.

Listen to yourself carefully as you say [aɪ]. If you go to [i] at the end, like this, [aɪ], you are gliding your tongue too high (which is usually caused by closing your jaw). Go only to [ɪ], like this, [aɪ].

Say the sound out loud. Sustain it for two counts.

[aɪ]... [aɪ]...

[aɪ]... [aɪ]...

Practice Words

Say the practice words out loud, then sing them on a comfortable pitch.

_I... I..._	_mine... mine..._	_pie... pie..._
aisle... aisle...	_nice... nice..._	_sigh... sigh..._
ice... ice...	_light... light..._	_high... high..._
ivy... ivy...	_ride... ride..._	_guy... guy..._
idea... idea...	_final... final..._	_ally... ally..._

Practice Sentences

Say the practice sentences slowly at first, then faster. In the beginning, accuracy is more important than speed.

Say them at a medium volume, then sing them on a comfortable pitch.

I like to pry smiled the spy.

Irene will drive the final mile.

Ice cream and pie widen your thigh.

Our guide will light the fire for night.

Daily Exercises—Diphthong #1 [aᴵ]

(1) Practice saying this sound and the other phonetic sounds you have learned with the Standard American Diction CDs.

(2) Read aloud from a newspaper, magazine or book until you feel and hear yourself say the [aᴵ] sound five times. Underline the words.

(3) Speak the following reading out loud, slowly at first, then faster. Right now accuracy is more important than speed. Underline the words with [aᴵ].

> Is it thy will thy image should keep open
> My heavy eyelids to the weary night?
> Dost thou desire my slumbers should be broken,
> While shadows like to thee do mock my sight?
> Is it thy spirit that thou send'st from thee
> So far from home into my deeds to pry,
> To find out shames and idle hours in me,
> The scope and tenor of thy jealousy?
> O no, thy love, though much, is not so great.
> It is my love that keeps mine eye awake,
> Mine own true love that doth my rest defeat,
> To play the watchman ever for thy sake.
>   For thee watch I, whilst thou dost wake elsewhere,
>   From me far off, with others all too near.
>   SHAKESPEARE, Sonnet 61

(4) Sing a short passage from one of your songs or arias that has the [aᴵ] in it. Repeat it several times, concentrating on singing [aᴵ] correctly.

(5) Repeat the entire section for [aᴵ] three times today.

(6) And make sure you're saying [aᴵ] correctly as you speak during the day.

Diphthong #2   [aᵁ]   "ouch"

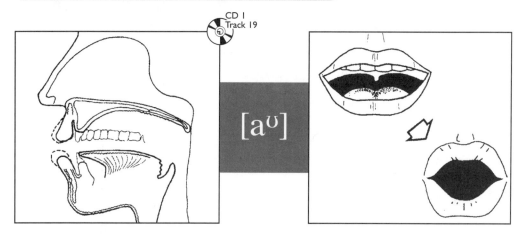

CD 1
Track 19

Beginning/Ending

Slide from Vowel #6, [a], to Vowel #11, [ᵁ].

Hearing

Listen carefully to this sound on the Standard American Diction CDs.

Jaw

Open your jaw about two finger widths or to a comfortable position almost two finger widths wide. (For speech and much of your singing, your jaw floats open about one finger width. But sometimes you need to open your jaw wider, so it's best to practice with a wide jaw.)

Tongue

Feel the blade of your tongue lightly touching the backs of your lower teeth and keep it there as you say the sound.

Feel the middle of your tongue raising up slightly to the [a] position before you begin the sound.

Lips

Begin the sound and immediately feel the corners of your lips moving forward to round your lips to the position of [u].

After you say the sound relax your lips and your tongue back to their normal positions. Say the sound out loud.

[aᵁ]... relax lips [aᵁ]... relax lips

[aᵁ]... relax lips [aᵁ]... relax lips

Now sing the sound at a medium volume, on a comfortable pitch.

[aᵁ]... relax lips [aᵁ]... relax lips

[aᵁ]... relax lips [aᵁ]... relax lips

Sustaining the Sound

When you sustain [aᵁ], the first sound of the diphthong, [a], is pronounced fully and is more strongly stressed than the second sound, [ᵁ]. The diphthong ends just as you say [ᵁ].

Say the sound out loud. Sustain it for two counts. (Hold the [a] for two counts and glide quickly to [ᵁ] at the end.)

[aᵁ]... relax lips [aᵁ]... relax lips

[aᵁ]... relax lips [aᵁ]... relax lips

Now sing the sound at a medium volume, on a comfortable pitch. Sustain it for two counts. (Hold the [a] for two counts and glide quickly to [ᵁ] at the end.)

[aᵁ]... relax lips [aᵁ]... relax lips

[aᵁ]... relax lips [aᵁ]... relax lips

Mirror Exercise

Now watch yourself in a mirror as you say [aᵁ].

Your jaw should stay open with your teeth approximately a finger width to two finger widths apart.

Say the sound out loud. Sustain it for two counts. (Hold the [a] for two counts and glide quickly to [u] at the end.)

[aᵁ]... relax lips [aᵁ]... relax lips

[aᵁ]... relax lips [aᵁ]... relax lips

Now sing the sound at a medium volume on a comfortable pitch. Sustain it for two counts. (Hold the [a] for two counts and glide quickly to [ᴜ] at the end.)

[aᵁ]... relax lips [aᵁ]... relax lips

[aᵁ]... relax lips [aᵁ]... relax lips

Possible Problems

Listen to yourself carefully as you say [aᵁ]. If you go to [u] at the end, like this, [aᵘ], you are rounding your lips too much. Only go to [ᴜ], like this, [aᵁ].

Say the sound out loud. Sustain it for two counts.

[aᵁ]... [aᵁ]...

[aᵁ]... [aᵁ]...

Another frequently heard problem with [aᵁ] is starting the sound at Vowel #5, [æ]. Start the sound with Vowel #6, [a].

Say the sound out loud. Sustain it for two counts.

[aᵁ]... [aᵁ]...

[aᵁ]... [aᵁ]...

Practice Words

Speak the practice words out loud, then sing them on a comfortable pitch.

out... out...	*loud... loud...*	*cow... cow...*
our... our...	*bout... bout...*	*how... how...*
owl... owl...	*mouse... mouse...*	*vow... vow...*
ouch... ouch...	*gown... gown...*	*allow... allow...*
oust... oust...	*foul... foul...*	*avow... avow...*

Practice Sentences

Say the practice sentences slowly at first, then faster. In the beginning, accuracy is more important than speed.

Speak the sentences out loud, then sing them on a comfortable pitch.

The brown cow is ours.

The owl and the mouse are out.

He plowed the ground around the house.

How loud the bounding hound howled.

Daily Exercises—Diphthong #2 [aᵁ]

(1) Practice saying this sound and the other phonetic sounds you have learned with the Standard American Diction CDs.

(2) Read aloud from a newspaper, magazine or book until you feel and hear yourself say the [aᵁ] sound five times. Underline the words.

(3) Speak the following reading out loud, slowly at first, then faster. Right now accuracy is more important than speed. Underline the words with [aᵁ].

> *Against my love shall be as I am now,*
> *With time's injurious hand crushed and o'erworn,*
> *When hours have drained his blood and filled his brow*
> *With lines and wrinkles, when his youthful morn*
> *Hath traveled on to age's steepy night,*
> *And all those beauties whereof now he's king*
> *Are vanishing, or vanished out of sight,*
> *Stealing away the treasure of his spring.*
> *For such a time do I now fortify*
> *Against confounding age's cruel knife,*
> *That he shall never cut from memory*
> *My sweet love's beauty, though my lover's life.*
> > *His beauty shall in these black lines be seen,*
> > *And they shall live, and he in them still green.*
> > *SHAKESPEARE, Sonnet 63.*

(4) Sing a short passage from one of your songs or arias that has the [aᵁ] in it. Repeat it several times, concentrating on singing [aᵁ] correctly.

(5) Repeat the entire section for [aᵁ] three times today.

(6) And make sure you're saying [aᵁ] correctly as you speak during the day.

Diphthong #3   [ɔɪ] "oil"

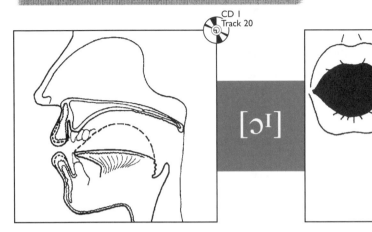

CD I
Track 20

Beginning/Ending
Slide from Vowel #9, [ɔ], to Vowel #2, [ɪ].

Hearing
Listen carefully to this sound on the Standard American Diction CDs.

Jaw
Open your jaw about two finger widths or to a comfortable position almost two finger widths wide. (For speech and much of your singing, your jaw floats open about one finger width. But sometimes you need to open your jaw wider, so it's best to practice with a wide jaw.)

Lips
Feel your lips moving to the [ɔ] position before you begin the sound.

Begin the sound and feel your lips relaxing open, as your tongue moves to the [ɪ] position.

Tongue
Feel the blade of your tongue lightly touching the backs of your lower teeth, as you say [ɔɪ].

Move your tongue to the [ɪ] position, as your lips relax open.

Relax your tongue back down to the floor of your mouth after you say the sound.

Say the sound out loud.

[ɔɪ]... tongue down [ɔɪ]... tongue down

[ɔɪ]... tongue down [ɔɪ]... tongue down

Now sing the sound at a medium volume, on a comfortable pitch.

[ɔɪ]... tongue down [ɔɪ]... tongue down

[ɔɪ]... tongue down [ɔɪ]... tongue down

Sustaining the Sound

When you sustain [ɔɪ], the first sound of the diphthong, [ɔ], is pronounced fully and is more strongly stressed than the second sound, [ɪ]. The diphthong ends just as you say the second sound.

Say the sound out loud. Sustain it for two counts. (Hold the [ɔ] for two counts and glide quickly to [ɪ] at the end.)

[ɔɪ]... [ɔɪ]...

[ɔɪ]... [ɔɪ]...

Now sing the sound at a medium volume, on a comfortable pitch. Sustain it for two counts. (Hold the [ɔ] for two counts and glide quickly to [ɪ] at the end.)

[ɔɪ]... [ɔɪ]...

[ɔɪ]... [ɔɪ]...

Mirror Exercise

Now watch yourself in a mirror as you say [ɔ^I].

Your jaw should stay open with your teeth approximately a finger width to two finger widths apart.

Say the sound out loud. Sustain it for two counts. (Hold the [ɔ] for two counts and glide quickly to [ɪ] at the end.)

[ɔ^I]... [ɔ^I]...

[ɔ^I]... [ɔ^I]...

Now sing the sound at a medium volume on a comfortable pitch. Sustain it for two counts. (Hold the [ɔ] for two counts and glide quickly to [ɪ] at the end.)

[ɔ^I]... [ɔ^I]...

[ɔ^I]... [ɔ^I]...

Possible Problems

Listen to yourself carefully as you say [ɔ^I]. If you go to [i] at the end, like this, [ɔⁱ], you are gliding your tongue too high. Only go to [ɪ], like this, [ɔ^I].

Say the sound out loud. Sustain it for two counts.

[ɔ^I]... [ɔ^I]...

[ɔ^I]... [ɔ^I]...

Practice Words

Say the practice words out loud, then sing them on a comfortable pitch.

oil... oil...	_coin... coin..._	_boy... boy..._
oink... oink...	_noise... noise..._	_joy... joy..._
oyster... oyster...	_spoil... spoil..._	_toy... toy..._
oilcloth... oilcloth...	_voice... voice..._	_decoy... decoy..._
ointment... ointment...	_poison... poison..._	_employ... employ..._

Practice Sentences

Say the practice sentences slowly at first, then faster. In the beginning, accuracy is more important than speed.

Speak the sentences out loud, then sing them on a comfortable pitch.

Coy oysters are not boy oysters.

Oil it and broil it in foil.

Lloyd rejoiced at the poise in Joy's voice.

The toy's noise was annoying to Roy.

Daily Exercises—Diphthong #3 [ɔ^I]

(1) Practice saying this sound and the other phonetic sounds you have learned with the Standard American Diction CDs.

(2) Read aloud from a newspaper, magazine or book until you feel and hear yourself say the [ɔ^I] sound five times. Underline the words.

(3) Speak the following reading out loud, slowly at first, then faster. Right now accuracy is more important than speed. Underline the words with [ɔ^I].

> Weary with toil, I haste me to my bed,
> The dear repose for limbs with travel tired,
> But then begins a journey in my head
> To work my mind, when body's work's expired.
> For then my thoughts, from far where I abide,
> Intend a zealous pilgrimage to thee,
> And keep my drooping eyelids open wide,
> Looking on darkness which the blind do see.
> Save that my soul's imaginary sight
> Presents thy shadow to my sightless view,
> Which like a jewel hung in ghastly night,
> Makes black night beauteous, and her old face new.
> Lo thus by day my limbs, by night my mind,
> For thee, and for myself, no quiet find.
>   SHAKESPEARE, Sonnet 27.

(4) Sing a short passage from one of your songs or arias that has the [ɔ^I] in it. Repeat it several times, concentrating on singing [ɔ^I] correctly.

(5) Repeat the entire section for [ɔ^I] three times today.

(6) And make sure you're saying [ɔ^I] correctly as you speak during the day.

Diphthong #4 [jᵘ] "you"

In some words, this diphthong and the next one, [ɪᵘ], are interchangable in Standard American Speech. If you are not sure which sound to use, look the word up in a pronunciation dictionary.

When you're singing with Standard American Diction, in most cases, you use diphthong #4, [jᵘ]. However, when singing a pop song or singing very fast, you might use Diphthong #5, [ɪᵘ].

CD 1
Track 21

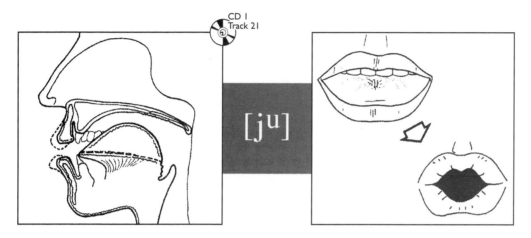

[jᵘ]

Beginning/Ending

Slide from Consonant Glide, [j], to Vowel #12, [u]. ([j] is the first sound in *yes*, not the same sound as the spelling alphabet j.)

Hearing

Listen carefully to this sound on the Standard American Diction CDs.

Jaw

Open your jaw about two finger widths or to a comfortable position almost two finger widths wide. (For speech and much of your singing, your jaw floats open about one finger width. But sometimes you need to open your jaw wider, so it's best to practice with a wide jaw.)

Tongue

Feel your tongue moving to a position approximately between [ɪ] and [ɛ].

Begin the sound and immediately feel your tongue relaxing down to the floor of your mouth (as your lips round to the [u] position).

Lips

Feel your lips relaxed open, as your tongue moves to the [j] position.

As you begin the sound, immediately move your lips to the [u] position (as your tongue relaxes down).

Relax your lips and tongue after you say the sound.

Say the sound out loud. (Glide immediately to [u] and hold it for the duration of the two counts.)

[jᵘ]... relax lips [jᵘ]... relax lips

[jᵘ]... relax lips [jᵘ]... relax lips

Now sing the sound at a medium volume, on a comfortable pitch.

[jᵘ]... relax lips [jᵘ]... relax lips

[jᵘ]... relax lips [jᵘ]... relax lips

If you have a choice of sounds, your best guide is listening to respected speakers and singers and, to some extent, your personal preference. It is important to listen to respected singers in the style you are singing.

Sustaining the Sound

When you sustain [jᵘ], glide immediately to the second sound of the diphthong, [u], and hold that sound to the end of the note.

Say the sound out loud. Sustain it for two counts.

[jᵘ]... [jᵘ]...

[jᵘ]... [jᵘ]...

Now sing the sound at a medium volume, on a comfortable pitch. Sustain it for two counts. (Glide immediately to [u].)

[jᵘ]... [jᵘ]...

[jᵘ]... [jᵘ]...

Mirror Exercise

Now watch yourself in a mirror as you say [jᵘ].

Your jaw should stay open with your teeth approximately a finger width to two finger widths apart.

Say the sound out loud. Sustain it for two counts. (Glide immediately to the [u].)

[jᵘ]... [jᵘ]...

[jᵘ]... [jᵘ]...

Now sing the sound at a medium volume on a comfortable pitch. Sustain it for two counts. (Glide immediately to the [u].)

[jᵘ]... [jᵘ]...

[jᵘ]... [jᵘ]...

Practice Words

Say the practice words out loud, then sing them on a comfortable pitch.

you... *you*...	*fuse*... *fuse*...	*few*... *few*...
use... *use*...	*cute*... *cute*...	*mew*... *mew*...
Europe... *Europe*...	*beauty*... *beauty*...	*hue*... *hue*...
union... *union*...	*bugle*... *bugle*...	*imbue*... *imbue*...
usual... *usual*...	*human*... *human*...	*review*... *review*...

Practice Sentences

Say the practice sentences slowly at first, then faster. In the beginning, accuracy is more important than speed.

Speak the sentences out loud, then sing them on a comfortable pitch.

You knew she was cute.

The evening news reviewed the situation.

The morning dew was beautiful on Tuesday.

The tuba played a tune that a few found humorous.

Daily Exercises—Diphthong #4 [j$^\text{u}$]

(1) Practice saying this sound and the other phonetic sounds you have learned with the Standard American Diction CDs.

(2) Read aloud from a newspaper, magazine or book until you feel and hear yourself say the [j$^\text{u}$] sound five times. Underline the words.

(3) Speak the following reading out loud, slowly at first, then faster. Right now accuracy is more important than speed. Underline the words with [j$^\text{u}$].

> *Music to hear, why hear'st thou music sadly?*
> *Sweets with sweets war not, joy delights in joy.*
> *Why lov'st thou that which thou receiv'st not gladly,*
> *Or else receiv'st with pleasure thine annoy?*
> *If the true concord of well-tuned sounds,*
> *By unions married, do offend thine ear,*
> *They do but sweetly chide thee, who confounds*
> *In singleness the parts that thou shouldst bear.*
> *Mark how one string, sweet husband to another,*
> *Strikes each in each by mutual ordering;*
> *Resembling sire, and child, and happy mother,*
> *Who all in one, one pleasing note do sing;*
>   *Whose speechless song, being many, seeming one,*
>   *Sings this to thee: "Thou single wilt prove none."*
>   SHAKESPEARE, Sonnet 8.

(4) Sing a short passage from one of your songs or arias that has the [j$^\text{u}$] in it. Repeat it several times, concentrating on singing [j$^\text{u}$] correctly.

(5) Repeat the entire section for [j$^\text{u}$] three times today.

(6) And make sure you're saying [j$^\text{u}$] correctly as you speak during the day.

Diphthong #5 [ɪᵘ] "n<u>ew</u>"

In some words, this diphthong and the previous one, [jᵘ], are interchangable in Standard American Speech. If you are not sure which sound to use, look the word up in a pronunciation dictionary.

When you're singing with Standard American Diction, in most cases, you use Diphthong #4, [jᵘ]. However, when you sing a pop song or if you are singing very fast, you might use [ɪᵘ].

When you have a choice, your best guide is listening to respected speakers and singers and, to some extent, your personal preference. It is important to listen to respected singers in the style you are singing.

CD I
Track 22

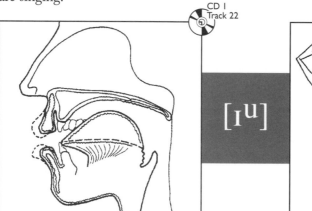

[ɪᵘ]

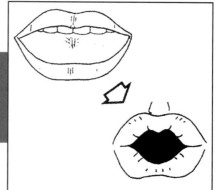

Beginning/Ending

Slide from Vowel #2, [ɪ], to Vowel #12, [u].

Hearing

Listen carefully to this sound on the Standard American Diction CDs.

Jaw

Open your jaw about two finger widths or to a comfortable position almost two finger widths wide. (For speech and much of your singing, your jaw floats open about one finger width. But sometimes you need to open your jaw wider, so it's best to practice with a wide jaw.)

Tongue

Feel your tongue move to the [ɪ] position before you begin the sound.

Begin the sound and immediately feel your tongue relaxing down, as your lips round to the [u] position.

Lips

Feel your lips relaxed open, as your tongue moves to the [ɪ] position.

As you begin the sound, immediately move your lips to the [u] position, as your tongue relaxes down.

Say the sound out loud.

[ɪᵘ]... relax lips [ɪᵘ]... relax lips

[ɪᵘ]... relax lips [ɪᵘ]... relax lips

Now sing the sound at a medium volume, on a comfortable pitch.

[ɪᵘ]... relax lips [ɪᵘ]... relax lips

[ɪᵘ]... relax lips [ɪᵘ]... relax lips

Sustaining the Sound

If you sing [ɪᵘ] on a sustained note, you may hold [ɪ] for part of the note and glide to [u] for the rest of the note. Divide it up in a way that sounds right to your ear for the style you are singing. (This is why it is important to listen to respected singers in the style you are singing.)

Say the sound out loud. Sustain it for two counts.

[ɪ^u]... [ɪ^u]...
[ɪ^u]... [ɪ^u]...

Now sing the sound at a medium volume, on a comfortable pitch.
Sustain it for two counts.

[ɪ^u]... [ɪ^u]...
[ɪ^u]... [ɪ^u]...

Mirror Exercise

Now watch yourself in a mirror as you sing [ɪ^u].

For a clear [ɪ^u] sound, your jaw should stay open with your teeth approximately a finger width to two finger widths apart.

Say the sound out loud. Sustain it for two counts.

[ɪ^u]... [ɪ^u]...
[ɪ^u]... [ɪ^u]...

Now sing the sound at a medium volume on a comfortable pitch.
Sustain it for two counts.

[ɪ^u]... [ɪ^u]...
[ɪ^u]... [ɪ^u]...

Comparison Exercise

Diphthong #4, [j^u], and Diphthong #5, [ɪ^u], are sometimes interchangable. If you have trouble recognizing the difference between them, repeat them carefully one after the other until you can clearly hear the difference between their sounds and feel the difference between their tongue movements and positions. Make sure you hear a difference between the beginning sounds. (These sounds are clearly demonstrated on the CDs.)

Speak, then sing, the sounds at a medium volume.

[j^u,ɪ^u,j^u,ɪ^u]... [j^u,ɪ^u,j^u,ɪ^u],
[j^u,ɪ^u,j^u,ɪ^u]... [j^u,ɪ^u,j^u,ɪ^u],

Practice Words

Say the practice words out loud, then sing them on a comfortable pitch.

new... new...	*duel... duel...*
mew... mew...	*cube... cube...*
few... few...	*humid... humid...*
	lieutenant... lieutenant

Practice Sentences

Say the practice sentences slowly at first, then faster. In the beginning, accuracy is more important than speed.

Speak the sentences out loud, then sing them on a comfortable pitch.

Few thought the lieutenant would duel.

The cube of ice melted in the humidity.

The new tune was played by the student on the tuba.

The duke rued the abuse of the accused.

Daily Exercises—Diphthong #5 $[\text{\textsc{i}}^\text{u}]$

(1) Practice saying this sound and the other phonetic sounds you have learned with the Standard American Diction CDs.

(2) Read aloud from a newspaper, magazine or book until you feel and hear yourself say the $[\text{\textsc{i}}^\text{u}]$ sound at least once. (There are not many words with the $[\text{\textsc{i}}^\text{u}]$ sound, so use your judgement on how long you spend on this exercise. Underline the words.)

(3) Speak the following reading out loud, slowly at first, then faster. Right now accuracy is more important than speed. Underline the words with $[\text{\textsc{i}}^\text{u}]$.

> *I grant thou wert not married to my muse,*
> *And therefore mayst without attaint o'erlook*
> *The dedicated words which writers use*
> *Of their subject, blessing every book.*
> *Thou art as fair in knowledge as in hue,*
> *Finding thy worth a limit past my praise,*
> *And therefore art enforced to seek anew*
> *Some fresher stamp of the time-bett'ring days.*
> *And do so, love; yet when they have devised*
> *What strained touches rhetoric can lend,*
> *Thou truly fair wert truly sympathized*
> *In true plain words by thy true-telling friend;*
> > *And their gross painting might be better used,*
> > *Where cheeks need blood; in thee it is abused*
> > *SHAKESPEARE, Sonnet 82.*

(4) Sing a short passage from one of your songs or arias that has the $[\text{\textsc{i}}^\text{u}]$ in it. Repeat it several times, concentrating on singing $[\text{\textsc{i}}^\text{u}]$ correctly.

(5) Repeat the entire section for $[\text{\textsc{i}}^\text{u}]$ three times today.

(6) And make sure you're saying $[\text{\textsc{i}}^\text{u}]$ correctly as you speak during the day.

Congratulations! You have learned to recognize and say all the **Vowel** and **Diphthong** sounds of **Standard American Speech.**

Review of Vowels and Diphthongs

Let's do a quick review. Speak, then sing, the sounds and the words at a medium volume.

Vowels

Tongue Vowels

(1) [i] *eel... even... need... easy...* [i]

(2) [ɪ] *in... big... fit... give...* [ɪ]

(3) [eᴵ] *aim... able... tail... bake...* [eᴵ] (diphthong)

(4) [ɛ] *edge... every... beg... enter...* [ɛ]

(5) [æ] *am... annual... bag ... add...* [æ]

(6) [a] *I... tie ... ice ... buy...* [a]

(7) [ɑ] *art... father... option... car...* [ɑ]

Lip Vowels

(8) [ɒ] *on... honest... bomb... cross...* [ɒ]

(9) [ɔ] *or... warm... hawk... before...* [ɔ]

(10) [oᵁ] *old... oak... moan... solo...* [oᵁ] (diphthong)

(11) [ʊ] *wool... book... put... could...* [ʊ]

(12) [u] *moon... ooze... loop... soon...* [u]

Other Vowels

(13) [ʌ] *up... above... custom... some...* [ʌ]

        [ʌ] (stressed symbol)

        [ə] (non-stressed symbol)

(14) [ɝ] *earn... germ... stir... firm...* [ɝ]

        [ɚ] (non-stressed symbol)

(15) [ɜ] *earn... world... furry... pearl...* [ɜ]

Diphthongs

(1) [aᴵ] *I... nine... light... try...* [aᴵ]

(2) [aᵁ] *out... loud... gown... cow...* [aᵁ]

(3) [ɔᴵ] *oil... boy... noise... joint...* [ɔᴵ]

(4) [jᵁ] *you... cue... beauty... music...* [jᵁ]

(5) [ɪᵁ] *new... few... juice... June...* [ɪᵁ]

Notice how much more clearly and easily you can say these sounds.

Exercise

(1) Record yourself saying the vowels and diphthongs, with their example words on the previous page.

(2) Compare this recording with your first recording.

(3) Notice the improvement in your diction.

Note: If you're still having trouble with any of the vowel and diphthong sounds, listen to the demonstrations on the Standard American Diction CDs and repeat the exercises for that sound until you can say it clearly and easily.

Notes:

vowel #2 eɪ "ai"

vowel #7 ɔ "uh"

consonant #8 ʃ "sh"

consonant #22 ɬ "t"

9 Consonants

"Today we're going to start learning how to make your singing clearer, more expressive and more beautiful, with consonants," announced the vocal coach.

"Consonants," moaned the singer. "I wish I didn't have to sing them. They just get in the way."

"Do they?" questioned the teacher.

"Yes. I get a beautiful tone going, just the way I want it, with my vowel—and I have to stop it, to say a consonant."

"Why do you have to put in the consonant?" asked the coach.

The singer looked up, startled. "Because they're part of the words. You can't sing without them."

This time the coach looked surprised. "You mean, you're complaining about something that you can't do without. Something that helps you in your singing?"

"Well, I guess so," admitted the singer.

"How do you feel about breathing?" asked the teacher.

"What do you mean?"

"Doesn't breathing interrupt the vocal tone?"

"Yes, but I have to breathe—to live and to sing well."

"And what about consonants?"

The student saw the connection. "Well, I guess I have to say consonants, too."

"Do you complain about breathing?"

"No."

The coach smiled. "Have you ever really thought about the role of consonants in your speech and singing? I mean, their advantages. What they do for you?

The singer took a deep breath. "No, I just never liked them."

"Because they were hard to sing," prompted the coach.

"Yes... and I don't like the sound of them."

"Because they don't sound like vowels," suggested the coach.

"I guess so... I don't know."

"Let's take a new look at consonants," said the coach, brightly. "I promise you, that when you realize what consonants do for your singing, and when you learn how to say them easily—with control and clarity—your attitude about consonants will change completely. You'll fall in love with them. You'll love singing them"

"You think so?"

"Would you like to sing without feeling that consonants are a drag on you?"

"Yes."

"Then let's do it."

What are Consonants?

Consonants are sounds of speech in which you bring two or more of your articulators together or very close together to make the sound.

Consonants are vital, fundamental components of speech, without which, your speech and singing would be unintelligible.

Say the following phrase out loud:

I love you.

Now say it with just the vowels:

I _o_e _ou. [aᴵ – ʌ– u]

Doesn't make much sense does it?

Now say it with just the consonants:

_ l_v_ y__. [__ l__ v j__]

It still isn't clear.

The point is, you need both vowels and consonants for intelligible speech and singing.

When properly used, consonants are dynamic, expressive sounds of speech. They add clarity, energy and character to your speaking and singing voice.

Consonants not only make your words understandable, they add elements of sensuality and beauty to your voice.

Are Consonants Obstacles to Speech and Singing?

Strangely enough, many singers and teachers feel that consonants are a bother and an obstacle to speaking and singing. They feel that consonants get in the way of beautiful singing and that they could get along without them very well.

This is a self-defeating attitude that stems from a basic misunderstanding of consonants.

Consonants evolved as part of our speech because they are necessary—as essential as vowels. There is no speech without consonants. And in their own way consonants are just as beautiful as vowels.

The Psychology of Singing Consonants

You put yourself at a physical and psychological disadvantage when you think of consonants as a necessary evil.

Rather than considering consonants to be an impedance to your singing, you should see them for what they actually are—an integral part of speech and singing—an essential part of your expressive communication.

Since it is impossible to sing without consonants, you should learn how to say them easily and incorporate them smoothly into your singing.

Singing is psychological in its operation—the way you think about it is the way you do it. Your articulation muscles operate primarily on an involuntary and habitual level. They are directed by your mental image of how your voice works. Thinking that consonants are difficult to produce and have negative effects on your singing becomes a self-fulfilling prophecy.

Improperly learned and articulated consonants make your speech and singing difficult to pronounce and hard to understand. And poorly pronounced consonants break up your vocal line and obscure the clarity of your voice.

Not being in control of consonants makes you wish you didn't have to say them.

On the other hand, learning how to pronounce consonants easily, clearly and dynamically puts you in control of your consonants. You find it easier to say them and your singing becomes more understandable to your audience. When you feel the consonants helping to release your voice to your audience, you will embrace them happily and appreciate them for helping you to be a better singer.

Starting now, you are going to learn how to incorporate consonants as natural and integral elements of your diction. You will learn how to pronounce them effortlessly and how to use them to help your voice project clearly, beautifully and easily to your audience.

Good Consonant Habits

When you're singing and speaking:

(1) sometimes you may say correct consonants,

(2) sometimes you may say consonants that are almost correct,

(3) sometimes you may say consonants that are hardly recognizable as the sound you meant to say,

(4) and sometimes you may not say certain consonants at all.

It all depends on the habits your articulators have learned. If you are having difficulty with consonants, you have not taught your articulators the right habits.

Learning to say consonants effortlessly and correctly is easy. Consonants, like vowels, are made by moving and placing your articulators in the right positions for the sounds.

For example, the only way you can say [p], as in *pup*, is to put your upper and lower lips together, build up a little air pressure behind them and then release them. Try saying [p] in any other way. Unless you put your articulators in the right place, you can't say the right sound.

But while you're talking or singing you don't have time to analyze the formation of each consonant. You don't have time to say to yourself,

"Well, for this sound I put my tongue here and my lips here." All the movements have to be done automatically, or habitually. You just think the word and let your articulators go to all the right positions by themselves.

How to Make Correct Consonants a Habit

In the following chapters, you will learn the correct consonant sounds of Standard American Speech and how to make saying them a habit.

Here is the learning method that works best:

First, practice the correct articulation for each consonant as a single sound.

Next, practice the consonant in words, first speaking, then singing.

Finally, practice the consonant in phrases, first speaking, then singing.

Until you've trained your articulators to move automatically to the right places, you'll need to be carefully conscious of where you are placing them and of the sounds you are making.

You'll also need to make frequent corrections.

But you'll only have to pay this kind of close attention for a short time. You'll be surprised at how quickly and easily your articulators learn to automatically say the correct sounds. In fact, you'll hear immediate improvement in your speaking and singing diction.

Neuro-sensory Conditioning™ The Natural Way to Learn Consonants

We described the natural way of learning to speak in Chapter One, *Introduction to Diction*. Go back and review that. You'll learn faster if you understand why you're learning this way.

We all learn to pronounce sounds by imitation. The easiest and most efficient method for learning consonants is by:

Hearing

Listen closely to people you feel are good speakers. In particular, listen to network radio and television announcers. Also, work with the Standard American Diction CDs that go along with this book.

Feeling

Pay close attention to the feel of the positions of your articulators as you follow the directions in the exercises.

Seeing

Work frequently with a mirror to see where you are placing your articulators. After a while, you can stop using the mirror and imagine the positions of your articulators.

Phonetic Alphabet Symbols

Consonant speech sounds, like the vowel speech sounds, have phonetic alphabet symbols, with one symbol for one sound.

As we said in Chapter Three, *Speech Sounds*, when you're learning to speak clearly, the phonetic alphabet is much easier and more convenient to use than the regular spelling alphabet.

Kinds of Consonant Sounds

There are twenty-five consonant speech sounds in Standard American Speech.

For study, it is convenient to divide them into six categories:

Fricatives

Fricatives are made by bringing two or three of your articulators close together and either blowing a little air between them to cause a friction-like sound or voicing a sound that vibrates strongly between them.

For example, *f*, as in *fun*; *v*, as in *van*.

There are nine fricative consonants.

Plosives

Plosives are made by bringing two of your articulators together to stop the flow of breath, building up a little air pressure against them and then releasing them to allow a little puff of air to escape.

For example, *b*, as in *ball*; *g*, as in *gum*.

There are six plosive consonants.

Affricatives

Affricatives are made by combining a fricative and a plosive consonant.

Examples: *dg*, as in *badge*; *ch*, as in *church*.

There are two affricative consonants.

Glides

Glides are made by starting with the articulators in one position and immediately gliding to the following vowel.

For example, *w*, as in *wall*; *y*, as in *yet*.

There are three glide consonants.

Semi-Vowels

Semi-Vowels are vowel-like in nature—that is, you voice a continuing sound and the sound comes out through the mouth.

They are, *l*, as in *lake*; *r*, as in *run*.

There are two semi-vowel consonants.

Nasals

Nasals are called nasals because the mouth passage is blocked by the articulators and the sound comes out through the nasal passage.

For example, *m*, as in *me*; *n*, as in *not*.

There are three nasal consonants.

In addition to the above categories, the fricatives and plosives may be either **voiced** or **voiceless**.

Voiced Consonants

When you say a voiced consonant, **your vocal cords vibrate as you say the sound**. You can also feel the articulators that form the consonant vibrating with the sound.

Here is an exercise to help you feel what a voiced consonant feels like.

Place your fingers lightly on the side of your throat.

Say *aaah*.

Feel the vibrations under your fingers.

This sound is **voiced**. Your vocal cords are **vibrating**.

Here is an example of a voiced consonant.

Say *v*, as in *voice*. Continue saying the sound out loud. Place your fingers lightly on the front of your neck as you say the sound. You can feel vibrations there. Those vibrations mean that your vocal cords are vibrating to create voiced sound.

You can also feel the vibrations of the sound on your lower lip and upper front teeth.

Voiceless Consonants

When you say a voiceless consonant, **your vocal cords are not vibrating as you say the sound**. All you hear is the friction-like sound of the breath escaping between the articulators.

Here is an exercise to help you feel what a voiceless consonant feels like.

Sigh *hhhh*, without any sound.

Touch your throat.

There are no vibrations under your fingers.

This sound is **voiceless**. Your vocal cords are **not vibrating**.

Here is an example of a voiceless consonant.

Say *f*, as in *fun*. Continue saying the sound out loud. Notice that you can't hear any vocal, or voiced, sound or feel any vibrations. All you can hear is the whispery sound of the breath. This is a voiceless sound.

The Consonant Sounds of Standard American Speech

These are all the consonant sounds of Standard American Speech, with example words.

Start your study of consonants by saying all of them out loud, just to get acquainted.

Listen carefully to yourself as you say them. They are demonstrated on the Standard American Diction CDs.

Fricatives

(1) [v] *van... veil... live...* [v]
(2) [f] *fun... far... if...* [f]
(3) [ð] *the... that... other...* [ð]
(4) [θ] *thank... thing... booth...* [θ]
(5) [z] *zoom... zip... buzz...* [z]
(6) [s] *song... sail... voice...* [s]
(7) [ʒ] *Asia... rouge... garage...* [ʒ]
(8) [ʃ] *she... shore... dash...* [ʃ]
(9) [h] *has... help... who...* [h]

Plosives

(10) [b] *ball... about... web...* [b]
(11) [p] *pull... apple... pop...* [p]
(12) [d] *dean... door... lad...* [d]
(13) [t] *tall... tend... lot...* [t]
(14) [g] *got... give... dog...* [g]
(15) [k] *can... call... look...* [k]

Affricatives

(16) [dʒ] *jar... joke... fudge...* [dʒ]
(17) [tʃ] *chair... chum... church...* [tʃ]

Glides

(18) [w] *will... were... awake...* [w]
(19) [ʍ] *while... when... what...* [ʍ]
(20) [j] *yes... yacht... loyal...* [j]

Semi-Vowels

(21) [l] *lake... laugh... all...* [l]
(22) [r] *rule... rain... are...* [r]

Nasals

(23) [m] *me... man... came...* [m]
(24) [n] *no... name... bin...* [n]
(25) [ŋ] *young... king... angle...* [ŋ]

Notes:

vowel #a ɒ "ah"

vowel #7 ə "uh"

consonant #8 ʃ "sh"

consonant #11 t "t"

10 Fricative Consonants

A fricative consonant has a slight hissing, or breathy sound.

How Do You Make a Fricative?

You make a fricative by bringing two or more of your articulators very close together or actually touching them lightly together and blowing a little breath between them. Blowing the breath through the small space creates a hissing, or friction-like, breathy sound.

Pairs of Fricatives

Fricative consonants come in pairs. That is, you place your articulators in the same position to make two different speech sounds.

The way you make the two sounds different is by adding vocal cord vibration (voiced sound) to one, but not to the other.

So one is called a **voiced** fricative and the other is called a **voiceless** fricative.

(The only fricative consonant that is not one of a pair is #9, [h].)

Voiced/Voiceless Fricatives

For a voiced fricative your vocal cords vibrate.

For a voiceless fricative your vocal cords do not vibrate.

Here is an exercise to help you feel and hear the difference between a voiced and voiceless sound.

Place your fingers lightly on your throat. Say *aaaah* and feel the vibrations. Continue saying *aaaah* and lift your lower lip up to touch your upper front teeth. You are saying the **voiced** fricative, [v]. Feel the vibrations on your lips and teeth.

Now say *hhhh* — there are no vibrations. Continue saying *hhhh* and lift your lower lip up to touch your upper front teeth. You are saying the **voiceless** fricative, [f].

Say the two sounds one after the other.

[v,f,v,f,v,f]... [v,f,v,f,v,f]...

[v,f,v,f,v,f]... [v,f,v,f,v,f]...

Nine Fricative Consonants

Say each sound out loud.

Voiced	Voiceless
(1) [v]... <u>v</u>an	(2) [f].... <u>f</u>un
(3) [ð]... <u>th</u>e	(4) [θ].... <u>th</u>ank
(5) [z]... <u>z</u>oom	(6) [s].... <u>s</u>ong
(7) [ʒ]... A<u>s</u>ia	(8) [ʃ].... <u>sh</u>e
	(9) [h].... <u>h</u>as

Consonant #1 [v] "van" (voiced fricative)

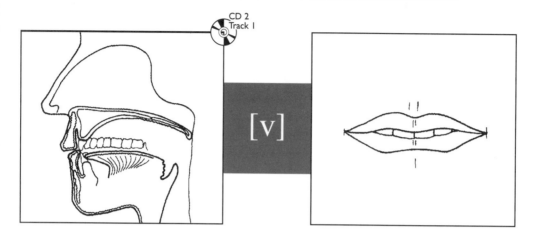

Hearing

Listen carefully to this sound on the Standard American Diction CDs.

Jaw

Open your jaw about a finger width. Leave your jaw open as you say the sound. (An open jaw allows you to maintain better resonance.)

Tongue

Feel your tongue relaxed down on the floor of your mouth. Leave it there as you say the sound.

Lips

Move your lower lip up to lightly touch your front upper teeth.

Your lip should not be tense and your jaw should stay open about a finger width.

Start the voiced sound.

Hear the sound and feel the vibrations on your lip and teeth.

After you say the sound, relax your lip back down to its normal position.

Say the sound out loud, sustaining it for two counts.

[v]... lip down [v]... lip down

[v]... lip down [v]... lip down

Now sing the sound out loud, on a comfortable pitch. Sustain it for two counts.

[v]... lip down [v]... lip down

[v]... lip down [v]... lip down

The vibrations will tickle your lip until you get used to saying [v] strongly, but don't stop. Practice the sound until you can sing it without the tickling bothering you.

Resonant Feel

Pay particular attention to the resonant feel of [v]. The character of its resonance is different from all the other speech sounds. Learn to love it and look forward to singing it.

Mirror Exercise

Now watch yourself in a mirror as you say [v].

For a clear [v] sound, your jaw should stay open, with your teeth about a finger width apart.

Lightly touch your jaw with your fingers to help keep it open.

Your lip should be relaxed and lightly touching your upper front teeth. Do not press your lip tightly against your teeth.

Say the sound out loud, sustaining it for two counts.

[v]... [v]...

[v]... [v]...

Now sing the sound out loud, on a comfortable pitch.
Sustain it for two counts.

[v]... [v]...

[v]... [v]...

Possible Problems

Listen to yourself carefully as you say [v]. If you hear the sound change right at the end, with a little [ə] (the vowel sound in *uh*), it means you're moving your lower lip before you finish saying the sound. Keep the sound pure, that is, a single sound. Notice that when your lip stays in place the sound doesn't change.

Speak, then sing the sound at a medium volume.

[v]... [v]...

[v]... [v]...

Saying Consonants in Words

When saying [v] in words, do not hold on to it. Say it quickly but clearly and move immediately to the vowel.

Do not leave a breathy space between the consonant and the vowel, start the vowel as soon as you release your lip. Think of the consonant as a springboard that bounces you powerfully into a clear, open vowel. You can feel the [v] well forward in your mouth, imagine bringing the vowel forward into that position as well.

Practice Words

In the following words say [v] clearly and strongly, but without any extra tension in your articulators.

Say the words out loud, then sing them on a comfortable pitch.

van... van...	*liver... liver...*	*dive... dive...*
voice... voice...	*never... never...*	*love... love...*
view... view...	*vivid... vivid...*	*live... live...*
very... very...	*even... even...*	*have... have...*
volume... volume...	*every... every...*	*receive... receive...*

Practice Sentences

In the following sentences feel your articulators moving and feel the resonance of each individual sound as you say the words.

Say them slowly at first, then faster. Right now accuracy is more important than speed.

Say the sentences out loud, then sing them on a comfortable pitch.

A vibrant voice reverberates vigorously.

The leaves above are a vivid hue.

Veronica viewed the vast vista of valley violets.

Virile Victor vanquished vain vendors.

Daily Exercises—Consonant #1 [v]

(1) Practice saying this sound and the other speech sounds you have learned with the Standard American Diction CDs.

(2) Read aloud from a newspaper, magazine or book until you feel and hear yourself say the [v] sound five times. Underline the words.

(3) Speak the following reading out loud, slowly at first, then faster. Right now accuracy is more important than speed. Underline the words with [v].

> Take all my loves, my love, yea take them all:
> What hast thou then more than thou hadst before?
> No love, my love, that thou mayst true love call;
> All mine was thine, before thou hadst this more.
> Then if for my love thou my love receivest,
> I cannot blame thee for my love thou usest;
> But yet be blamed, if thou thyself deceivest
> By wilful taste of what thyself refusest.
> I do forgive thy robb'ry, gentle thief,
> Although thou steal thee all my poverty;
> And yet love knows it is a greater grief
> To bear love's wrong than hate's known injury.
>> Lascivious grace, in whom all ill well shows,
>> Kill me with spites, yet we must not be foes.
>> SHAKESPEARE, Sonnet 40.

(4) Sing a short passage from one of your songs or arias that has the [v] in it. Repeat it several times, concentrating on saying [v] correctly.

(5) Repeat the entire section for [v] three times today.

(6) And make sure you're saying [v] correctly as you speak during the day.

Consonant #2   [f] "**f**un" (voiceless fricative)

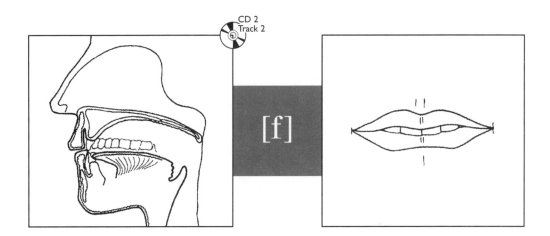

Hearing

Listen carefully to this sound on the Standard American Diction CDs.

Jaw

Open your jaw about a finger width.

Leave your jaw open as you say the sound.

(An open jaw allows you to maintain better resonance.)

Tongue

Feel your tongue relaxed down on the floor of your mouth. Leave it there as you say the sound.

Lips

Move your lower lip up to lightly touch your upper teeth.

Your lip should not be tense and your jaw should stay slightly open.

Blow a tiny amount of breath between your lip and teeth, so that you can barely hear a quiet [f] sound.

Don't blow hard. (Don't let the breath pressure expand your cheeks.)

After you say the sound, relax your lip back down to its normal position.

Say the sound out loud, sustaining it for two counts.

[f]... lip down [f]... lip down

[f]... lip down [f]... lip down

Resonant Feel

Pay particular attention to the feel of [f]. Its character is different from all the other speech sounds. Learn to love it and look forward to singing it.

Mirror Exercise

Now watch yourself in a mirror as you say [f].

For a clear [f] sound, your jaw should stay open, with your teeth about a finger width apart. Lightly touch your jaw with your fingers to help keep it open. Your lip should be lightly touching your upper front teeth, not pressed tightly against them.

Say the sound out loud.

[f]... [f]...

[f]... [f]...

Comparison Exercise

Here is a comparison exercise to help you differentiate between [v] and [f].

Repeat them one after the other until you can clearly hear and feel the difference between them.

Say the sounds out loud.

[v,f,v,f,v,f]... [v,f,v,f,v,f]...
[v,f,v,f,v,f]... [v,f,v,f,v,f]...

Saying Consonants In Words

When saying [f] in words, do not hold on to it. Say it quickly but clearly and move immediately to the vowel.

Do not leave a breathy space between the consonant and the vowel, start the vowel as soon as you release your lip. Think of the consonant as a springboard that bounces you powerfully into a clear, open vowel. You can feel the [f] well forward in your mouth, imagine bringing the vowel forward into that position as well.

Note: When you say a voiceless consonant, like [f], your vocal cords are apart, that is, not vibrating. So when you move from the consonant to the vowel make a special effort to start the vowel clearly and strongly—*a breathy vowel cannot be blamed on a voiceless consonant*. If you have trouble moving from a voiceless consonant to the vowel, practice the transition until the vowel is clear every time you say it.

Practice Words

In the following words say [f] clearly and strongly, but without any extra tension in your articulators.

Say the words out loud, then sing them on a comfortable pitch.

fan... fan...	*often... often...*	*off... off...*
fuss... fuss...	*coffee... coffee...*	*deaf... deaf...*
feel... feel...	*effect... effect...*	*calf... calf...*
fought... fought...	*refuse... refuse...*	*tough... tough...*
fowl... fowl...	*swift... swift...*	*enough... enough...*

Practice Sentences

In the following sentences feel your articulators moving and the resonance of each individual sound as you say the words.

Say them slowly at first, then faster. Right now accuracy is more important than speed.

Say the sentences out loud, then sing them on a comfortable pitch.

Fierce fowl ruffle their feathers.

Falling flat on rough turf is foolish.

Five frantic fat frogs fled from fifty fierce fishes.

Four fat friers frying forty-five flat fish.

Daily Exercises—Consonant #2 [f]

(1) Practice saying this sound and the other speech sounds you have learned with the Standard American Diction CDs.

(2) Read aloud from a newspaper, magazine or book until you feel and hear yourself say the [f] sound five times. Underline the words.

(3) Speak the following reading out loud, slowly at first, then faster. Right now accuracy is more important than speed. Underline the words with [f].

> *When in disgrace with fortune and men's eyes,*
> *I all alone beweep my outcast state,*
> *And trouble deaf heav'n with my bootless cries,*
> *And look upon myself and curse my fate,*
> *Wishing me like to one more rich in hope,*
> *Featured like him, like him with friends possessed,*
> *Desiring this man's art, and that man's scope,*
> *With what I most enjoy contented least;*
> *Yet in these thoughts myself almost despising,*
> *Haply I think on thee, and then my state,*
> *Like to the lark at break of day arising*
> *From sullen earth, sings hymns at heaven's gate;*
> > *For thy sweet love rememb'red such wealth brings,*
> > *That then I scorn to change my state with kings.*
> > SHAKESPEARE, Sonnet 29.

(4) Sing a short passage from one of your songs or arias that has the [f] in it. Repeat it several times, concentrating on saying [f] correctly.

(5) Repeat the entire section for [f] three times today.

(6) And make sure you're saying [f] correctly as you speak during the day.

Consonant #3   [ð]   "that" (voiced fricative)

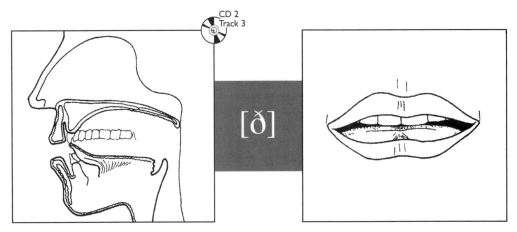

CD 2
Track 3

Hearing

Listen carefully to this sound on the Standard American Diction CDs.

Jaw

Open your jaw about a finger width. Leave your jaw open as you say the sound. (An open jaw allows you to maintain better resonance.)

Lips

Feel your lips relaxed and open.

Tongue

Touch the edge of the blade of your tongue lightly to the cutting edges of your upper front teeth.

Do not tense your tongue or press it hard against your teeth.

The sides of your tongue touch your upper molars and stop breath from escaping around the sides.

Start the voiced sound.

Hear the sound and feel the vibrations on your tongue and teeth. (The vocal sound should be louder than the sound of the breath escaping between your tongue and teeth.)

After you say the sound, relax your tongue back down to its normal position.

Say the sound out loud, sustaining it for two counts.

[ð]... tongue down [ð]... tongue down

[ð]... tongue down [ð]... tongue down

Now sing the sound out loud, on a comfortable pitch. Sustain it for two counts.

[ð]... [ð]...

[ð]... [ð]...

The vibrations will tickle your tongue and you may have difficulty keeping your tongue in the correct position at first, but don't stop. Practice the sound until you can sing it easily and comfortably.

Resonant Feel

Pay particular attention to the resonant feel of [ð]. The character of its resonance is different from all the other speech sounds. Learn to love it and look forward to singing it.

Mirror Exercise

Now watch yourself in a mirror as you say [ð].

For a clear [ð] sound, your jaw should stay open, with your teeth about a finger width apart. Lightly touch your jaw with your fingers to help keep it open.

Your tongue should lightly touch the cutting edges of your upper front teeth. Do not press your tongue tightly against your teeth. Your tongue should not stick out of your mouth past your teeth.

Say the sound out loud.

[ð]... relax tongue... [ð]... relax tongue...

[ð]... relax tongue... [ð]... relax tongue...

Now sing the sound out loud, on a comfortable pitch.
Sustain it for two counts.

[ð]... relax tongue... [ð]... relax tongue...

[ð]... relax tongue... [ð]... relax tongue...

Possible Problems

Listen to yourself carefully as you say [ð]. If you hear the sound change right at the end, with a little [ə] (the vowel sound in *uh*), it means you're moving your tongue before you finish saying the sound. Keep the sound pure, that is, a single sound. Notice that when your tongue stays in place the sound doesn't change.

Speak, then sing the sound at a medium volume.

[ð]... [ð]... [ð]... [ð]...

Saying Consonants In Words

When saying [ð] in words, do not hold on to it. Say it clearly but quickly and move immediately to the vowel.

Do not leave a breathy space between the consonant and the vowel, start the vowel as soon as you release your lip. Think of the consonant as a springboard that bounces you powerfully into a clear, open vowel. You can feel the [ð] well forward in your mouth, imagine bringing the vowel forward into that position as well.

Practice Words

In the following words say [ð] clearly and strongly, but without any extra tension in your articulators.

Say the words out loud, then sing them on a comfortable pitch.

the... the...	*other... other...*	*with... with...*
these... these...	*either... either...*	*lathe... lathe...*
those... those...	*feather... feather...*	*soothe... soothe...*
than... than...	*although... although...*	*teethe... teethe...*
there... there...	*worthy... worthy...*	*smooth... smooth...*

Practice Sentences

In the following sentences feel your articulators moving and feel the resonance of each individual sound as you say the words.

Say them slowly at first, then faster. Right now accuracy is more important than speed.

Say the sentences out loud, then sing them on a comfortable pitch.

There are those that like smooth leather.

They loathed bathing in cold weather.

They gathered together in the heather.

Smog bothers those that breathe.

Daily Exercises—Consonant #3 [ð]

(1) Practice saying this sound and the other speech sounds you have learned with the Standard American Diction CDs.

(2) Read aloud from a newspaper, magazine or book until you feel and hear yourself say the [ð] sound five times. Underline the words.

(3) Speak the following reading out loud, slowly at first, then faster. Right now accuracy is more important than speed. Underline the words with [ð].

> *Unthrifty loveliness, why dost thou spend*
> *Upon thyself thy beauty's legacy?*
> *Nature's bequest gives nothing but doth lend,*
> *And being frank she lends to those are free.*
> *Then beauteous niggard why dost thou abuse*
> *The bounteous largess given the to give?*
> *Profitless usurer, why dost thou use*
> *So great a sum of sums yet canst not live?*
> *For having traffic with thyself alone,*
> *Thou of thy sweet self dost deceive.*
> *Then how when nature calls thee to be gone,*
> *What acceptable audit canst thou leave?*
> > *Thy unused beauty must be tombed with thee,*
> > *Which used lives th'executor to be.*
> > > *SHAKESPEARE, Sonnet 4.*

(4) Sing a short passage from one of your songs or arias that has the [ð] in it. Repeat it several times, concentrating on saying [ð] correctly.

(5) Repeat the entire section for [ð] three times today.

(6) And make sure you're saying [ð] correctly as you speak during the day.

Consonant #4 [θ] "th̲ank" (voiceless fricative)

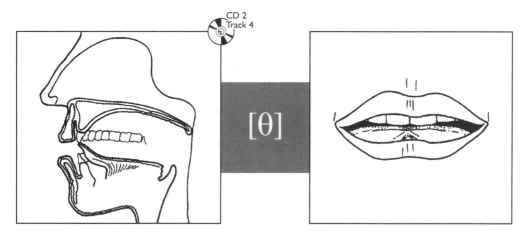

CD 2
Track 4

Hearing

Listen carefully to this sound on the Standard American Diction CDs.

Jaw

Open your jaw about a finger width. Leave your jaw open as you say the sound. (An open jaw allows you to maintain better resonance.)

Lips

Feel your lips relaxed and open.

Tongue

Touch the edge of the blade of your tongue lightly to the cutting edges of your upper front teeth.

Do not tense your tongue or press it hard against your teeth.

The sides of your tongue touch your upper molars and prevent breath from escaping between your tongue and teeth at the sides.

Blow a tiny amount of breath between your tongue and front teeth, so that you can barely hear a quiet [θ] sound. Don't blow hard.

After you say the sound, relax your tongue back down to its normal position.

Say the sound out loud, sustaining it for two counts.

[θ]... tongue down. [θ]... tongue down.

[θ]... tongue down. [θ]... tongue down.

Resonant Feel

Pay particular attention to the feel of [θ]. Its character is different from all the other speech sounds. Learn to love it and look forward to singing it.

Mirror Exercise

Now watch yourself in a mirror as you say [θ].

For a clear [θ] sound, your jaw should stay open, with your teeth about a finger width apart. Lightly touch your jaw with your fingers to help keep it open.

Your tongue should lightly touch the cutting edges of your upper front teeth. Do not press your tongue tightly against your teeth. Your tongue should not stick out of your mouth past your teeth.

Say the sound out loud.

[θ]... [θ]...

[θ]... [θ]...

Comparison Exercise

Here is a comparison exercise to help you differentiate between [ð] and [θ].

Repeat them one after the other until you can clearly hear and feel the difference between them.

Say the sounds out loud.

[ð,θ,ð,θ,ð,θ]... [ð,θ,ð,θ,ð,θ]...
[ð,θ,ð,θ,ð,θ]... [ð,θ,ð,θ,ð,θ]...

Saying Consonants in Words

When saying [θ] in words, do not hold on to it. Say it clearly but quickly and move immediately to the vowel.

Do not leave a breathy space between the consonant and the vowel, start the vowel as soon as you release your lip.

Think of the consonant as a springboard that bounces you powerfully into a clear, open vowel. You can feel the [θ] well forward in your mouth, imagine bringing the vowel forward into that position as well.

Note: When you say a voiceless consonant, like [θ], your vocal cords are apart, that is, not vibrating. So when you move from the consonant to the vowel make a special effort to start the vowel clearly and strongly—*a breathy vowel cannot be blamed on a voiceless consonant*.

If you have trouble moving from a voiceless consonant to the vowel, practice the transition until the vowel is clear every time you say it.

Practice Words

In the following words say [θ] clearly and strongly, but without any extra tension in your articulators.

Say the words out loud, then sing them on a comfortable pitch.

three... three...	*author... author...*	*faith... faith...*
think... think...	*nothing... nothing...*	*teeth... teeth...*
thirst... thirst...	*birthday... birthday...*	*booth... booth...*
thigh... thigh...	*anything... anything...*	*mouth... mouth...*
thumb... thumb...	*lengthen... lengthen...*	*tenth... tenth...*

Practice Sentences

In the following sentences feel your articulators moving and feel the resonance of each individual sound as you say the words.

Say them slowly at first, then faster. Right now accuracy is more important than speed.

Say the sentences out loud, then sing them on a comfortable pitch.

He thought he saw three thin panthers.

Any theory of warmth at the south pole is a myth.

A thin little boy picked six thick thistle sticks.

She is a thistle sifter and she has a sieve of sifted thistles and a sieve of unsifted thistles, and the sieve of unsifted thistles she sieves into the sieve of sifted thistles, because she is a thistle sifter.

Daily Exercises—Consonant #4 [θ]

(1) Practice saying this sound and the other speech sounds you have learned with the Standard American Diction CDs.

(2) Read aloud from a newspaper, magazine or book until you feel and hear yourself say the [θ] sound five times. Underline the words.

(3) Speak the following reading out loud, slowly at first, then faster. Right now accuracy is more important than speed. Underline the words with [θ].

> *My love is as a fever, longing still*
> *For that which longer nurseth the disease,*
> *Feeding on that which doth preserve the ill,*
> *Th'uncertain sickly appetite to please.*
> *My reason, the physician to my love,*
> *Angry that his prescriptions are not kept,*
> *Hath left me, and I desp'rate now approve*
> *Desire is death, which physic did except.*
> *Past cure I am, now reason is past care,*
> *And frantic mad with evermore unrest,*
> *My thoughts and my discourse as madmen's are,*
> *At random from the truth vainly expressed;*
> > *For I have sworn thee fair, and thought thee bright,*
> > *Who art as black as hell, as dark as night.*
> > > *SHAKESPEARE, Sonnet 147.*

(4) Sing a short passage from one of your songs or arias that has the [θ] in it. Repeat it several times, concentrating on saying [θ] correctly.

(5) Repeat the entire section for [θ] three times today.

(6) And make sure you're saying [θ] correctly as you speak during the day.

Consonant #5 [Z] "zoom" (voiced fricative)

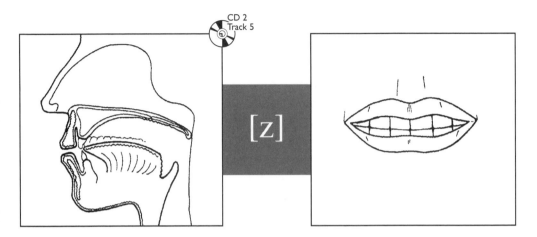

CD 2
Track 5

[z]

Hearing

Listen carefully to this sound on the Standard American Diction CDs.

Jaw

Bring the cutting edges of your front teeth very close together, so that they are almost touching edge to edge and slightly overlapping.

Lips

Feel your lips relaxed and open.

Tongue

Feel the sides of your tongue lightly touching your upper molars.

Feel the front edge of the blade of your tongue very close to the cutting edges of your front teeth.

Start the voiced sound.

Hear the sound and feel the vibrations on your tongue and teeth. The vocal sound should be louder than the sound of the breath moving between your teeth.

After you say the sound, relax your tongue back down to its normal position and let your jaw relax open.

Say the sound out loud, sustaining it for two counts.

[z]... relax [z]... relax

[z]... relax [z]... relax

Now sing the sound out loud, on a comfortable pitch. Sustain it for two counts.

[z]... relax [z]... relax

[z]... relax [z]... relax

Resonant Feel

Pay particular attention to the resonant feel of [z]. The character of its resonance is different from all the other speech sounds. Learn to love it and look forward to singing it.

Mirror Exercise

Now watch yourself in a mirror as you say [z].

See the position of your teeth and hear the sound you make.

Your teeth should be almost edge to edge, with your upper teeth slightly overlapping your lower teeth. If the sound isn't quite right, adjust the position of your teeth to bring them more edge to edge or slightly more overlapping.

To get the right sound you may also need to move your tongue closer to or further away from your front teeth.

You may also need to move the front edge of the blade of your tongue slightly up or down.

It should feel like you're aiming the sound right at the space between the cutting edges of your front teeth.

Your lower lip should be down low enough to allow you to see the space between your teeth, so that it doesn't obstruct the flow of air.

> Say the sound out loud.
> [z]... [z]...
> [z]... [z]...
> Now sing the sound out loud, on a comfortable pitch.
> Sustain it for two counts.
> [z]... [z]...
> [z]... [z]...

Possible Problems

Listen carefully to the sound of your [z]. If it does not sound like the examples on the Standard American Diction CDs, try some of the following adjustments.

Teeth

The problem may be with the position of your teeth. Your upper and lower teeth should be very close together in the front, with a tiny space between them.

They should be almost edge to edge, with the upper teeth slightly overlapping the lower teeth.

Look in a mirror to check their position.

Tongue

The problem may also be with the position of your tongue.

Move the front edge of the blade of your tongue slightly up or down.

It should feel like you're aiming the sound right at the space between the cutting edges of your front teeth.

Lips

Sometimes your lower lip can lift up too high and get in the way of the [z] sound.

Your lower lip should be down low enough so that you can see the space between your teeth.

Listen to yourself carefully as you say [z]. If you hear the sound change right at the end, with a little [ə] (the vowel sound in *uh*), it means you're moving your tongue or your jaw, or both, before you finish saying the sound. Keep the sound pure, that is, a single sound. Notice that when your tongue and jaw stay in place the sound doesn't change.

> Speak, then sing the sound at a medium volume.
> [z]... [z]...
> [z]... [z]...

Saying Consonants in Words

When saying [z] in words, do not hold on to it. Say it clearly but quickly and move immediately to the vowel.

Do not leave a breathy space between the consonant and the vowel, start the vowel as soon as you release your lip. Think of the consonant as a springboard that bounces you powerfully into a clear, open vowel. You can feel the [z] well forward in your mouth, imagine bringing the vowel forward into that position as well.

Practice Words

In the following words say [z] clearly and strongly, but without any extra tension in your articulators.

Say the words out loud, then sing them on a comfortable pitch.

zoo... zoo...	*using... using...*	*has... has...*
zip... zip...	*busy... busy...*	*was... was...*
zero... zero...	*music... music...*	*buzz... buzz...*
zone... zone...	*hazard... hazard...*	*doze... doze...*
zany... zany...	*buzzard... buzzard...*	*browse... browse...*

Practice Sentences

In the following sentences feel your articulators moving and feel the resonance of each individual sound as you say the words.

Say them slowly at first, then faster. Right now accuracy is more important than speed.

Say the sentences out loud, then sing them on a comfortable pitch.

The zebras were dozing at the zoo.

His teasing was pleasing the maids.

His head was dizzy from zooming around.

Suzie's husband closed his nose in the closet doors.

Daily Exercises—Consonant #5 [z]

(1) Practice saying this sound and the other speech sounds you have learned with the Standard American Diction CDs.

(2) Read aloud from a newspaper, magazine or book until you feel and hear yourself say the [z] sound five times. Underline the words.

(3) Speak the following reading out loud, slowly at first, then faster. Right now accuracy is more important than speed. Underline the words with [z].

> *Music to hear, why hear'st thou music sadly?*
> *Sweets with sweets war not, joy delights in joy.*
> *Why lov'st thou that which thou receiv'st not gladly,*
> *Or else receiv'st with pleasure thine annoy?*
> *If the true concord of well-tuned sounds,*
> *By unions married, do offend thine ear,*
> *They do but sweetly chide thee, who confounds*
> *In singleness the parts that thou shouldst bear.*
> *Mark how one string, sweet husband to another,*
> *Strikes each in each by mutual ordering;*
> *Resembling sire, and child, and happy mother,*
> *Who all in one, one pleasing note do sing;*
> > *Whose speechless song being many, seeming one,*
> > *Sings this to thee: "Thou single wilt prove none."*
> > *SHAKESPEARE, Sonnet 8.*

(4) Sing a short passage from one of your songs or arias that has the [z] in it. Repeat it several times, concentrating on saying [z] correctly.

(5) Repeat the entire section for [z] three times today.

(6) And make sure you're saying [z] correctly as you speak during the day.

Consonant #6 [s] "sale" (voiceless fricative)

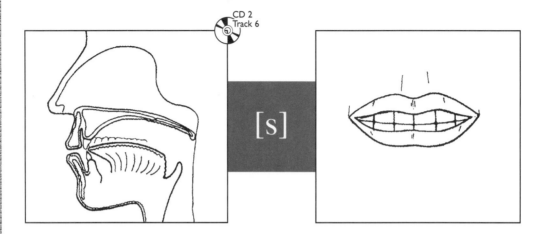

CD 2
Track 6

[s]

Hearing

Listen carefully to this sound on the Standard American Diction CDs.

Jaw

Bring the cutting edges of your front teeth very close together, so that they are almost touching edge to edge and slightly overlapping.

Lips

Feel your lips relaxed and open.

Tongue

Feel the sides of your tongue lightly touching your upper molars.

Feel the front edge of the blade of your tongue very close to the cutting edges of your front teeth.

Blow a little air out between your front teeth. No air should escape around the sides.

Hear the high-pitched whispery sound of [s].

After you say the sound, relax your tongue back down to its normal position and let your jaw relax open.

Say the sound out loud, sustaining it for two counts.

[s]... relax [s]... relax

[s]... relax [s]... relax

Resonant Feel

Pay particular attention to the feel of [s]. Its character is different from all the other speech sounds. Learn to love it and look forward to singing it.

Mirror Exercise

Now watch yourself in a mirror as you say [s].

Hear the sound you make. If it doesn't sound the same as the examples on the Standard American Diction CDs, adjust the position of your teeth or the position of your tongue.

Your teeth should be almost edge to edge, with your upper teeth slightly overlapping your lower teeth. If the sound isn't quite right, adjust the position of your teeth to bring them more edge to edge or slightly more overlapping.

To get the right sound you may need to move your tongue closer to or further away from your front teeth.

You may also need to move the front edge of the blade of your tongue slightly up or down.

It should feel like you're aiming the stream of air that makes the sound right at the space between the cutting edges of your front teeth.

Your lower lip should be down low enough to allow you to see the space between your teeth, so that it doesn't obstruct the flow of air.

> Say the sound out loud.
>
> [s]... [s]...
>
> [s]... [s]...

Possible Problems

Listen carefully to the sound of your [s]. If it does not sound like the examples on the Standard American Diction CDs, try some of the following adjustments.

Teeth

The problem may be with the position of your teeth. Your upper and lower teeth should be very close together in the front, with a very narrow space between them, through which you blow the air.

They should be almost edge to edge or the upper teeth slightly overlapping the lower teeth.

Look in a mirror to see where you are positioning your teeth when you say [s].

Tongue

The problem may also be with the position of your tongue.

Move your tongue closer to or further away from your front teeth to change the sound.

You may also need to move the front edge of the blade of your tongue slightly up or down.

It should feel like you're aiming the stream of air right at the space between the cutting edges of your front teeth.

Sometimes people press their tongue too hard against their teeth. Your tongue should touch your teeth very lightly and leave a tiny space between your teeth and the very front of your tongue, through which you blow the air.

Another problem is moving your tongue as you say the [s]. Some people press their tongue against their teeth, blocking the flow of air, then release their tongue as they start the sound. This creates a kind of lisping sound, [ts]. Your tongue should lightly touch just the right place, without any movement or obstruction of the stream of air.

Lips

Another problem may be the position of your lower lip. Sometimes your lower lip can lift up too high and get in the way of the [s] sound.

Your lower lip should be down low enough so that you can see the space between your teeth.

Comparison Exercise

Here is a comparison exercise to help you differentiate between [z] and [s].

Repeat them one after the other until you can clearly hear and feel the difference between them.

Say the sounds out loud.

[z,s,z,s,z,s]... [z,s,z,s,z,s]...

[z,s,z,s,z,s]... [z,s,z,s,z,s]...

Saying Consonants in Words

When saying [s] in words, do not hold on to it. Say it clearly but quickly and move immediately to the vowel.

Do not leave a breathy space between the consonant and the vowel, start the vowel as soon as you release your lip. Think of the consonant as a springboard that bounces you powerfully into a clear, open vowel. You can feel the [s] well forward in your mouth, imagine bringing the vowel forward into that position as well.

Note: When you say a voiceless consonant, like [s], your vocal cords are apart, that is, not vibrating. So when you move from the consonant to the vowel make a special effort to start the vowel clearly and strongly—*a breathy vowel cannot be blamed on a voiceless consonant*. If you have trouble moving from a voiceless consonant to the vowel, practice the transition until the vowel is clear every time you say it.

Practice Words

In the following words say [s] clearly and strongly, but without any extra tension in your articulators.

Say the words out loud, then sing them on a comfortable pitch.

see... see...	*lesson... lesson...*	*less... less...*
say... say...	*past... past...*	*guess... guess...*
some... some...	*essay... essay...*	*crease... crease...*
stay... stay...	*classic... classic...*	*mouse... mouse...*
sleep... sleep...	*assign... assign...*	*tricks... tricks...*

Practice Sentences

In the following sentences feel your articulators moving and feel the resonance of each individual sound as you say the words.

Say them slowly at first, then faster. Right now accuracy is more important than speed.

Say the sentences out loud, then sing them on a comfortable pitch.

Sleek seals swim in the icy sea.

It's seldom said the sun sets in the East.

Sister Suzie's sewing shirts for soldiers by the sea shore.

Six steaming shopkeepers sitting stitching sheets.

Daily Exercises—Consonant #6 [s]

(1) Practice saying this sound and the other speech sounds you have learned with the Standard American Diction CDs.

(2) Read aloud from a newspaper, magazine or book until you feel and hear yourself say the [s] sound five times. Underline the words.

(3) Speak the following reading out loud, slowly at first, then faster. Right now accuracy is more important than speed. Underline the words with [s].

> *When to the sessions of sweet silent thought*
> *I summon up remembrance of things past,*
> *I sigh the lack of many a thing I sought,*
> *And with old woes new wail my dear times waste.*
> *Then can I drown an eye, unused to flow,*
> *For precious friends hid in death's dateless night,*
> *And weep afresh love's long since cancelled woe,*
> *And moan th'expense of many a vanished sight.*
> *Then can I grieve at grievances foregone,*
> *And heavily from woe to woe tell o'er*
> *The sad account of fore-bemoaned moan,*
> *Which I new pay as if not paid before.*
> > *But if the while I think on thee, dear friend,*
> > *All losses are restored, and sorrows end.*
> > *SHAKESPEARE, Sonnet 30*

(4) Sing a short passage from one of your songs or arias that has the [s] in it. Repeat it several times, concentrating on saying [s] correctly.

(5) Repeat the entire section for [s] three times today.

(6) And make sure you're saying [s] correctly as you speak during the day.

How to Avoid Excessive Sibilance

The [s] sound is a sibilant sound, that is, it sounds like a hiss. When the [s] becomes too loud or prominent, it is annoying to listen to and is called excessive **sibilance**.

There are three reasons for excessive sibilance.

Let's take quick look at how you can eliminate each of these problems.

Shorten the duration of the [s].

If your [s] is too loud because you hold on to it too long, you need to decrease the length of time you blow the air between your teeth.

Here is an exercise to learn to control your breath on a [s].

Alternate holding the [s] for two counts and for one count.

[s] (two counts)... [s] (1 count)...

[s] (two counts)... [s] (1 count)...

Again.

[s] (two counts)... [s] (1 count)...

[s] (two counts)... [s] (1 count)...

You can control the length of time that you hold the [s] sound.

Blow the air more lightly between your teeth.

If your [s] is too loud because you blow the air too forcefully between your teeth, learn to blow the air more lightly.

Practicing saying a very light [s], so light that you can hardly hear it.
Then connect the light [s] to a strong, resonant vowel.

Alternate between a loud [s] and a light [s].

[s] (strong)... [s] (light)...

[s] (strong)... [s] (light)...

Again.

[s] (strong)... [s] (light)...

[s] (strong)... [s] (light)...

Now let's add a strong, resonant vowel to the light, short [s].

[sɑ]... [sɑ]...

[sɑ]... [sɑ]...

Again.

[sɑ]... [sɑ]...

[sɑ]... [sɑ]...

Usually, when you say the vowel forcefully, you also tend to say the [s] forcefully, so the trick is to keep the vowel strong while you pull back on the force of the [s].

Say [z] where you should say [z].

If you have a habit of saying [s] where you should say [z], your speech and singing will sound too sibilant.

The solution is to pay more attention to saying the correct sound—and don't let the spelling fool you.

For example, words such as *has*, *because*, *bands*, *is* and *as* are pronounced with [z], not with [s].

There are two guidelines that may help you know when to say [s] and when to say [z].

[z] follows a voiced consonant—*dogs* [dɑgz]

[s] follows a voiceless consonant—*cats* [kæts].

There are some exceptions to these two rules, but they generally hold true.

Be sure you know the correct pronunciation of the word and be careful to say it correctly.

Consonant #7   [ʒ]   "leisure"   (voiced fricative)

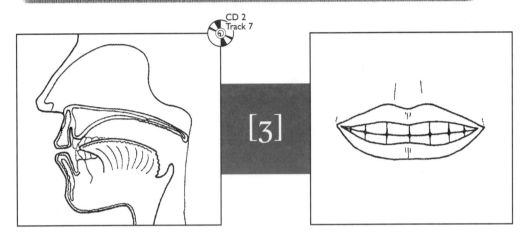

CD 2
Track 7

[ʒ]

Hearing

Listen carefully to this sound on the Standard American Diction CDs.

Jaw

Bring the cutting edges of your front teeth very close together, so that they are almost touching edge to edge and slightly overlapping.

Lips

Feel your lips relaxed and open.

Tongue

Feel the sides of your tongue lightly touching your upper molars.

Feel the front edge of the blade of your tongue close to your front teeth, but a little further away than it is for [ʒ].

Start the voiced sound.

Hear the sound and feel the vibrations on your tongue and teeth. The vocal sound should be louder than the sound of the breath.

After you say the sound, relax your tongue back down to its normal position and let your jaw relax open.

Say the sound out loud, sustaining it for two counts.

[ʒ]... relax [ʒ]... relax

[ʒ]... relax [ʒ]... relax

Now sing the sound out loud, on a comfortable pitch. Sustain it for two counts.

[ʒ]... [ʒ]...

[ʒ]... [ʒ]...

Resonant Feel

Pay particular attention to the resonant feel of [ʒ]. The character of its resonance is different from all the other speech sounds. Learn to love it and look forward to singing it.

Mirror Exercise

Now watch yourself in a mirror as you say [ʒ].

Hear the sound. If it doesn't sound the same as the examples on the Standard American Diction CDs, adjust the position of your teeth or the position of your tongue.

Your teeth should be almost edge to edge, with your upper teeth slightly overlapping your lower teeth. If the sound isn't quite right, adjust the position of your teeth to bring them more edge to edge or slightly more overlapping.

To get just the right sound, you may need move your tongue closer to or further away from your front teeth.

You may also need to move the front edge of the blade of your tongue slightly up or down. It should feel like you're moving the sound over the blade of your tongue and through the space between the cutting edges of your front teeth.

Your lower lip should be down low enough to allow you to see the space between your teeth, so that it doesn't obstruct the flow of air.

Say the sound out loud.

[ʒ]... [ʒ]...
[ʒ]... [ʒ]...

Now sing the sound out loud, on a comfortable pitch.
Sustain it for two counts.

[ʒ]... [ʒ]...
[ʒ]... [ʒ]...

Possible Problems

Listen to yourself carefully as you say [ʒ]. If you hear the sound change right at the end, with a little [ə] (the vowel sound in *uh*), it means you're moving your tongue or your jaw, or both, before you finish saying the sound. Keep the sound pure, that is, a single sound. Notice that when your tongue and jaw stay in place the sound doesn't change.

Speak, then sing the sound at a medium volume.

[ʒ]... [ʒ]... [ʒ]... [ʒ]...

Comparison Exercise

Here is a comparison exercise to help you differentiate between [z] and [ʒ].

Feel the difference in the position of your tongue for each sound.

Repeat the sounds one after the other until you can clearly hear and feel the difference between them.

Say the sounds out loud.

[z,ʒ,z,ʒ,z,ʒ]... [z,ʒ,z,ʒ,z,ʒ]...
[z,ʒ,z,ʒ,z,ʒ]... [z,ʒ,z,ʒ,z,ʒ]...

Saying Consonants in Words

When saying [ʒ] in words, do not hold on to it. Say it clearly but quickly and move immediately to the vowel.

Do not leave a breathy space between the consonant and the vowel, start the vowel as soon as you release your lip. Think of the consonant as a springboard that bounces you powerfully into a clear, open vowel. You can feel the [ʒ] well forward in your mouth, imagine bringing the vowel forward into that position as well.

Practice Words

In the following words say [ʒ] clearly and strongly, but without any extra tension in your articulators.

Say the words out loud, then sing them on a comfortable pitch.

u*s*ual... u*s*ual...	rou*g*e... rou*g*e...
vi*s*ion... vi*s*ion...	bei*g*e... bei*g*e...
a*z*ure... a*z*ure...	gara*g*e... gara*g*e...
mea*s*ure... mea*s*ure...	corsa*g*e... corsa*g*e..
preci*s*ion... preci*s*ion...	presti*g*e... presti*g*e...

Practice Sentences

In the following sentences feel your articulators moving and feel the resonance of each individual sound as you say the words.

Say them slowly at first, then faster. Right now accuracy is more important than speed.

Say the sentences out loud, then sing them on a comfortable pitch.

> *The mirage was a delusion of his vision.*
> *They measured the treasure with precision.*
> *The division's prestige came under derision.*
> *Visions of treasure bring measureless pleasure.*

Daily Exercises—Consonant #7 [ʒ]

(1) Practice saying this sound and the other speech sounds you have learned with the Standard American Diction CDs.

(2) Read aloud from a newspaper, magazine or book until you feel and hear yourself say the [ʒ] sound five times. Underline the words.

(3) Speak the following reading out loud, slowly at first, then faster. Right now accuracy is more important than speed. Underline the words with [ʒ].

> *So am I as the rich whose blessed key*
> *Can bring him to his sweet up-locked treasure,*
> *The which he will not every hour survey,*
> *For blunting the fine point of seldom pleasure.*
> *Therefore are feasts so solemn and so rare,*
> *Since seldom coming in the long year set,*
> *Like stones of worth they thinly placed are,*
> *Or captain jewels in the carcanet.*
> *So is the time that keeps you as my chest,*
> *Or as the wardrobe which the robe doth hide*
> *To make some special instant special blest,*
> *By new unfolding his imprisoned pride.*
> > *Blessed are you whose worthiness gives scope,*
> > *Being had to triumph, being lacked to hope.*
> > SHAKESPEARE, Sonnet 52.

(4) Sing a short passage from one of your songs or arias that has the [ʒ] in it. Repeat it several times, concentrating on saying [ʒ] correctly.

(5) Repeat the entire section for [ʒ] three times today.

(6) And make sure you're saying [ʒ] correctly as you speak during the day.

Consonant #8 [ʃ] "<u>sh</u>e" (voiceless fricative)

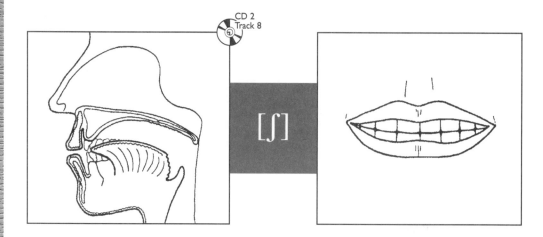

Hearing

Listen carefully to this sound on the Standard American Diction CDs.

Jaw

Bring the cutting edges of your front teeth very close together, so that they are almost touching edge to edge and slightly overlapping.

Lips

Feel your lips relaxed and open.

Tongue

Feel the sides of your tongue lightly touching your upper molars.

Feel the edge of the blade of your tongue very close to the edges of your front teeth, but a little further away than it is for [s].

Blow a small amount of breath out between the front edges of your teeth. No air should escape around the sides.

Hear the whispery, friction-like sound of [ʃ].

After you say the sound, relax your tongue back down to its normal position and let your jaw relax open.

Say the sound out loud, sustaining it for two counts.

[ʃ]... relax [ʃ]... relax

[ʃ]... relax [ʃ]... relax

Resonant Feel

Pay particular attention to the feel of [ʃ]. Its character is different from all the other speech sounds. Learn to love it and look forward to singing it.

Mirror Exercise

Now watch yourself in a mirror as you say [ʃ].

Hear the sound. If it doesn't sound the same as the examples on the Standard American Diction CDs, adjust the positions of your teeth or your tongue.

Your teeth should be almost edge to edge, with your upper teeth slightly overlapping your lower teeth. If the sound isn't quite right, adjust the position of your teeth to bring them more edge to edge or slightly more overlapping.

To get just the right sound, you may need move your tongue closer to or further away from your front teeth.

You may also need to move the front edge of the blade of your tongue slightly up or down.

It should feel like you're moving the sound over the blade of your tongue and through the space between the cutting edges of your front teeth.

Your lower lip should be down low enough to allow you to see the space between your teeth, so that it doesn't obstruct the flow of air.

Say the sound out loud.

[ʃ]... [ʃ]...
[ʃ]... [ʃ]...

Comparison Exercises

Here is a comparison exercise to help you differentiate between [s] and [ʃ].

Feel the difference in the position of your tongue for each sound.

Repeat them one after the other until you can clearly hear and feel the difference between them.

Say the sounds out loud.

[s,ʃ,s,ʃ,s,ʃ]... [s,ʃ,s,ʃ,s,ʃ]...
[s,ʃ,s,ʃ,s,ʃ]... [s,ʃ,s,ʃ,s,ʃ]...

Here is a comparison exercise to help you differentiate between [ʒ] and [ʃ].

Repeat the sounds one after the other until you can clearly hear and feel the difference between them.

Say the sounds out loud.

[ʒ,ʃ,ʒ,ʃ,ʒ,ʃ]... [ʒ,ʃ,ʒ,ʃ,ʒ,ʃ]...
[ʒ,ʃ,ʒ,ʃ,ʒ,ʃ]... [ʒ,ʃ,ʒ,ʃ,ʒ,ʃ]...

Saying Consonants in Words

When saying [ʃ] in words, do not hold on to it. Say it clearly but quickly and move immediately to the vowel.

Do not leave a breathy space between the consonant and the vowel, start the vowel as soon as you release your lip. Think of the consonant as a springboard that bounces you powerfully into a clear, open vowel. You can feel the [ʃ] well forward in your mouth, imagine bringing the vowel forward into that position as well.

Note: When you say a voiceless consonant, like [ʃ], your vocal cords are apart, that is, not vibrating. So when you move from the consonant to the vowel make a special effort to start the vowel clearly and strongly—*a breathy vowel cannot be blamed on a voiceless consonant*. If you have trouble moving from a voiceless consonant to the vowel, practice the transition until the vowel is clear every time you say it.

Practice Words

In the following words say [ʃ] clearly and strongly, but without any extra tension in your articulators.

Say the words out loud, then sing them on a comfortable pitch.

sure... sure...	*ocean... ocean...*	*dash... dash...*
shade... shade...	*passion... passion...*	*push... push...*
shut... shut...	*caution... caution...*	*leash... leash...*
shack... shack...	*precious... precious...*	*harsh... harsh...*
shambles... shambles...	*conscience... conscience...*	*vanish... vanish...*

Practice Sentences

In the following sentences feel your articulators moving and feel the resonance of each individual sound as you say the words.

Say them slowly at first, then faster. Right now accuracy is more important than speed.

Say the sentences out loud, then sing them on a comfortable pitch.

> Such <u>sh</u>abby sa<u>sh</u>es are <u>sh</u>ameful.
>
> A lu<u>sh</u> blu<u>sh</u> is more than a flu<u>sh</u>.
>
> <u>Sh</u>y <u>Sh</u>eila sat <u>sh</u>ivering in her slim <u>sh</u>iny <u>sh</u>ot-silk smock.
>
> <u>Sh</u>e sells sea-<u>sh</u>ells, <u>sh</u>erry and sand<u>sh</u>oes on the sea <u>sh</u>ore.

Daily Exercises—Consonant #8 [ʃ]

(1) Practice saying this sound and the other speech sounds you have learned with the Standard American Diction CDs.

(2) Read aloud from a newspaper, magazine or book until you feel and hear yourself say the [ʃ] sound five times. Underline the words.

(3) Speak the following reading out loud, slowly at first, then faster. Right now accuracy is more important than speed. Underline the words with [ʃ].

> Shall I compare thee to a summer's day?
> Thou art more lovely and more temperate:
> Rough winds do shake the darling buds of May,
> And summer's lease hath all too short a date;
> Sometime too hot the eye of heaven shines,
> And often is his gold complexion dimmed;
> And every fair from fair sometime declines,
> By chance or nature's changing course untrimmed:
> But thy eternal summer shall not fade,
> Nor lose possession of that fair thou ow'st,
> Nor shall death brag thou wand'rest in his shade,
> When in eternal lines to time thou grow'st.
> > So long as men can breathe or eyes can see,
> > So long lives this, and this gives life to thee.
> > > SHAKESPEARE, Sonnet 18.

(4) Sing a short passage from one of your songs or arias that has the [ʃ] in it. Repeat it several times, concentrating on saying [ʃ] correctly.

(5) Repeat the entire section for [ʃ] three times today.

(6) And make sure you're saying [ʃ] correctly as you speak during the day.

Consonant #9 [h] "have" (voiceless fricative)

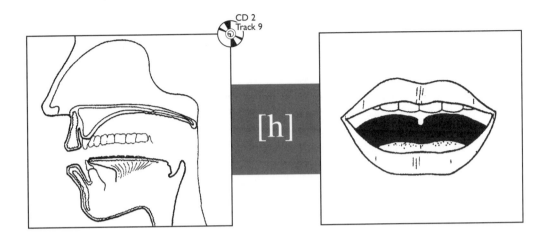

CD 2
Track 9

Hearing

Listen carefully to this sound on the Standard American Diction CDs.

Jaw

Open your jaw about a finger width.

Leave your jaw open as you say the sound.

(An open jaw allows you to maintain better resonance.)

Tongue

Feel your tongue relaxed down on the floor of your mouth. Leave it there as you say the sound.

Lips

Feel your lips relaxed and open.

Do not tighten your throat.

Expel a tiny amount of breath.

Hear a very quiet breathy sound.

Say the sound out loud.

[h]... [h]...

[h]... [h]...

When you say this sound your articulators are always in position for the vowel sound that follows. For example:

Feel your articulators in place for [i] and say *he*.

Feel your articulators in place for [u] and say *who*.

Possible Problems

This consonant is so quiet, it is almost inaudible and you should not try to make it loud.

But even though [h] is not loud, you can tell if it is being said or not.

For example, say the following words with and without [h]. If you listen carefully, you can tell by the sound when you are not saying [h].

Say the words out loud.

he... _e... *him*... _im... *who*... _o...

The only problems you might have with this sound are:

(1) Blowing too much air.

(2) Trying to make it too loud.

Saying Consonants in Words

When saying [h] in words, do not hold on to it. Say it quickly but clearly and move immediately to the vowel.

Do not leave a space between the consonant and the vowel. Think of the consonant as a springboard that bounces you powerfully into a clear, open vowel. You can feel the [h] well forward in your mouth, imagine bringing the vowel forward into that position as well.

Note: When you say a voiceless consonant, like [h], your vocal cords are apart, that is, not vibrating. So when you move from the consonant to the vowel make a special effort to start the vowel clearly and strongly—*a breathy vowel cannot be blamed on a voiceless consonant*. If you have trouble moving from a voiceless consonant to the vowel, practice the transition until the vowel is clear every time you say it.

Practice Words

Say the words out loud, then sing them on a comfortable pitch.

has... has...	*behind... behind...*
home... home...	*rehearse... rehearse...*
help... help...	*ahead... ahead...*
haven... haven...	*perhaps... perhaps...*
haughty... haughty...	*anyhow... anyhow...*

Practice Sentences

In the following sentences feel your articulators moving and feel the resonance of each individual sound as you say the words.

Say them slowly at first, then faster. Right now accuracy is more important than speed.

Say the sentences out loud, then sing them on a comfortable pitch.

He has his habits.

Perhaps he'll rehearse anyhow.

How high his highness holds his haughty head.

Holly hoped her hat hung happily.

Daily Exercises—Consonant #9 [h]

(1) Practice saying this sound and the other speech sounds you have learned with the Standard American Diction CDs.

(2) Read aloud from a newspaper, magazine or book until you feel and hear yourself say the [h] sound five times. Underline the words.

(3) Speak the following reading out loud, slowly at first, then faster. Right now accuracy is more important than speed. Underline the words with [h].

> *Thy bosom is endeared with all hearts,*
> *Which I by lacking have supposed dead.*
> *And there reigns love and all love's loving parts,*
> *And all those friends which I thought buried.*
> *How many a holy and obsequious tear*
> *Hath dear religious love stol'n from mine eye,*
> *As interest of the dead, which now appear*
> *But things removed that hidden in thee lie.*
> *Thou art the grave where buried love doth live,*
> *Hung with the trophies of my lovers gone,*
> *Who all their parts of me to thee did give;*
> *That due of many now is thine alone.*
> > *Their images I loved I view in thee,*
> > *And thou, all they, hast all the all of me.*
> > *SHAKESPEARE, Sonnet 31.*

(4) Sing a short passage from one of your songs or arias that has the [h] in it. Repeat it several times, concentrating on saying [h] correctly.

(5) Repeat the entire section for [h] three times today.

(6) And make sure you're saying [h] correctly as you speak during the day.

Congratulations! You've learned to recognize and say all the **Fricative Consonant** sounds of **Standard American Speech**.

Review of Fricatives

Let's do a quick review of the fricative consonants.

Speak, then sing, the sounds and the words out loud.

(1) [v] *van... veil... live...* [v]
(2) [f] *fun... far... if...* [f]
(3) [ð] *the... that... other...* [ð]
(4) [θ] *thank... thing... booth...* [θ]
(5) [z] *zoom... zip... buzz...* [z]
(6) [s] *song... sail... voice...* [s]
(7) [ʒ] *Asia... rouge... garage...* [ʒ]
(8) [ʃ] *she... shore... dash...* [ʃ]
(9) [h] *has... help... who...* [h]

Notice how much more clearly and easily you can say these sounds.

Notes:

vowel #3 eɪ "ai"

vowel #7 ə "uh"

consonant #8 ʃ "sh"

consonant #21 l "t"

11 Plosive Consonants

A plosive consonant is a consonant formed by building up breath pressure behind your articulators, then releasing it with the sound.

Sometimes plosives are also called stop-plosives, or simply stops.

How Do You Make a Plosive?

You make a plosive by bringing two of your articulators together, building up a little air pressure behind them, then opening them to release a quiet, little puff of air.

Pairs of Plosives

Plosives come in pairs. That is, you place your articulators in the same position to make two different phonetic sounds.

The way you make the sounds different is by adding **vocal cord vibration** (**voiced** sound) to one, but not to the other.

So one is a **voiced plosive** and the other is a **voiceless plosive**.

Voiced/Voiceless Plosives

For a **voiced** plosive your **vocal cords vibrate**.

For a voiceless plosive your **vocal cords do not vibrate**.

Here is an exercise to help you feel and hear the difference between a voiced and voiceless sound.

To feel a **voiced** plosive:

Place your fingers lightly on your throat.

Say *aaaah* and feel the vibrations.

Continue saying *aaaah* and touch your upper and lower lips together, as if you are saying *b*.

Feel the vibrations on your lips and teeth.

(You can only sustain the sound for a moment, because you have blocked off the air passage.)

Now release your lips.

You have just said the **voiced** plosive [b].

Notice that when you release a voiced plosive you have to say a vowel, because you are already voicing a sound.

In your practice exercises, say the neutral vowel, [ə], when you release your articulators after a voiced plosive.

To feel a **voiceless** plosive:

Place your fingers lightly on your throat.

Say *hhhh*.

There are no vibrations.

Continue saying *hhhh* and touch your upper and lower lips together.

(This blocks off the air passage and stops the *hhhh*.)

Now release your lips.

There is a slight puff of air released and no vocal sound.

You have just said the **voiceless** plosive [p].

To hear and feel the difference between the voiced and voiceless plosive, say the two sounds one after the other.

[b,p,b,p,b,p]...

[b,p,b,p,b,p]...

Here are the pairs of voiced and voiceless plosive consonants.

Say the consonants and the words out loud.

Voiced	Voiceless
(10) [b]... *ball*...	(11) [p]... *pull*...
(12) [d]... *dean*...	(13) [t]... *tall*...
(14) [g]... *got*...	(15) [k]... *can*...

Consonant #10 [b] "<u>b</u>all" (voiced plosive)

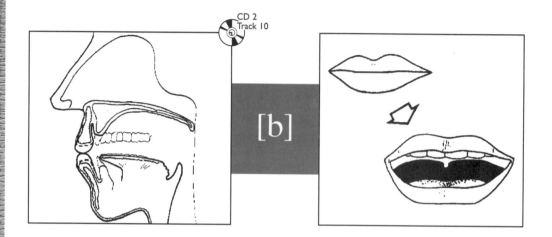

CD 2
Track 10

Hearing

Listen carefully to this sound on the Standard American Diction CDs.

Jaw

Open your jaw a little more than one finger width. (For speech and much of your singing, your jaw floats open about one finger width. But sometimes you need to open your jaw wider, so it's best to practice with a wide jaw.)

Tongue

Feel your tongue relaxed down on the floor of your mouth. Leave it there as you say the sound.

Lips

Bring your upper and lower lips lightly together. Do not close your jaw. (An open jaw helps you to maintain better resonance.)

Begin the vocal sound and feel the vibrations on your lips.

Feel a little breath pressure build up behind your lips. (Do not let the breath pressure puff out your cheeks.)

Relax your lips open.

Feel like you're bouncing into a strong vowel sound.

Say the sound out loud—open up to the neutral vowel, [ə].

[b]... [b]...

[b]... [b]...

Now sing the sound at a medium volume, on a comfortable pitch—release into the neutral vowel, [ə].

[b]... [b]...

[b]... [b]...

Resonant Feel

Pay particular attention to the resonant feel of [b]. The character of its resonance is different from all the other phonetic sounds. Learn to love it and look forward to singing it.

Mirror Exercise

Watch yourself in a mirror as you say [b].

For a clear [b], your jaw should stay open, with your teeth about a finger width apart. Touch your jaw to help it stay open.

Say the sound out loud.

[b]... [b]...

[b]... [b]...

Now sing the sound at a medium volume, on a comfortable pitch—use the neutral vowel, [ə].

[b]... [b]...

[b]... [b]...

Saying Consonants in Words

Do not leave a breathy space between the consonant and the vowel, start the vowel as soon as you release your lips. Think of the consonant as a springboard that bounces you powerfully into a clear, open vowel. You can feel the [b] well forward in your mouth, imagine bringing the vowel forward into that position as well.

Practice Words

In the following words, say [b] clearly and strongly, but without any extra tension in your articulators.

Say the words out loud, then sing them on a comfortable pitch.

ball... ball...	*about... about...*	*dab... dab...*
bone... bone...	*nibble... nibble...*	*tube... tube...*
bare... bare...	*number... number...*	*robe... robe...*
bark... bark...	*ribbon... ribbon...*	*garb... garb...*
begin... begin...	*rabbit... rabbit...*	*rhubarb... rhubarb...*

Practice Sentences

In the following sentences, feel your articulators moving and feel the resonance of each individual sound as you say the words.

Say the sentences slowly at first, then faster. Right now accuracy is more important than speed.

Speak them out loud, then sing them on a comfortable pitch.

The baby burbled bubbles in the crib.

The rubber bands began to break.

Rubber baby buggy bumpers.

Billy bit a bite of butter,

But it was a bitter bit:

Billy bought some better butter

And had a bite of it.

Daily Exercises—Consonant #10 [b]

(1) Practice saying this sound and the other phonetic sounds you have learned with the Standard American Diction CDs.

(2) Read aloud from a newspaper, magazine or book until you feel and hear yourself say the [b] sound five times. Underline the words.

(3) Speak the following reading out loud, slowly at first, then faster. Right now accuracy is more important than speed. Underline the words with [b].

> *In the old age black was not counted fair,*
> *Or if it were it bore not beauty's name.*
> *But now is black beauty's successive heir,*
> *And beauty slandered with a bastard shame;*
> *For since each hand hath put on nature's pow'r,*
> *Fairing the foul with art's false borrowed face,*
> *Sweet beauty hath no name, no holy bow'r,*
> *But is profaned, if not lives in disgrace.*
> *Therefore my mistress' eyes are raven black,*
> *Her eyes so suited, and they mourners seem*
> *At such who, not born fair, no beauty lack,*
> *Sland'ring creation with a false esteem.*
> > *Yet so they mourn becoming of their woe,*
> > *That every tongue says beauty should look so.*
> > SHAKESPEARE, Sonnet 129.

(4) Sing a short passage from one of your songs or arias that has the [b] in it. Repeat it several times, concentrating on saying [b] correctly.

(5) Repeat the entire section for [b] three times today.

(6) And make sure you're saying [b] correctly as you speak during the day.

Consonant #11   [p]   "pop"   (voiceless plosive)

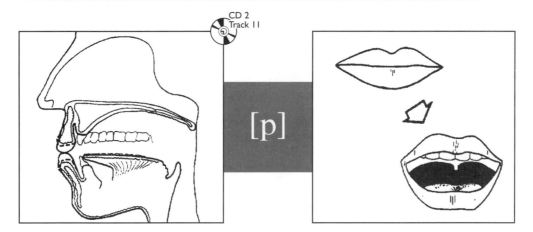

CD 2
Track 11

Hearing

Listen carefully to this sound on the Standard American Diction CDs.

Jaw

Open your jaw a little more than one finger width. (For speech and much of your singing, your jaw floats open about one finger width. But sometimes you need to open your jaw wider, so it's best to practice with a wide jaw.)

Tongue

Feel your tongue relaxed down on the floor of your mouth. Leave it there as you say the sound.

Lips

Bring your upper and lower lips lightly together. Do not close your jaw. (An open jaw helps you to maintain better resonance.)

Feel a little breath pressure build up behind your lips. (Do not let the breath pressure puff out your cheeks.)

Relax your lips open.

Feel and hear the release of a light puff of air.

Say the sound out loud. Do not try to make it loud.

[p]... [p]...
[p]... [p]...

Now sing the sound at a medium volume, on a comfortable pitch— release into the neutral vowel, [ə].

[p]... [p]...
[p]... [p]...

Resonant Feel

Pay particular attention to the feel of [p]. It is different from all the other phonetic sounds. Learn to love it and look forward to singing it.

Mirror Exercise

Watch yourself in a mirror as you say [p].

Don't press your lips tightly against each other and don't close your jaw when you bring your lips together.

Touch your jaw to help it stay open.

Hear and feel the release of a tiny, almost inaudible puff of breath—don't try to make it loud.

Say the sound out loud.
[p]... [p]...
[p]... [p]...

Possible Problems

Blowing too much air: Generally, the only problem with making this sound is allowing too much breath to escape between it and the following vowel. Be sure that you start the vowel sound as soon as you open your lips.

Say the sound, opening out to the neutral vowel, [ə].

[p]... [p]...
[p]... [p]...

Now sing [p] at a medium volume, on a comfortable pitch.

[p]... [p]...
[p]... [p]...

Comparison Exercise

Here is an exercise to help you differentiate between [b] and [p].

Feel the difference in the resonance for each sound.

Repeat them one after the other until you can clearly hear and feel the difference between them.

Say the sounds out loud.

[b,p,b,p,b,p]...
[b,p,b,p,b,p]...

Saying Consonants in Words

Do not leave a breathy space between the consonant and the vowel, start the vowel as soon as you release your lips.

Think of the consonant as a springboard that bounces you powerfully into a clear, open vowel. You can feel the [p] well forward in your mouth, imagine bringing the vowel forward into that position as well.

Note: When you say a voiceless consonant, like [p], your vocal cords are apart, that is, not vibrating. So when you move from the consonant to the vowel make a special effort to start the vowel clearly and strongly—*a breathy vowel cannot be blamed on a voiceless consonant.* If you have trouble moving from a voiceless consonant to the vowel, practice the transition until the vowel is clear every time you say it.

Practice Words

In the following words, say [p] clearly and strongly, but without any extra tension in your articulators.

Do not blow air between the consonant and the vowel.

Speak the words out loud, then sing them on a comfortable pitch.

peace... peace...	appeal...appeal...	up... up...
pull... pull...	open... open...	tape... tape...
park... park...	apple... apple...	shop... shop...
pile... pile...	span... span...	deep... deep...
poem... poem...	apron... apron...	stop... stop...

Practice Sentences

In the following sentences, feel your articulators moving and feel the resonance of each individual sound as you say the words.

Say the sentences slowly at first, then faster. Right now accuracy is more important than speed.

Speak them out loud, then sing them on a comfortable pitch.

A piece of apple pie puts on a couple of pounds.

Peter hoped to prime the pump.

Playful Polly always pauses for appropriate applause.

Peter Piper picked a peck of pickled peppers,

A peck of pickled peppers, Peter Piper picked.

If Peter Piper picked a peck of pickled peppers,

Where's the peck of pickled peppers Peter Piper picked?

Daily Exercises—Consonant #11 [p]

(1) Practice saying this sound and the other phonetic sounds you have learned with the Standard American Diction CDs.

(2) Read aloud from a newspaper, magazine or book until you feel and hear yourself say the [p] sound five times. Underline the words.

(3) Speak the following reading out loud, slowly at first, then faster. Right now accuracy is more important than speed. Underline the words.with [p].

> *Not from the stars do I my judgement pluck,*
> *And yet methinks I have astronomy;*
> *But not to tell of good or evil luck,*
> *Of plagues, of dearths, or season's quality;*
> *Nor can I fortune to brief minutes tell,*
> *Pointing to each his thunder, rain, and wind,*
> *Or say with princes if it shall go well,*
> *By oft predict that I in heaven find.*
> *But from thine eyes my knowledge I derive,*
> *And, constant stars, in them I read such art*
> *As truth and beauty shall together thrive,*
> *If from thyself to store thou wouldst convert;*
> > *Or else of thee this I prognosticate,*
> > *Thy end is truth's and beauty's doom and date.*
> > > *SHAKESPEARE, Sonnet 14.*

(4) Sing a short passage from one of your songs or arias that has the [p] in it. Repeat it several times, concentrating on saying [p] correctly.

(5) Repeat the entire section for [p] three times today.

(6) And make sure you're saying [p] correctly as you speak during the day.

Consonant #12 [d] "<u>d</u>oll" (voiced plosive)

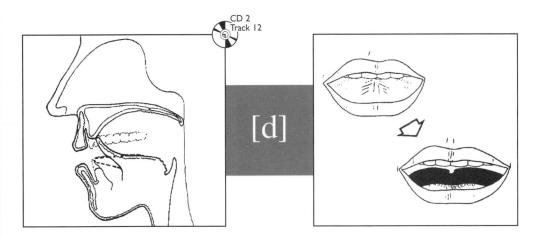

CD 2
Track 12

Hearing

Listen carefully to this sound on the Standard American Diction CDs.

Jaw

Open your jaw about two finger widths. (For speech and much of your singing, your jaw floats open about one finger width. But sometimes you need to open your jaw wider, so it's best to practice with a wide jaw.)

Lips

Feel your lips relaxed open as you say this sound.

Tongue

Lightly touch the edge of the blade of your tongue to your upper gum ridge.

Feel the sides of your tongue touching your upper teeth all the way around, blocking the flow of air.

Start the vocal sound and feel the vibrations on the blade of your tongue and upper gum ridge.

Feel a little breath pressure build up on your tongue, then let your tongue drop down.

Feel like you're bouncing into a strong vowel sound.

Say the sound out loud—open up to the neutral vowel, [ə].

[d]... [d]...

[d]... [d]...

Now sing the sound at a medium volume, on a comfortable pitch— release into the neutral vowel, [ə].

[d]... [d]...

[d]... [d]...

Resonant Feel

Pay particular attention to the resonant feel of [d]. The character of its resonance is different from all the other phonetic sounds. Learn to love it and look forward to singing it.

Mirror Exercise

Watch yourself in a mirror as you say [d].

Don't close your jaw when you touch your tongue to your upper gum ridge. Touch your jaw to help it stay open.

Don't press the top surface of the blade of your tongue against your front teeth or against the roof of your mouth. Touch only the front edge of your tongue lightly to your upper gum ridge.

When you drop your tongue down, let your tongue touch the backs of your lower teeth.

Say the sound out loud.

[d]... [d]...

[d]... [d]...

Now sing the sound at a medium volume, on a comfortable pitch—
use the neutral vowel, [ə].

[d]... [d]...

[d]... [d]...

Saying Consonants in Words

Do not leave a breathy space between the consonant and the vowel, start the vowel as soon as you release your tongue. Think of the consonant as a springboard that bounces you powerfully into a clear, open vowel. You can feel the [d] well forward in your mouth, imagine bringing the vowel forward into that position as well.

Practice Words

In the following words, say [d] clearly and strongly, but without any extra tension in your articulators.

Speak the words out loud, then sing them on a comfortable pitch.

duck... duck...	*advance... advance...*	*odd... odd...*
door... door...	*edict... edict...*	*and... and...*
day... day...	*body... body...*	*red... red...*
dollar... dollar..	*hinder... hinder...*	*made... made...*
dazzle... dazzle...	*sudden... sudden...*	*needed... needed...*

Practice Sentences

In the following sentences, feel your articulators moving and feel the resonance of each individual sound as you say the words.

Say the sentences slowly at first, then faster. Right now accuracy is more important than speed.

Speak them out loud, then sing them on a comfortable pitch.

At dawn the docks are cold.

Loud discussions are seldom dull.

Undoubtably Dan was a dangerous dancer.

Dimpled Delilah declined to dance with Dan.

Daily Exercises—Consonant #12 [d]

(1) Practice saying this sound and the other phonetic sounds you have learned with the Standard American Diction CDs.

(2) Read aloud from a newspaper, magazine or book until you feel and hear yourself say the [d] sound five times. Underline the words.

(3) Speak the following reading out loud, slowly at first, then faster. Right now accuracy is more important than speed. Underline the words with [d].

> *When forty winters shall besiege thy brow*
> *And dig deep trenches in thy beauty's field,*
> *Thy youth's proud livery, so gazed on now,*
> *Will be a tottered weed of small worth held.*
> *Then being asked where all thy beauty lies,*
> *Where all the treasure of thy lusty days;*
> *To say within thine own deep-sunken eyes*
> *Were and all-eating shame and thriftless praise.*
> *How much more praise deserved thy beauty's use,*
> *If thou couldst answer, "This fair child of mine*
> *Shall sum my count and make my old excuse,"*
> *Proving his beauty by succession thine.*
> > *This were to be new made when thou art old,*
> > *And see thy blood warm when thou feel'st it cold.*
> >   *SHAKESPEARE, Sonnet 2.*

(4) Sing a short passage from one of your songs or arias that has the [d] in it. Repeat it several times, concentrating on saying [d] correctly.

(5) Repeat the entire section for [d] three times today.

(6) And make sure you're saying [d] correctly as you speak during the day.

Consonant #13   [t]   "<u>t</u>op" (voiceless plosive)

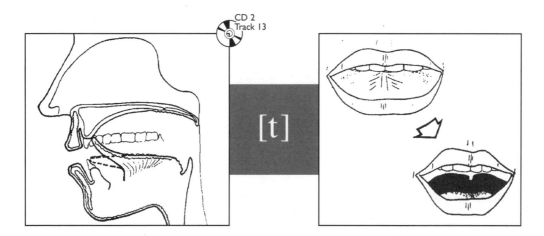

CD 2
Track 13

Hearing

Listen carefully to this sound on the Standard American Diction CDs.

Jaw

Open your jaw a little more than a finger width. (When you are actually speaking, your jaw will almost close as you say [t], but for practice, keep your jaw more open—between one to two finger widths.)

Lips

Feel your lips relaxed open as you say this sound.

Tongue

Lightly touch the edge of the blade of your tongue to your upper gum ridge.

Feel the sides of your tongue touching your upper teeth all the way around, blocking the passage of air.

Feel a little breath pressure build up on your tongue, then let your tongue drop down.

You'll hear a very quiet sound as the air is released.

Say the sound. Do not try to make it loud.

[t]... [t]...

[t]... [t]...

Now sing the sound at a medium volume, on a comfortable pitch— release into the neutral vowel, [ə].

[t]... [t]...

[t]... [t]...

<u>Resonant Feel</u>

Pay particular attention to the feel of [t]. It is different from all the other phonetic sounds. Learn to love it and look forward to singing it.

<u>Mirror Exercise</u>

Watch yourself in a mirror as you say [t].

Don't close your jaw when you touch your tongue to your upper gum ridge. Leave your teeth approximately one finger width apart. Touch your jaw to help it stay open.

Don't press the top surface of the blade of your tongue against your front teeth or against the roof of your mouth. Touch only the front edge of your tongue lightly to your upper gum ridge.

Hear and feel the release of a tiny, almost inaudible puff of breath—don't try to make it loud.

Say the sound out loud.

[t]... [t]...

[t]... [t]...

Now sing the sound at a medium volume, on a comfortable pitch— release into the neutral vowel, [ə].

[t]... [t]...

[t]... [t]...

Possible Problems

Blowing too much air: One of the problems with making this sound is blowing out too much breath between it and the following vowel. Be sure that you start the vowel sound as soon as you release your tongue.

Too much sibilance: Although there is usually a slight sibilant sound with [t], be careful not to add too much sibilant sound, like [ts]. A [s] sound is caused by keeping the edge of the blade of your tongue too close to your upper gum ridge as you release the puff of air.

To avoid the sibilant sound, let your tongue drop away cleanly and quickly. Do not pull it up and back to release the puff of air.

The tendency to add [s] is increased when your teeth are close together as you say [t]. Leave your teeth approximately a finger width apart.

Say the sound out loud—open out to the neutral vowel, [ə].

[t]... [t]...

[t]... [t]...

Now sing the sound at a medium volume, on a comfortable pitch.

[t]... [t]...

[t]... [t]...

Comparison Exercise

Here is an exercise to help you differentiate between [d] and [t].

Feel the difference in the resonance for each sound.

Repeat them one after the other until you can clearly hear and feel the difference between them.

Say the sounds out loud.

[d,t,d,t,d,t]...

[d,t,d,t,d,t]...

Saying Consonants in Words

Do not leave a breathy space between the consonant and the vowel, start the vowel as soon as you release your tongue. Think of the consonant as a springboard that bounces you powerfully into a clear, open vowel. You can feel the [t] well forward in your mouth, imagine bringing the vowel forward into that position as well.

Note: When you say a voiceless consonant, like [t], your vocal cords are apart, that is, not vibrating. So when you move from the consonant to the vowel make a special effort to start the vowel clearly and strongly—*a breathy vowel cannot be blamed on a voiceless consonant.* If you have trouble moving from a voiceless consonant to the vowel, practice the transition until the vowel is clear every time you say it.

Practice Words

In the following words, say [t] clearly and strongly, but without any extra tension in your articulators.

Say the words out loud, then sing them on a comfortable pitch.

too... too...	*letter... letter...*	*not... not...*
time... time...	*water... water...*	*cat... cat...*
taste... taste...	*party... party...*	*just... just...*
table... table...	*metal... metal...*	*count... count...*
today... today...	*notable... notable...*	*basket... basket...*

Practice Sentences

In the following sentences, feel your articulators moving and feel the resonance of each individual sound as you say the words.

Say the sentences slowly at first, then faster. Right now accuracy is more important than speed.

Speak them out loud, then sing them on a comfortable pitch.

The table took ten coats of paint.

Tennis racket strings are tightly strung.

Terrible Terry ate twenty tiny tomatoes.

A tutor who tooted the flute

Tried to tutor two tooters to toot.

Said the two to the tutor

Is it easier to toot

Or to tutor two tooters to toot.

Daily Exercises—Consonant #13 [t]

(1) Practice saying this sound and the other phonetic sounds you have learned with the Standard American Diction CDs.

(2) Read aloud from a newspaper, magazine or book until you feel and hear yourself say the [t] sound five times. Underline the words.

(3) Speak the following reading out loud, slowly at first, then faster. Right now accuracy is more important than speed. Underline the words with [t].

> *Against that time (if ever that time come)*
> *When I shall see thee frown on my defects,*
> *Whenas thy love hath cast his utmost sum,*
> *Called to that audit by advised respects;*
> *Against that time when thou shalt strangely pass,*
> *When love converted from the the thing it was*
> *Shall reasons find of settled gravity;*
> *Against that time do I ensconce me here*
> *Within the knowledge of mine own desert,*
> *And this my hand against myself uprear*
> *To guard the lawful reasons on thy part;*
>> *To leave poor me thou hast the strength of laws,*
>> *Since why to love I can allege no cause.*
>> *SHAKESPEARE, Sonnet 49.*

(4) Sing a short passage from one of your songs or arias that has the [t] in it. Repeat it several times, concentrating on saying [t] correctly.

(5) Repeat the entire section for [t] three times today.

(6) And make sure you're saying [t] correctly as you speak during the day.

Consonant #14   [g]   "give" (voiced plosive)

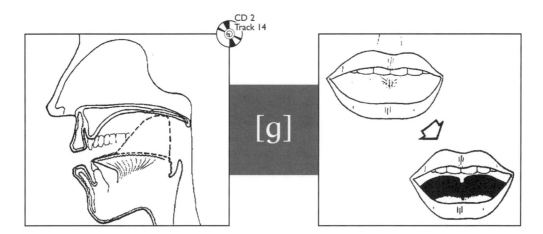

CD 2
Track 14

[g]

Hearing

Listen carefully to this sound on the Standard American Diction CDs.

Jaw

Open your jaw about two finger widths. (For speech and much of your singing, your jaw floats open about one finger width. But sometimes you need to open your jaw wider, so it's best to practice with a wide jaw.)

Lips

Feel your lips relaxed open as you say this sound.

Tongue

Lightly touch the back of your tongue to your soft palate.

Leave the blade of your tongue lightly touching the backs of your lower front teeth.

Start the vocal sound and feel the vibrations on the back of your tongue.

Feel a little breath pressure build up behind your tongue, then let your tongue drop down.

Feel like you're bouncing into a strong vowel sound.

Say the sound out loud, open up to the neutral vowel, [ə].

[g]... [g]...
[g]... [g]...

Now sing the sound at a medium volume, on a comfortable pitch— release into the neutral vowel, [ə].

[g]... [g]...
[g]... [g]...

Resonant Feel

Pay particular attention to the resonant feel of [g]. The character of its resonance is different from all the other phonetic sounds. Learn to love it and look forward to singing it.

Mirror Exercise

Watch yourself in a mirror as you say [g].

Don't close your jaw when you touch your tongue to your soft palate. Touch your jaw to help it stay open.

Leave the blade of your tongue lightly touching your front teeth.

Feel as if the back of your tongue is lifting up and a little toward the front. Do not pull your tongue backwards toward the back of your throat.

Say the sound out loud.

[g]... [g]...

[g]... [g]...

Now sing the sound at a medium volume, on a comfortable pitch — use the neutral vowel, [ə].

[g]... [g]...

[g]... [g]...

Saying Consonants in Words

Do not leave a breathy space between the consonant and the vowel, start the vowel as soon as you release your tongue. Think of the consonant as a springboard that bounces you powerfully into a clear, open vowel. Imagine bringing both the [g] and the vowel forward into the front of your mouth.

Practice Words

In the following words, say [g] clearly and strongly, but without any extra tension in your articulators.

Say the words out loud, then sing them on a comfortable pitch.

go... go...	*ago... ago...*	*dig... dig...*
game... game...	*again... again...*	*log... log...*
guard... guard...	*buggy... buggy...*	*bug... bug...*
guest... guest...	*beggar... beggar...*	*shrug... shrug...*
gamble... gamble...	*vanguard... vanguard...*	*league... league...*

Practice Sentences

In the following sentences, feel your articulators moving and feel the resonance of each individual sound as you say the words.

Say the sentences slowly at first, then faster. Right now accuracy is more important than speed.

Speak them out loud, then sing them on a comfortable pitch.

The grinning dog giggled gleefully.

He gave his beagle a doggy bag.

A glowing gleam glowing green.

Gary's gray goose greedily gobbled granny's grain.

Daily Exercises—Consonant #14 [g]

(1) Practice saying this sound and the other phonetic sounds you have learned with the Standard American Diction CDs.

(2) Read aloud from a newspaper, magazine or book until you feel and hear yourself say the [g] sound five times. Underline the words.

(3) Speak the following reading out loud, slowly at first, then faster. Right now accuracy is more important than speed. Underline the words with [g].

> *Full many a glorious morning have I seen*
> *Flatter the mountain tops with sovereign eye,*
> *Kissing with golden face the meadows green,*
> *Gilding pale streams with heav'nly alchemy,*
> *Anon permit the basest clouds to ride*
> *With ugly rack on his celestial face,*
> *And from the forlorn world his visage hide,*
> *Stealing unseen to west with this disgrace.*
> *Ev'n so my sun one early morn did shine*
> *With all triumphant splendor on my brow;*
> *But out alack, he was but one hour mine,*
> *The region cloud hath masked him from me now.*
> > *Yet him for this my love no whit disdaineth;*
> > *Suns of the world may stain when heav'n's sun staineth.*
> > > *SHAKESPEARE, Sonnet 33.*

(4) Sing a short passage from one of your songs or arias that has the [g] in it. Repeat it several times, concentrating on saying [g] correctly.

(5) Repeat the entire section for [g] three times today.

(6) And make sure you're saying [g] correctly as you speak during the day.

Consonant #15   [k]   "cat" (voiceless plosive)

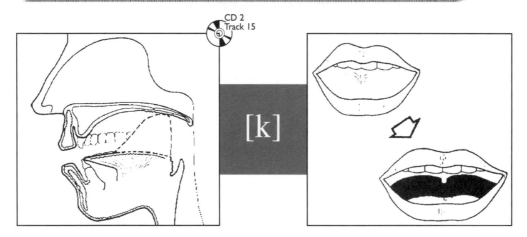

CD 2
Track 15

Hearing

Listen carefully to this sound on the Standard American Diction CDs.

Jaw

Open your jaw about two finger widths. (For speech and much of your singing, your jaw floats open about one finger width. But sometimes you need to open your jaw wider, so it's best to practice with a wide jaw.)

Lips

Feel your lips relaxed open as you say this sound.

Tongue

Lightly touch the back of your tongue to your soft palate.

Leave the blade of your tongue touching the backs of your lower front teeth.

Feel a little breath pressure build up behind your tongue, then let your tongue drop down.

You'll hear a very quiet sound as the air is released.

Say the sound out loud.

[k]... [k]...
[k]... [k]...

Now sing the sound at a medium volume, on a comfortable pitch— release into the neutral vowel, [ə].

[k]... [k]...
[k]... [k]...

Resonant Feel

Pay particular attention to the feel of [k]. It is different from all the other phonetic sounds. Learn to love it and look forward to singing it.

Mirror Exercise

Watch yourself in a mirror as you say [k]. Don't close your jaw when you touch your tongue to your soft palate. Touch your jaw to help it stay open.

Leave the blade of your tongue lightly touching your front teeth.

Feel as if the back of your tongue is lifting up and a little toward the front. Do not pull your tongue backwards toward the back of your mouth.

Say the sound out loud.

[k]... [k]...
[k]... [k]...

Now sing the sound at a medium volume, on a comfortable pitch— release into the neutral vowel, [ə].

[k]... [k]...
[k]... [k]...

Possible Problems

Releasing too much air: Some people release too much breath between [k] and the following vowel. Be sure that you start the vowel sound as soon as you open your lips.

Say the sound, opening up to the neutral vowel, [ə].

[k]... [k]...

[k]... [k]...

Now sing the sound at a medium volume, on a comfortable pitch— use the neutral vowel, [ə].

[k]... [k]...

[k]... [k]...

Comparison Exercise

Here is an exercise to help you differentiate between [g] and [k].

Feel the difference in the resonance for each sound.

Repeat them one after the other until you can clearly hear and feel the difference between them.

Say the sounds out loud.

[g,k,g,k,g,k]...

[g,k,g,k,g,k]...

Saying Consonants in Words

Do not leave a breathy space between the consonant and the vowel, start the vowel as soon as you release your tongue. Think of the consonant as a springboard that bounces you powerfully into a clear, open vowel. Imagine bringing both [k] and the vowel forward into the front of your mouth.

Note: When you say a voiceless consonant, like [k], your vocal cords are apart, that is, not vibrating. So when you move from the conso-

nant to the vowel make a special effort to start the vowel clearly and strongly—*a breathy vowel cannot be blamed on a voiceless consonant.* If you have trouble moving from a voiceless consonant to the vowel, practice the transition until the vowel is clear every time you say it.

Practice Words

In the following words, say [k] clearly and strongly, but without any extra tension in your articulators.

Say the words out loud, then sing them on a comfortable pitch.

come... come...	*okay... okay...*
like... like...	*keep... keep...*
tackle... tackle...	*quick... quick...*
cost... cost...	*because... because..*
shock... shock...	*crave... crave...*
basket... basket...	*talk... talk...*
common... common...	*second... second...*
prank... prank...	

Practice Sentences

In the following sentences, feel your articulators moving and feel the resonance of each individual sound as you say the words.

Say the sentences slowly at first, then faster. Right now accuracy is more important than speed.

Speak them out loud, then sing them on a comfortable pitch.

Cookies and biscuits crumble when crushed.
Acting and cooking are crafts.
The critical critic cried at the comedy.
How many cuckoos could a good cook cook
If a good cook could could cuckoos?
If a good cook could cook cuckoos so fine,
If a good cook could cook cuckoos all the time,
How many cuckoos could a good cook cook
If a good cook could cook cuckoos?

Daily Exercises—Consonant #15 [k]

(1) Practice saying this sound and the other phonetic sounds you have learned with the Standard American Diction CDs.

(2) Read aloud from a newspaper, magazine or book until you feel and hear yourself say the [k] sound five times. Underline the words.

(3) Speak the following reading out loud, slowly at first, then faster. Right now accuracy is more important than speed. Underline the words with [k].

> *When I do count the clock that tells the time,*
> *And see the brave day sunk in hideous night,*
> *When I behold the violet past prime,*
> *And sable curls all silvered o'er with white,*
> *When lofty trees I see barren of leaves,*
> *Which erst from heat did canopy the herd,*
> *And summer's green all girded up in sheaves*
> *Borne on the bier with white and bristly beard;*
> *Then of thy beauty do I question make*
> *That thou among the wastes of time must go,*
> *Since sweets and beauties do themselves forsake,*
> *And die as fast as they see others grow,*
> > *And nothing 'gainst time's scythe can make defence*
> > *Save breed to brave him when he takes thee hence.*
> >   *SHAKESPEARE, Sonnet 12.*

(4) Sing a short passage from one of your songs or arias that has the [k] in it. Repeat it several times, concentrating on saying [k] correctly.

(5) Repeat the entire section for [k] three times today.

(6) And make sure you're saying [k] correctly as you speak during the day.

Congratulations! You have learned to recognize and say the **Plosive Consonants** of **Standard American Speech**.

Review of Plosives

Let's do a quick review of the plosive consonants.

Speak, then sing, the sounds and the words at a medium volume.

(10) [b] **ball**... a**b**out... we**b**... [b]
(11) [p] **p**ull... a**pp**le... **p**o**p**... [p]
(12) [d] **d**ean... **d**oor... la**d**... [d]
(13) [t] **t**all... **t**end... lo**t**... [t]
(14) [g] **g**ot... **g**ive... do**g**... [g]
(15) [k] **c**an... **c**all... loo**k**... [k]

Notice how much more clearly and easily you can say these sounds.

12 Affricative Consonants

An affricative consonant is a single consonant sound, created by combining a plosive consonant and a fricative consonant.

How Do You Make an Affricative?

To make an affricative, you bring two of your articulators together to form a plosive and as you release your articulators you slide smoothly into a fricative sound.

Voiced/Voiceless Affricatives

There are two affricatives—one **voiced** and the other **voiceless**.

(If you're not sure what voiced and voiceless consonants are, you will find an explanation at the beginning of the chapters on *Fricative Consonants* and *Plosive Consonants*.)

Say the consonants and the words out loud.

Voiced	Voiceless
(16) [dʒ]...*j*ump	(17) [tʃ]...*ch*amp

Consonant #16 [dʒ] "jump" (voiced affricative)

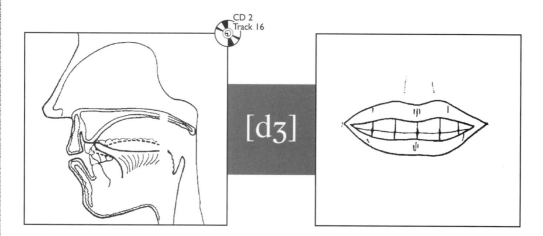

CD 2
Track 16

[dʒ]

Hearing

Listen carefully to this sound on the Standard American Diction CDs.

Jaw

Bring your upper and lower teeth almost together, in the position for [ʒ].

Lips

Feel your lips relaxed and open.

Tongue

Feel the blade of your tongue touching your upper gum ridge for [d].

Start the vocal sound.

Feel a little breath pressure build up behind your tongue.

Feel the vibrations on your tongue.

Feel the blade of your tongue release from the upper gum ridge and slide back slightly for the [ʒ] sound.

Hear the sound change as you make the slide.

Say the sound out loud, sustaining it for two counts.

[dʒ]... [dʒ]...

[dʒ]... [dʒ]...

Now sing the sound at a medium volume, on a comfortable pitch. sustain it for two counts.

[dʒ]... [dʒ]...

[dʒ]... [dʒ]...

Consonant Combination

This sound is a combination of the voiced consonants #12, [d], and #7, [ʒ]. You slide your articulators from the position for [d] to the position for [ʒ].

Resonant Feel

Pay particular attention to the resonant feel of [dʒ]. The character of its resonance is different from all the other speech sounds. Learn to love it and look forward to singing it.

Mirror Exercise

Now watch yourself in a mirror as you say [dʒ].

See and feel your jaw almost closed and your teeth almost touching, in the position for [ʒ].

Feel that your tongue is not pressed hard against your upper gum ridge, as you start [dʒ]. Your tongue should touch lightly and move relaxed.

Say the sound out loud.

[dʒ]... [dʒ]...

[dʒ]... [dʒ]...

Saying Consonants in Words

When saying [dʒ] in words, do not hold on to it. Say it clearly, but quickly, and move immediately to the vowel.

Do not leave a breathy space between the consonant and the vowel. Think of the consonant as a springboard that bounces you powerfully into a clear, open vowel. You can feel the [dʒ] well forward in your mouth, imagine bringing the vowel forward into that position as well.

Note: Your teeth are close together as you say [dʒ], so your jaw will have to drop open quickly for the following vowel.

Practice Words

In the following practice words, say [dʒ] clearly and strongly, but without any extra tension.

Say the words out loud, then sing them on a comfortable pitch.
(Make sure your jaw drops open for the vowel.)

jump... jump...	*agent... agent...*	*age... age...*
joke... joke...	*magic... magic...*	*judge... judge...*
juice... juice...	*pigeon... pigeon...*	*badge... badge...*
just... just...	*imagine... imagine...*	*sponge... sponge...*
giraffe... giraffe...	*register... register...*	*emerge... emerge...*

Practice Sentences

In the following sentences, feel your articulators moving and feel the resonance of each individual sound as you say the words.

Say them slowly at first, then faster. Right now accuracy is more important than speed.

Speak the sentences out loud, then sing them on a comfortable pitch.
(Make sure your jaw drops open for the vowel.)

The gem was larger than our budget.

The giant genii was orange.

Joan, James and John joyously jumped and jigged.

How many jeeps could a jeep jack jack,
If a jeep jack could jack jeeps?
If a jeep jack could jack jeeps okay,
If a jeep jack could jack jeeps all day.
How many jeeps could a jeep jack jack,
If a jeep jack could jack jeeps?

Daily Exercises—Consonant #16 [dʒ]

(1) Practice saying this sound and the other speech sounds you have learned with the Standard American Diction CDs.

(2) Read aloud from a newspaper, magazine or book until you feel and hear yourself say the [dʒ] sound five times. Underline the words.

(3) Speak the following reading out loud, slowly at first, then faster. Right now accuracy is more important than speed. Underline the words with [dʒ].

> *Th'expense of spirit in a waste of shame*
> *Is lust in action, and till action lust*
> *Is perjured, murd'rous, bloody, full of blame,*
> *Savage, extreme, rude, cruel, not to trust,*
> *Enjoyed no sooner but despised straight,*
> *Past reason hunted, and no sooner had,*
> *Past reason hated as a swallowed bait,*
> *On purpose laid to make the taker mad;*
> *Mad in pursuit, and in possession so,*
> *Had, having, and in quest to have, extreme,*
> *A bliss in proof, and proved, a very woe,*
> *Before a joy proposed, behind, a dream.*
> > *All this the world well knows, yet none knows well*
> > *To shun the heav'n that leads men to this hell.*
> > SHAKESPEARE, Sonnet 129.

(4) Sing a short passage from one of your songs or arias that has [dʒ] in it. Repeat it several times, concentrating on saying [dʒ] correctly.

(5) Repeat the entire section for [dʒ] three times today.

(6) And make sure you're saying [dʒ] correctly as you speak during the day.

Consonant #17 [tʃ] "<u>ch</u>amp." (voiceless affricative)

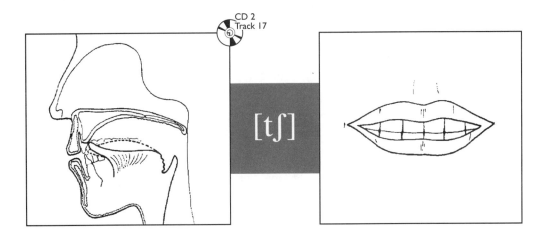

CD 2
Track 17

[tʃ]

Hearing

Listen carefully to this sound on the Standard American Diction CDs.

Jaw

Bring your upper and lower teeth almost together, in the [ʃ] position.

Lips

Feel your lips relaxed and open.

Tongue

Feel the blade of your tongue touching your upper gum ridge for [t].

Feel a little breath pressure build up behind your tongue.

Feel the blade of your tongue release from the upper gum ridge and slide back slightly for the [ʃ] sound.

Hear the sound change as you make the slide.

Say the sound out loud, sustaining it for two counts.

[tʃ]... [tʃ]...
[tʃ]... [tʃ]...

Consonant Combination

This sound is a combination of the voiceless Consonants #13, [t], and #8, [ʃ]. You slide your articulators from the position for [t] to the position for [ʃ].

Resonant Feel

Pay particular attention to the feel of [tʒ]. It is different from all the other speech sounds. Learn to love it and look forward to singing it.

Mirror Exercise

Now watch yourself in a mirror as you say [tʒ].

See and feel your jaw almost closed and your teeth almost touching in the position for [ʃ].

Feel that your tongue is not pressed hard against your upper gum ridge, as you say [tʃ]. Your tongue should touch lightly and move relaxed.

Say the sound out loud.

[tʃ]... [tʃ]...
[tʃ]... [tʃ]...

Comparison Exercise

Here is a comparison exercise to help you differentiate between [dʒ], and [tʃ].

Feel the difference in the resonance of each sound.

Repeat them one after the other until you can clearly hear and feel the difference between them.

Say the sounds out loud.

[dʒ, tʃ, dʒ, tʃ, dʒ, tʃ]...

[dʒ, tʃ, dʒ, tʃ, dʒ, tʃ]...

Saying Consonants in Words

When saying [tʃ] in words, do not hold on to it. Say it clearly, but quickly, and move immediately to the vowel.

Do not leave a breathy space between the consonant and the vowel. Think of the consonant as a springboard that bounces you powerfully into a clear, open vowel. You can feel the [tʃ] well forward in your mouth, imagine bringing the vowel forward into that position as well.

Note: When you say a voiceless consonant, like [tʃ], your vocal cords are apart, that is, not vibrating. So when you move from the consonant to the vowel make a special effort to start the vowel clearly and strongly—*a breathy vowel cannot be blamed on a voiceless consonant*. If you have trouble moving from a voiceless consonant to the vowel, practice the transition until the vowel is clear every time you say it.

Note: Your teeth are close together as you say [tʃ], so your jaw will have to drop open quickly for the following vowel.

Practice Words

In the following practice words, say [tʃ] clearly and strongly, but without any extra tension in your articulators.

Speak the words out loud, then sing them on a comfortable pitch.
(Make sure your jaw drops open for the vowel.)

choose... choose...	*kitchen... kitchen...*	*church... church...*
change... change...	*butcher... butcher...*	*batch... batch...*
chance... chance...	*orchard... orchard...*	*lurch... lurch...*
chuckle... chuckle...	*exchange... exchange...*	*squelch... squelch...*
chowder... chowder...	*bachelor... bachelor...*	*research... research...*

Practice Sentences

In the following sentences, feel your articulators moving and feel the resonance of each individual sound as you say the words.

Say them slowly at first, then faster. Right now accuracy is more important than speed.

Say the sentences out loud, then sing them on a comfortable pitch.
(Make sure your jaw drops open for the vowel.)

The children chatted as they marched to church.

The witch in the orchard chewed and chuckled.

Cherry's cheap chip shop sells cheap chips.

How much wood could a woodchuck chuck,

If a woodchuck could chuck wood,

If a woodchuck could chuck wood so fine,

If a woodchuck could chuck wood all the time,

How much wood would a woodchuck chuck

If a woodchuck could chuck wood?

Daily Exercises—Consonant #17 [tʃ]

(1) Practice saying this sound and the other speech sounds you have learned with the Standard American Diction CDs.

(2) Read aloud from a newspaper, magazine or book until you feel and hear yourself say the [tʃ] sound five times. Underline the words.

(3) Speak the following reading out loud, slowly at first, then faster. Right now accuracy is more important than speed. Underline the words with [tʃ].

When I consider everything that grows
Holds in perfection but a little moment,
That this huge stage presenteth nought but shows
Whereon the stars in secret influence comment;
When I perceive that men as plants increase,
Cheered and checked ev'n by the selfsame sky,
Vaunt in their youthful sap, at height decrease,
And wear their brave state out of memory;
Then the conceit of this inconstant stay
Sets you most rich in youth before my sight,
Where wasteful time debateth with decay
To change your day of youth to sullied night;
*   And all in war with time for love of you,*
*   As he takes from you, I engraft you new.*
SHAKESPEARE, Sonnet 15.

(4) Sing a short passage from one of your songs or arias that has [tʃ] in it. Repeat it several times, concentrating on saying [tʃ] correctly.

(5) Repeat the entire section for [tʃ] three times today.

(6) And make sure you're saying [tʃ] correctly as you speak during the day.

Congratulations! You have learned to recognize and say all the **Affricative Consonants** of **Standard American Speech**.

Because this is a short chapter, we will review the **Affricatives** with the **Glides** in the next chapter.

Notes:

13　Glide Consonants

A glide consonant is a single speech sound that glides from its starting position to the following vowel.

How Do You Make A Glide Consonant?

You say a glide consonant by placing your articulators in the starting position for the consonant and immediately sliding to the position for the following vowel.

Voiced/Voiceless Glides

There are three glides. Two are **voiced** and one is **voiceless**.

(If you're not sure what voiced and voiceless consonants are, you will find an explanation at the beginning of the chapters on Fricatives and Plosives.)

Say the consonants and the words out loud.

Voiced	**Voiceless**
(18) [w]... will	(19) [ʍ]... while
(20) [j]... yes	

Consonant #18 [w] "will" (voiced glide)

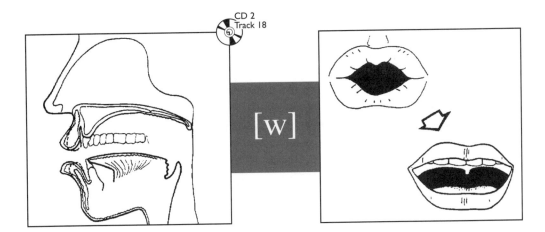

CD 2
Track 18

Hearing

Listen carefully to this sound on the Standard American Diction CDs.

Jaw

Open your jaw a little more than a finger width. (For speech and much of your singing, your jaw floats open about one finger width. But sometimes you need to open your jaw wider, so it's best to practice with a wider jaw.)

Tongue

Feel your tongue relaxed on the floor of your mouth, touching the backs of your lower teeth.

Lips

Feel your lips move forward and round slightly. The position is similar to, but not as rounded as the position for vowel #12, [u].

Start the voiced sound.

As you begin the sound immediately release your lips and slide to the following vowel.

For practice use [ə] as the following vowel.

Say the sound out loud.

[wə]... [wə]...

[wə]... [wə]...

Now sing the sound out loud, on a comfortable pitch.

[wə]... [wə]...

[wə]... [wə]...

Resonant Feel

Pay particular attention to the resonant feel of [w]. The character of its resonance is different from all the other phonetic sounds. Learn to love it and look forward to saying it.

Mirror Exercise

Now watch yourself in a mirror as you say [w].

For a clear [w] sound, your jaw should stay open, with your teeth about a finger width apart.

Your lips should round in a relaxed way, not tensed, and move to the vowel as soon as you start the sound.

Say the sound out loud and open up to the neutral vowel, [ə].

[wə]... [wə]...
[wə]... [wə]...

Now sing the sound out loud on a comfortable pitch.

[wə]... [wə]...
[wə]... [wə]...

Saying Consonants in Words

Think of the consonant as a springboard that bounces you powerfully into a clear, open vowel. You can feel the [w] well forward in your mouth, imagine bringing the vowel forward into that position as well.

Practice Words

In the following words, say [w] clearly and strongly, but without any extra tension.

Speak the words out loud, then sing them on a comfortable pitch.

will... will...	*bewitch... bewitch...*
want... want...	*awake... awake...*
week... week...	*quick... quick...*
wish... wish...	*reward... reward...*
water... water...	*sandwich... sandwich...*
	wow... wow...

Practice Sentences

In the following sentences, feel your articulators moving and feel the resonance of each individual sound as you say the words.

Say the sentences slowly at first, then faster. Right now accuracy is more important than speed.

Speak them out loud, then sing them on a comfortable pitch.

We would always walk by the water.
The queen requested a sandwich by the well.
Will you wash Willy's windows with warm water.
Wishy-washy Wilfred wished to win a wager.

Daily Exercises—Consonant #18 [w]

(1) Practice saying this sound and the other phonetic sounds you have learned with the Standard American Diction CDs.

(2) Read aloud from a newspaper, magazine or book until you feel and hear yourself say the [w] sound five times. Underline the words.

(3) Speak the following reading out loud, slowly at first, then faster. Right now accuracy is more important than speed. Underline the words with [w].

> *Is it for fear to wet a widow's eye*
> *That thou consum'st thyself in single life?*
> *Ah, if thou issueless shalt hap to die,*
> *The world will wail thee like a makeless wife;*
> *The world will be thy widow and still weep,*
> *That thou no form of thee hast left behind,*
> *When every private widow well may keep,*
> *By children's eyes, her husband's shape in mind.*
> *Look what an unthrift in the world doth spend*
> *Shifts but his place, for still the world enjoys it;*
> *But beauty's waste hath in the world an end,*
> *And kept unused, the user so destroys it.*
>   *No love toward others in that bosom sits*
>   *That on himself such murd'rous shame commits.*
>   *SHAKESPEARE, Sonnet 9.*

(4) Sing a short passage from one of your songs or arias that has [w] in it. Repeat it several times, concentrating on saying [w] correctly.

(5) Repeat the entire section for [w] three times today.

(6) And make sure you're saying [w] correctly as you speak during the day.

Consonant # 19 [ʍ] "<u>while</u>" (voiceless glide)

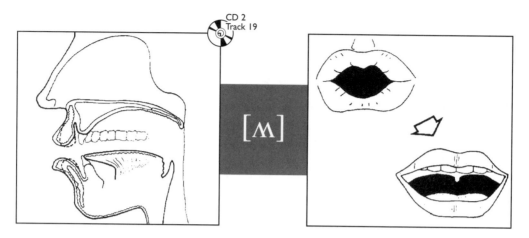

Hearing

Listen carefully to this sound on the Standard American Diction CDs.

Jaw

Open your jaw a little more than a finger width. (For speech and much of your singing, your jaw floats open about one finger width. But sometimes you need to open your jaw wider, so it's best to practice with a wider jaw.)

Tongue

Feel your tongue relaxed on the floor of your mouth, touching the backs of your lower teeth.

Lips

Feel your lips move forward and round slightly. The position is similar to, but not as rounded as the position for vowel #12, [u].

Blow a tiny amount of breath between your lips and at the same time release your lips and slide to the following vowel sound.

For practice use [ə] as the following vowel. Say the sound out loud.

[ʍə]... [ʍə]...

[ʍə]... [ʍə]...

Now sing the sound out loud, on a comfortable pitch.

[ʍə]... [ʍə]...

[ʍə]... [ʍə]...

Resonant Feel

Pay particular attention to the feel of [ʍ]. Its character is different from all the other phonetic sounds. Learn to love it and look forward to saying it.

Mirror Exercise

Watch yourself in a mirror as you say [ʍ].

For a clear [ʍ] sound, your jaw should stay open, with your teeth about a finger width apart.

Your lips should round in a relaxed way, not tensed, and move to the vowel as soon as you start to blow a little air.

Say the sound out loud, open up to the neutral vowel, [ə].

[ʍə]... [ʍə]...

[ʍə]... [ʍə]...

Now sing the sound out loud on a comfortable pitch.

[ʍə]... [ʍə]...

[ʍə]... [ʍə]...

Possible Problems

[ʍ] is a voiceless consonant. It's so quiet, it's almost inaudible and you shouldn't try to make it loud.

But even though it's not loud, you can tell if it's being said or not.

For example, say the following words with and without [ʍ]. If you listen carefully, you can tell by the sound when you are saying [ʍ] and when you're not.

Say the words out loud.

when... __en.....

while... __ile.....

what... __at.....

The other problem you might have with this sound is blowing too much air. Release only a tiny amount of air and begin saying the following vowel immediately.

Comparison Exercise

Here is a comparison exercise to help you differentiate between Glides [w] and [ʍ].

Repeat them one after the other until you can clearly hear and feel the difference between them.

Say the sounds out loud.

[wə, ʍə, wə, ʍə, wə, ʍə]...

[wə, ʍə, wə, ʍə, wə, ʍə]...

Saying Consonants in Words

Do not leave a breathy space between the consonant and the vowel. Think of the consonant as a springboard that bounces you powerfully into a clear, open vowel. You can feel the [ʍ] well forward in your mouth, imagine bringing the vowel forward into that position as well.

Note: When you say a voiceless consonant, like [ʍ], your vocal cords are apart, that is, not vibrating. So when you move from the consonant to the vowel make a special effort to start the vowel clearly and strongly—*a breathy vowel cannot be blamed on a voiceless consonant.* If you have trouble saying a clear vowel after a voiceless consonant, practice the transition until the vowel is clear every time you say it.

Practice Words

In the following words, say [ʍ] clearly and strongly, but without any extra tension in your articulators.

Speak the words out loud, then sing them on a comfortable pitch.

whip... whip...	*awhile... awhile...*
wheat... wheat...	*nowhere... nowhere...*
whale... whale...	*buckwheat... buckwheat...*
whiff... whiff...	*meanwhile... meanwhile...*
whisker... whisker...	*anywhere... anywhere...*

Practice Sentences

In the following practice sentences, feel your articulators moving and feel the resonance of each individual sound as you say the words.

Say them slowly at first, then faster. Right now accuracy is more important than speed.

Speak them out loud, then sing them on a comfortable pitch.

Which wheel whistles while it whirls.
When wheat waves it whispers.
The white waves whipped in the wind.
Whether, weather; what, watt; which, witch; where, wear.

Daily Exercises—Consonant #19　[ʍ]

(1) Practice saying this sound and the other phonetic sounds you have learned with the Standard American Diction CDs.

(2) Read aloud from a newspaper, magazine or book until you feel and hear yourself say the [ʍ] sound five times. Underline the words.

(3) Speak the following reading out loud, slowly at first, then faster. Right now accuracy is more important than speed. Underline the words with [ʍ].

Thou blind fool love, what dost thou to mine eyes,
That they behold and see not what they see?
They know what beauty is, see where it lies,
Yet what the best is take the worst to be.
If eyes corrupt by over partial looks
Be anchored in the bay where all men ride,
Why of eyes' falsehood hast thou forged hooks,
Whereto the judgement of my heart is tied?
Why should my heart think that a several plot,
Which my heart knows the wide world's common place?
Or mine eyes, seeing this, say this is not
To put fair truth upon so foul a face?
In things right true my heart and eyes have erred,
And to this false plague are they now transferred.
　　　SHAKESPEARE, Sonnet 137.

(4) Sing a short passage from one of your songs or arias that has [ʍ] in it. Repeat it several times, concentrating on saying [ʍ] correctly.

(5) Repeat the entire section for [ʍ] three times today.

(6) And make sure you're saying [ʍ] correctly as you speak during the day.

Consonant #20   [j]   "yes" (voiced glide)

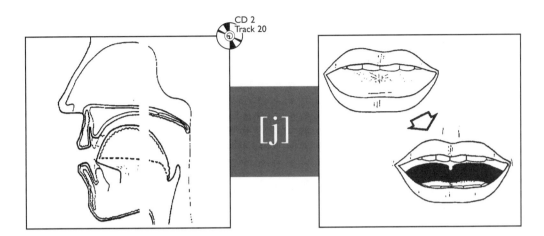

CD 2
Track 20

[j]

Hearing

Listen carefully to this sound on the Standard American Diction CDs.

Jaw

Open your jaw two finger widths. (For speech and much of your singing, your jaw floats open about one finger width. But sometimes you need to open your jaw wider, so it's best to practice with a wide jaw.)

Lips

Feel your lips relaxed open as you say this sound.

Tongue

Feel your tongue in a position approximately between Vowel #1, [i], and Vowel #2, [ɪ].

Begin the sound.

Immediately slide your tongue to the position for the following vowel.

For practice, we will use [ə] as the following vowel.

Say the sounds out loud.

[jə]... [jə]...

[jə]... [jə]...

Now sing the sound out loud, on a comfortable pitch.

[jə]... [jə]...

[jə]... [jə]...

Resonant Feel

Pay particular attention to the resonant feel of [j]. The character of its resonance is different from all the other phonetic sounds. Learn to love it and look forward to saying it.

Mirror Exercise

Watch yourself in a mirror as you say [j].

For a clear [j] sound, your jaw should stay open, with your teeth approximately one to two finger widths apart.

Feel your tongue relaxed, not tensed.

Feel your tongue slide to the position for the following vowel as soon as you start the sound.

Say [j] out loud and open up to the neutral vowel, [ə].

[jə]... [jə]...

[jə]... [jə]...

Now sing [j] out loud on a comfortable pitch.

[jə]... [jə]...

[jə]... [jə]...

Saying Consonants in Words

Think of the consonant as a springboard that bounces you powerfully into a clear, open vowel. You can feel the [j] well forward in your mouth, imagine bringing the vowel forward into that position as well.

Practice Words

In the following words, say [j] clearly and strongly, but without any extra tension.

Speak the words out loud, then sing them on a comfortable pitch.

yes... yes...	*canyon... canyon...*
year... year...	*loyal... loyal...*
yacht... yacht...	*senior... senior...*
young... young...	*valiant... valiant...*
yonder... yonder...	*billiard... billiard...*

Practice Sentences

In the following sentences, feel your articulators moving and feel the resonance of each individual sound as you say the words.

Say them slowly at first, then faster. Right now accuracy is more important than speed.

Speak them out loud, then sing them on a comfortable pitch.

The value of the yacht was over a million.

Yonder lies the canyon said the senior.

Yummy, yummy yellow yams.

Yarn is valued by the yard.

Daily Exercises—Consonant #20   [j]

(1) Practice saying this sound and the other phonetic sounds you have learned with the Standard American Diction CDs.

(2) Read aloud from a newspaper, magazine or book until you feel and hear yourself say the [j] sound five times. Underline the words.

(3) Speak the following reading out loud, slowly at first, then faster. Right now accuracy is more important than speed. Underline the words with [j].

> *From you have I been absent in the spring,*
> *When proud-pied April, dressed in all his trim,*
> *Hath put a spirit of youth in everything,*
> *That heavy Saturn laughed and leapt with him.*
> *Yet not the lays of birds, nor the sweet smell*
> *Of different flow'rs in odor and in hue,*
> *Could make me any summer's story tell,*
> *Or from their proud lap pluck them where they grew.*
> *Nor did I wonder at the lily's white,*
> *Nor praise the deep vermilion in the rose;*
> *They were but sweet, but figures of delight,*
> *Drawn after you, you pattern of all those.*
> > *Yet seemed it winter still, and, you away,*
> > *As with your shadow I with these did play.*
> > *SHAKESPEARE, Sonnet 98.*

(4) Sing a short passage from one of your songs or arias that has [j] in it. Repeat it several times, concentrating on saying [j] correctly.

(5) Repeat the entire section for [j] three times today.

(6) And make sure you're saying [j] correctly as you speak during the day.

Congratulations! You've learned to recognize and say all the **Affricative Consonants** and **Glide Consonants** of **Standard American Speech.**

Review of Affricatives and Glides

Let's do a quick review of **Affricatives** and **Glides**.

Speak the sounds and words out loud, then sing them on a comfortable pitch.

Affricatives

(16) [dʒ] *jar... joke... fudge...* [dʒ]

(17) [tʃ] *chair... chum... church...* [tʃ]

Glides

(18) [w] *will... were... awake...* [w]

(19) [ʍ] *while... when... what...* [ʍ]

(20) [j] *yes... yacht... loyal...* [j]

Notes:

vowel #x eɪ "ai"

vowel #y ɔ "uh"

consonant #z ʃ "sh"

consonant #21 l "l"

14 Semi-Vowel Consonants

A semi-vowel is a consonant that resembles a vowel in its production. It is voiced, with no fricative sound, and the sound is resonated through the mouth.

Two Semi-Vowel Consonants

There are two semi-vowel consonants.

Say them out loud.

(21) [l]... *lake*

(22) [r]... *run*

Consonant #21 [l] "lake" (semi-vowel)

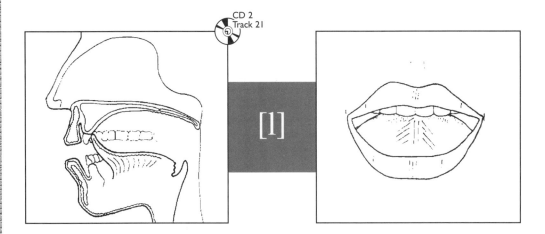

CD 2
Track 21

[l]

Hearing

Listen carefully to this sound on the Standard American Diction CDs.

Jaw

Open your jaw about two finger widths. (For speech and much of your singing, your jaw floats open about one finger width. But sometimes you need to open your jaw wider, so it's best to practice with a wide jaw.)

Lips

Feel your lips relaxed and open as you say this sound.

Tongue

Touch the edge of the blade of your tongue lightly to your upper gum ridge.

Feel the middle of your tongue dropped down so that there is space between the sides of your tongue and your upper molars.

Start the sound.

Hear the sound and feel the vibrations where your tongue touches your gum ridge.

Your tongue should not be tense or pressed hard against your gum ridge.

After the sound relax your tongue back down to the floor of your mouth.

Say the sound out loud. Hold it for two counts.

[l]... tongue down [l]... tongue down

[l]... tongue down [l]... tongue down

Now sing the sound at a medium volume, on a comfortable pitch. Sustain it for two counts.

[l]... tongue down [l]... tongue down

[l]... tongue down [l]... tongue down

Resonant Feel

Pay particular attention to the resonant feel of [l]. The character of its resonance is different from all the other phonetic sounds. Learn to love it and look forward to singing it.

Mirror Exercise

Watch yourself in a mirror as you say [l].

For a clear [l] sound, your jaw should stay open, with your teeth approximately one to two finger widths apart.

Your tongue should lightly touch your upper gum ridge. Don't stick your tongue out of your mouth past your teeth.

Say the sound out loud, sustaining it for two counts.

[l]... [l]...

[l]... [l]...

Now sing the sound at a medium volume, on a comfortable pitch. Sustain it for two counts.

[l]... [l]...

[l]... [l]...

Possible Problems

Back or Dark *l*

Some American dialects use a variety of *l* that is made by raising the back or middle of the tongue towards the roof of the mouth, a movement which may also cause the blade of the tongue to lose contact with the upper gum ridge.

This is called a "back *l*" or a "dark *l*," as opposed to the "front *l*" used in Standard American Speech.

When the back *l* is pronounced, it is usually said in the middle of a word or at the end of a word.

In Standard American Speech never use the back *l*. Always use the front *l*.

Saying Consonants in Words

When saying [l] in words, do not hold on to it. Say it quickly, but clearly, and move immediately to the vowel.

Do not leave a breathy space between the consonant and the vowel, start the vowel as soon as you release your tongue. Think of the consonant as a springboard that bounces you powerfully into a clear, open vowel. You can feel the [l] well forward in your mouth, imagine bringing the vowel forward into that position as well.

Practice Words

In the following words, say [l] clearly and strongly, but without any extra tension.

Speak the words out loud, then sing them on a comfortable pitch.

lark... lark...	*alive... alive...*	*doll... doll...*
lost... lost...	*collar... collar...*	*sale... sale...*
leave... leave...	*alright... alright...*	*table... table...*
live... live..	*delay... delay...*	*earl... earl...*
labor... labor...	*absolute... absolute...*	*beguile... beguile...*

Practice Sentences

In the following practice sentences, feel your articulators moving and feel the resonance of each individual sound as you say the words.

Say the sentences slowly at first, then faster. Right now accuracy is more important than speed.

Speak them out loud, then sing them on a comfortable pitch.

__L__ove__l__y __l__i__l__ies fi__ll__ed the fie__l__d.

Un__l__ucky __L__uther was eaten by crocodi__l__es.

A __l__ibrary __l__itera__ll__y __l__ittered with __l__iterature.

Red __l__eather, ye__ll__ow __l__eather, red __l__eather, ye__ll__ow __l__eather.

Daily Exercises—Consonant #21 [l]

CD 2
Track 22

(1) Practice saying this sound and the other phonetic sounds you have learned with the Standard American Diction CDs.

(2) Read aloud from a newspaper, magazine or book until you feel and hear yourself say the [l] sound five times. Underline the words.

(3) Speak the following reading out loud, slowly at first, then faster. Right now accuracy is more important than speed. Underline the words with [l].

> *Lo, in the orient when the gracious light*
> *Lifts up his burning head, each under eye*
> *Doth homage to his new-appearing sight,*
> *Serving with looks his sacred majesty;*
> *And having climbed the steep-up heav'nly hill,*
> *Resembling strong youth in his middle age,*
> *Yet mortal looks adore his beauty still,*
> *Attending on his golden pilgrimage.*
> *But when from highmost pitch, with weary car,*
> *Like feeble age he reeleth from the day,*
> *The eyes ('fore duteous) now converted are*
> *From his low tract and look another way.*
>   *So thou, thyself outgoing in thy noon,*
>   *Unlooked on diest unless thou get a son.*
>   SHAKESPEARE, Sonnet 7.

(4) Sing a short passage several times, concentrating on saying [l] correctly.

(5) Repeat the entire section for [l] three times today.

(6) And make sure you're saying [l] correctly as you speak during the day.

Consonant #22 $[r]$ "<u>r</u>un" (semi-vowel)

The Standard American $[r]$ is sometimes called a "soft *r*", to distinguish it from the "hard" or "retroflex *r*," common in many American dialects. (See *Notes on Variations*, at the end of this chapter.)

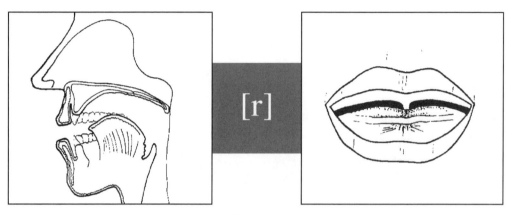

Tongue position for $[r]$ in middle or end of word.

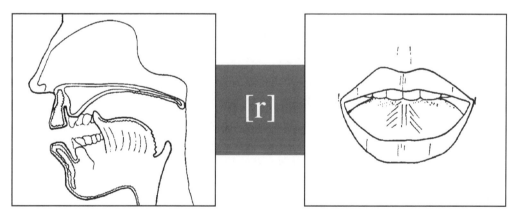

Tongue position for $[r]$ at the beginning of a word.

Hearing

Listen carefully to this sound on the Standard American Diction CDs.

Jaw

Open your mouth a little more than a finger width. (For speech and much of your singing, your jaw floats open about one finger width. But sometimes you need to open your jaw wider, so it's best to practice with a wide jaw.)

Lips

Feel your lips relaxed open as you say this sound.

Your lips may round slightly, but they should not interfere with or change the production of the sound.

Tongue

Feel the sides of your tongue raise up to lightly touch your upper molars, just a little further back than the position for [ə].

Feel the blade of your tongue lift up to about midway between the roof and the floor or your mouth and pull back slightly to about the middle of your mouth.

Feel the blade of your tongue aiming toward the front of your mouth, not lifted toward the roof of your mouth.

(When you actually say [r] the blade of your tongue and the sides of your tongue move into position simultaneously.)

Release your tongue back down to the floor of your mouth after you say the sound.

Say the sound out loud. Sustain it for two counts.

[r]... tongue down [r]... tongue down

[r]... tongue down [r]... tongue down

Now sing [r] at a medium volume, on a comfortable pitch. You don't usually sustain [r] but for this exercise, hold it for two counts.

[r]... tongue down [r]... tongue down

[r]... tongue down [r]... tongue down

Resonant Feel

Pay particular attention to the resonant feel of [r]. The character of its resonance is different from all the other phonetic sounds. Learn to love it and look forward to saying it.

Mirror Exercise

Now watch yourself in a mirror and see the position of your tongue as you say [r].

See and feel the blade of your tongue raise up to about the middle of your mouth and pull back slightly with the blade still aiming toward the front.

Don't let the blade lift high and curl backwards towards the back of your mouth.

Say [r] out loud, sustaining it for two counts.

[r]... [r]...
[r]... [r]...

Now sing [r] at a medium volume, on a comfortable pitch.

[r]... [r]...
[r]... [r]...

Two Exercises to Find the Position for [r]

If you're still having some trouble making a relaxed [r], practice saying it with the following exercises.

(1) To teach your tongue to remain relaxed as it moves to the correct position, practice sliding from [ɜ] to [r]. Keep the flat blade of your tongue pointing toward the front.

Say the sounds out loud.

[ɜ,r]... relax tongue down [ɜ,r]... relax tongue down

[ɜ,r]... relax tongue down [ɜ,r]... relax tongue down

(2) Another good way of learning the correct position of the tongue for [r] is to say [ɜ], then open your jaw without changing the position of your tongue. (This method is described by Daniel Jones, in *The Pronunciation of English*, p. 109.)

Try it. Make sure you open your jaw without tensing your tongue.

Say the sounds out loud.

[ɜ,r]... [ɜ,r]...

[ɜ,r]... [ɜ,r]...

Possible Problems

Excessive lip rounding is a common problem associated with saying [r]. If you round your lips too much, you mix a kind of [w] sound in with your [r], which obscures the clear, pure [r] sound.

However, don't worry about a little lip rounding. It's normal for your lips to round slightly for the [r] sound.

The tendency to round your lips is greatest when [r] is the first sound in the word, e.g., *road*. When [r] is in the middle of a word or at the end of a word, e.g., *very*, your lips generally stay more relaxed. Excessive lip movement is a holdover from your baby days, when you couldn't say [r] and had to substitute [w]. (Sometimes this is called "infantile perseveration.")

Practice saying [r] without rounding your lips.

Say the sound out loud.

[r]... [r]...

[r]... [r]...

You will find some other [r] varieties in *Notes on Variations*, at the end of this chapter.

Saying Consonants in Words

When saying [r] in words, do not hold on to it. Say it quickly, but clearly, and move immediately to the vowel.

Do not leave a breathy space between the consonant and the vowel, start the vowel as soon as you release your tongue. Think of the consonant as a springboard that bounces you powerfully into a clear, open vowel. You can feel the [r] well forward in your mouth, imagine bringing the vowel forward into that position as well.

Practice Words

In the following words, say [r] clearly and strongly, but without any extra tension.

Speak the words out loud, then sing them on a comfortable pitch.

run... run...	*around... around...*	*are... are...*
rose... rose...	*warm... warm...*	*dear... dear...*
repeat... repeat...	*crowd... crowd...*	*care... care...*
rascal... rascal...	*morning... morning...*	*cure... cure...*
ripple... ripple...	*street... street...*	*buccaneer... buccaneer...*

Practice Sentences

In the following practice sentences, feel your articulators moving and feel the resonance of each individual sound as you say the words.

Say them slowly at first, then faster. Right now accuracy is more important than speed.

Speak them out loud, then sing them on a comfortable pitch.

> *Red roses grow in the orchard.*
> *Harry's fervor was hard to ignore.*
> *Rascally ruffians robbed the regent.*
> *Round and round the rugged rock the ragged rascal ran.*

Daily Exercises—Consonant #22 [r]

(1) Practice saying this sound and the other phonetic sounds you have learned with the Standard American Diction CDs.

(2) Read aloud from a newspaper, magazine or book until you feel and hear yourself say the [r] sound five times. Underline the words.

(3) Speak the following reading out loud, slowly at first, then faster. Right now accuracy is more important than speed. Underline the words with [r].

> *From fairest creatures we desire increase,*
> *That thereby beauty's rose might never die,*
> *But as the riper should by time decease*
> *His tender heir might bear his memory:*
> *But thou, contracted to thine own bright eyes,*
> *Feed'st thy light's flame with self-substantial fuel,*
> *Making a famine where abundance lies,*
> *Thyself thy foe, to thy sweet self too cruel.*
> *Thou that art now the world's fresh ornament*
> *And only herald to the gaudy spring*
> *Within thin own bud buriest thy content,*
> *And tender churl, mak'st waste in niggarding.*
> > *Pity the world, or else this glutton be,*
> > *To eat the world's due, by the grave and thee.*
> > > *SHAKESPEARE, Sonnet 1*

(4) Sing a short passage several times, concentrating on saying [r] correctly.

(5) Repeat the entire section for [r] three times today.

(6) And make sure you're saying [r] correctly as you speak during the day.

Notes on Variations of "r"

Consonant [r] and Vowel [ɝ]

The r sound is classified as a consonant when you pronounce a vowel in the same syllable as the r, as in h**a**rd, [hɑrd]. (Compare with the vowel [ɝ], page 100.)

The consonant [r] and the vowel [ɝ] sound alike.

There is little or no difference in the positions of your articulators when you say the vowel r or the consonant r in the middle or at the end of a word. However, when you say r at the beginning of a word, the front edge of your tongue raises a little toward the roof of your mouth. (Compare the r figures, p. 203.)

Retroflex r

Many Americans pronounce a "retroflex r," or a "hard r," which sounds different from the Standard American r, or "soft r."

The retroflex r is the result of:

(1) Tensing and bunching up your tongue, pressing its sides hard against your upper molars and pulling it far back in your mouth.

(2) Lifting the front edge of your tongue high and curling the blade so that it points upward and toward the back of your mouth.

It is possible for these two tongue conditions to occur separately, but usually you'll find them in combination.

The retroflex r was called a "snarling" sound by Madeleine Marshall (*The Singers Manual of English Diction*, p. 9) and she appears to speak for most voice teachers in that respect.

In addition to it not being a pleasant sound, when you articulate a retroflex r your tongue is very tense , so it is also a difficult sound to pronounce.

Because of its tension and unpleasant sound you should not use a retroflex r when speaking or singing with Standard American Diction. We are showing it to you so that you can avoid it.

The One Place You Should Use a Semi-Retroflex r

When r begins the word (as in **r**ain) the blade of your tongue lifts a little higher so that it aims toward the roof of your mouth. But your tongue should still be relaxed. It should not curl backwards, nor should it be bunched up, pulled far back in your mouth or tense. (Compare the r figures, p. 203.)

r Coloring

The term "r coloring" describes what happens when your tongue tries to articulate r at the same time you are saying a vowel.

r coloring may occur in words that have a vowel followed by an r, (ba**r**, fai**r**). Your tongue pulls back a little and bunches up during the production of the vowel.

Sometimes your tongue may try to move to the r position before it has finished saying the vowel. Moving your tongue too soon distorts the sound of the vowel.

In severe r coloring cases, the tongue takes the retroflex r position right at the start of the vowel. The tongue bunches up in the back of the mouth and distorts the whole vowel.

People who habitually say a retroflex r are also likely to say most of their vowels with at least some r coloring.

To prevent r coloring, make sure you say a pure vowel by itself. Then make your move to the following r quickly and deftly.

Needless to say, r coloring should not be heard in Standard American Speech. However, if you are singing with a dialect that uses r coloring, you may use it as part of the sound of the style or character.

Flipped and Trilled *r*

There are two other varieties of *r*:

(1) The "tapped," "flipped" or "flapped" *r*.

(2) The "trilled" or "rolled" *r*.

You use these varieties primarily when you sing Classical repertoire, such as opera, sacred songs and art songs.

You seldom hear a flipped or a trilled *r* in Pop music.

Flipped *r*

The flipped *r* is made by lightly tapping the front edge of the blade of your tongue once against your upper gum ridge. It sounds something like a very fast [d], but with a lighter touch.

Sometimes, the flipped *r* may be written in dialect as two *dd*'s, i.e., *veddy* for *very*.

The flipped *r* is not normally used in Standard American Speech. However, sometimes, but not always, it is naturally pronounced after [θ] (as in *three*).

Instances in which you might use (but are not required to use) the flipped *r* are:

Classical acting: The flipped *r* is frequently heard as a traditional characteristic of classical speech. Sometimes it is mistakenly described as or even pronounced as a rolled *r*.

Opera, sacred music and art songs: Use of the flipped *r* is traditional when you sing opera and you frequently hear it used in sacred music and art songs. Some artists prefer its sound over the Standard American *r*.

The reasons usually given for preferring the flipped *r* are:

(1) It has greater carrying power, or projection, than the Standard American *r*.

(2) It sounds more dignified or sophisticated.

(3) On high notes the flipped r is easier to sing.

Although singing a flipped *r* is not mandatory, the force of tradition carries considerable weight in deciding what *r* to use. If you decide to use the flipped *r*, be consistent and follow the rules for using the flipped *r* given below.

Rules for Singing the Flipped *r*

If you use the flipped *r*, you must be careful to follow the rules. Indiscriminate or haphazard substitution of the flipped *r* for the regular Standard American *r* makes you sound like an amateur actor speaking a bad British dialect. Or it makes you sound like you are singing English with a foreign accent.

(1) Use the flipped *r* between vowels.

(A) In words: *oral, carry, foreign, herald*.

(B) In linking words: *far away, here I am, tear up*.

(2) Do not use a flipped *r* before a consonant. Use the Standard American, or soft, *r*:

(A) In words: *thirty, farm, park, turn*.

(B) In linking words: *fear not, dare to, for me*.

(3) Do not use a flipped *r* after a consonant, use the Standard American, or soft, *r*: *from, drill, pray, crown*.

Exception: You might you use a flipped *r* in the *thr* combination, as in *three*.

(You may hear some classical singers use the flipped *r* in all but the *tr* and *dr* combinations (*true, drop*). But that practice does not seem to be universal.)

Trilled or Rolled *r*

The trilled, or rolled, *r* is a series of flipped *r*'s, usually not exceeding two or three taps.

To learn how to make the trilled *r*, touch the blade of your tongue lightly against your hard palate just behind your upper gum ridge and touch the sides of your tongue to your upper molars. Relax the blade of your tongue and allow it to flap loosely against your gum ridge as you blow a stream of breath between your hard palate and the blade of your tongue.

If the trill doesn't happen easily for you, you might also try saying a series of fast *dddd*'s, while you blow air out between the blade of your tongue and your gum ridge. Gradually relax the blade of your tongue and let it begin flapping from the force of your breath.

The trilled, or rolled, *r* is heard in a number of dialects, such as Scots and Spanish.

Dropping the *r*

The English people in the London area started dropping their *r*'s before consonants around the fifteenth century. But dropping the *r*'s before all consonants and pauses did not become a distinctive part of the speech of the British upper class until the late eighteenth century (about the time of the American Revolution). (See *Introduction*)

As we discussed in the *Introduction*, dropping the *r*'s never really caught on in America and today Standard American Speech does not drop the *r*.

Nevertheless, it is traditional to sing opera, sacred music and art songs in English with dropped *r*'s. Usually the reasons given for dropping the *r*'s are that it sounds better and it's easier to sing.

Before deciding to drop or not to drop your *r*'s, you should consider some of the reasons for and against it.

You have already seen that a retroflex *r* creates tension problems in your tongue. But the Standard American [r] or [ɜˠ/ɚˠ] is no more difficult to sing than any other vowel or consonant.

The tradition of dropping the *r*'s when singing opera, sacred music and art songs in English carries a lot of weight. Audiences are used to hearing classical singers drop their *r*'s. Combined with other pronunciations, such as the Boston *a*, it is considered to be elegant speech, associated with culture and sophistication.

On the negative side, some people consider it to be snobbish, elitist speech.

Today, American actors and well-known public speakers (e.g., network newscasters) generally pronounce their *r*'s. So your audience is used to hearing an *r* in the normal pronunciation of a word. Pronouncing the word without the *r* sometimes makes it difficult for them to understand it.

For example, depending upon your pronunciation of the vowel, *tu*r*n*, without an *r*, might be difficult to distinguish from *ton*, or *ma*r*k*, without an *r*, might sound like *mock*.

You should also keep in mind that in the United States dropping the *r* gives an East coast or Southern dialect sound to your pronunciation. Some listeners may even mistake it for a British dialect. There is nothing wrong with that if you are playing a character who is supposed to sound like he or she is from the Southern or Eastern states or from England. But, usually, unless a dialect is specified for a character, Standard American Dialect, which is not identified with any specific region, is the preferred stage dialect.

Of course, if you are singing a style of pop music that is sung with a dialect that drops *r*'s, you should drop them.

In the final analysis, dropping or not dropping your *r*'s is a matter of choice, taste and clarity. The overriding considerations are the force of tradition, vocal aesthetics and the need to be understood.

Rules for Dropping the *r*

If you do drop your *r*'s, you should do it according to the rules. As with the flipped *r*, indiscriminate or haphazard dropping of *r* sounds amateurish.

(1) Drop the *r* before consonants.

    (A) Drop *r* before a consonant when the vowel in the syllable is pronounced. (Be sure to keep the pronunciation of the vowel the same):

(1) In words: *la(r)k, to(r)n, sta(r)t.*

(2) In linking words: *fo(r) me, fa(r) gone.*

    (B) In **stressed** syllables that have the vowel sound [ɝ], change the [ɝ] to [ɜ] (Kenyon & Knott, *A Pronouncing Dictionary of American English*, p. xvii.): *perfect,* [pɜfɪkt], *turn*, [tɜn], *pearl*, [pɜl].

    (C) In **nonstressed** syllables that have the vowel sound [ɚ], change the [ɚ] to [ə] (Kenyon & Knott, *A Pronouncing Dictionary of American English*, p. xvii.): *father*, [fɑðə], *further*, [fɜðə], *cater*, [keɪtə].

(2) Drop *r* when it is the final sound before a pause.

    (A) Drop *r* before a pause as long as the word remains recognizable: *Oh bright sta(r). What a pai(r). I am poo(r).*

    (B) But change [r] to [ə] when the word would be unrecognizable unless you pronounced either [r] or [ə]: For example, *Do not fear,* would sound like *Do not fee;* or *No, never,* would sound like *No, nev.*

(3) Always pronounce *r* before a vowel.

    (A) In opera it is traditional to use the flipped *r* (except in *tr* and *dr* combinations (*trap, dream*), where the Standard American *r* is used.)

(Madeleine Marshall, *The Singers Manual of English Diction*, p. 16.) However, as we stated under *Rules for Singing the Flipped r*, #3, singing the flipped *r* is not as prevalent as it once was.

    (B) In sacred songs and art songs it has been traditional to use the Standard American *r*, with three exceptions:

(1) Use the flipped *r* between vowels: i.e., *terrible; for a while.*

(2) Use the flipped *r* on very high pitches.

(3) Use the flipped *r* in *cr* and *gr* combinations: i.e., *crush, great.* (Madeleine Marshall, *The Singers Manual of English Diction*, p. 16.)

    (C) In styles of singing other than opera, sacred songs and art songs use only the Standard American *r*.

Although rules such as these presented here are useful as guidelines, in practice, even the best professional singers do not always follow rules or conventions.

Choices about what kind of *r* to use and whether or not to drop the *r* are many times made unconsciously and according to what is easiest to sing or what sounds best to the singer's ear. You'll probably make your own choices in much the same way.

But knowing what choices you have can take away much of the confusion about what to do with an *r*—and making a confident choice reduces tension in your articulators.

Congratulations! You have learned to recognize and say the **Semi-Vowels** of **Standard American Speech**.

We will combine the review of the Semi-Vowels with the review of the Nasals at the end of the next chapter.

15 Nasal Consonants

A nasal consonant is a speech sound which resonates out through your nasal passages, or your nose, instead of through your mouth.

How Do You Make a Nasal Consonant?

For the sound to resonate freely through your nose, you stop the sound from coming out through your mouth by closing your lips or closing off the mouth passage with your tongue and you drop your soft palate down to open up the passage into the nasal area. The position of your soft palate is difficult to feel, but it's the same position it takes to allow you to breathe through your nose.

Three Nasal Consonants

There are three nasal consonants.

Say them out loud.

(23) [m]... *me*

(24) [n]... *no*

(25) [ŋ]... *king*

Consonant #23 [m] "me" (nasal)

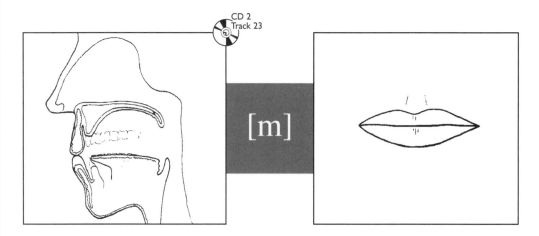

CD 2
Track 23

Hearing

Listen carefully to this sound on the Standard American Diction CDs.

Jaw

Open your jaw about a finger width. (For speech and much of your singing, your jaw floats open about one finger width. But sometimes you need to open your jaw wider, so it's best to practice with a wide jaw.)

Tongue

Feel your tongue relaxed down on the floor of your mouth, not touching the roof of your mouth.

Soft Palate

Feel your soft palate open, so that you can breathe through your nose.

Lips

Without closing your jaw touch your upper and lower lips together.

Start the vocal sound.

Feel the vibrations strongly across the bridge of your nose and on your lips.

After saying the sound, relax your lips open.

Say the sound out loud, sustaining it for two counts.

[m]... open lips, [m]... open lips.

[m]... open lips, [m]... open lips.

Now sing the sound at a medium volume, on a comfortable pitch. Sustain it for two counts.

[m]... open lips, [m]... open lips.

[m]... open lips, [m]... open lips.

Resonant Feel

Pay particular attention to the resonant feel of [m]. The character of its resonance is different from all the other phonetic sounds. Learn to love it and look forward to saying it.

Mirror Exercise

Watch yourself in a mirror as you say [m].

For a clear, resonant [m], your jaw should stay open with your teeth approximately a finger width apart. Do not close your jaw when you bring your lips together.

Your lips should touch lightly together.

Your tongue should remain in the floor of your mouth, not touching the roof of your mouth.

Say the sound out loud, sustaining it for two counts.

[m]... open lips, [m]... open lips.

[m]... open lips, [m]... open lips.

Now sing the sound at a medium volume, on a comfortable pitch.
Sustain it for two counts.

[m]... open lips, [m]... open lips.

[m]... open lips, [m]... open lips.

Possible Problems

There are two potential problems in saying this sound:

(1) **Closing your jaw as you bring your lips together.** You should keep your
jaw slightly open so that the sound can resonate in the mouth chamber,
as well as in the nasal cavity.

(2) **Raising your tongue to block off the mouth resonance.** Do not let the
middle of your tongue lift up to touch the roof of your mouth and do not
let the back of your tongue lift up to touch your soft palate. Both these
positions stop the sound from resonating in your mouth.

Make sure that your tongue is relaxed down on the floor or your mouth and that your
mouth cavity is open. When the sound is resonating in your mouth, you will feel strong
vibrations on your lips.

Saying Consonants in Words

When saying [m] in words, do not hold on to it. Say it quickly, but clearly, and move
immediately to the vowel.

Occasionally, singers will linger on [m] a little longer than they do on other consonants.
This is a stylistic or dramatic choice that at times is effective.

Start the vowel as soon as you release your lips. Think of the consonant as a springboard
that bounces you powerfully into a clear, open vowel. You can feel the [m] well forward in
your mouth, imagine bringing the vowel into that position as well.

Practice Words

In the following words, say [m] clearly and strongly, but without any
extra tension.

Speak the words out loud, then sing them on a comfortable pitch.

me... me...	*amount... amount...*	*beam... beam...*
may... may..	*common... common...*	*atom... atom...*
more... more...	*empty... empty...*	*rhythm... rhythm...*
mask... mask...	*almost... almost...*	*climb... climb...*
message... message...	*famous... famous...*	*phantom... phantom...*

Practice Sentences

In the following practice sentences, feel your articulators moving and feel the resonance of each individual sound as you say the words.

Say them slowly at first, then faster. Right now accuracy is more important than speed.

Speak them out loud, then sing them on a comfortable pitch.

> *<u>M</u>emories are <u>m</u>o<u>m</u>ents to re<u>m</u>e<u>m</u>ber.*
>
> *<u>M</u>onday <u>m</u>orning the far<u>m</u>er ca<u>m</u>e ho<u>m</u>e.*
>
> *<u>M</u>any <u>m</u>incing <u>m</u>aidens <u>m</u>aking for the <u>m</u>oor.*
>
> *<u>M</u>r. <u>M</u>ather <u>m</u>akes <u>m</u>agnificent <u>m</u>arsh<u>m</u>allow <u>m</u>acaroons.*

Daily Exercises—Consonant #23 [m]

(1) Practice saying this sound and the other phonetic sounds you have learned with the Standard American Diction CDs.

(2) Read aloud from a newspaper, magazine or book until you feel and hear yourself say the [m] sound five times. Underline the words.

(3) Speak the following reading out loud, slowly at first, then faster. Right now accuracy is more important than speed. Underline the words with [m].

> *My mistress' eyes are nothing like the sun,*
> *Coral is far more red than her lips' red,*
> *If snow be white, why then her breasts are dun,*
> *If hairs be wires, black wires grow on her head:*
> *I have seen roses damasked red and white,*
> *But no such roses see I in her cheeks,*
> *And in some perfumes is there more delight*
> *Than in the breath that from my mistress reeks.*
> *I love to hear her speak, yet well I know*
> *That music hath a far more pleasing sound.*
> *I grant I never saw a goddess go;*
> *My mistress when she walks treads on the ground.*
> >   *And yet by heav'n I think my love as rare*
> >   *As any she belied with false compare.*
> >   *SHAKESPEARE, Sonnet 130.*

(4) Sing a short passage from one of your songs or arias that has the [m] in it. Repeat it several times, concentrating on saying [m] correctly.

(5) Repeat the entire section for [m] three times today.

(6) And make sure you're saying [m] correctly as you speak during the day.

Consonant #24 [n] "<u>n</u>o" (nasal)

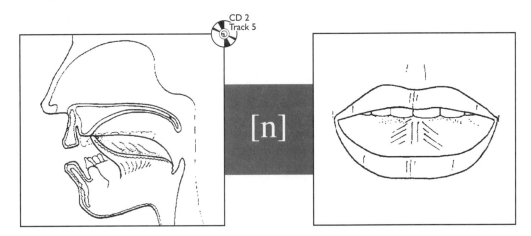

CD 2
Track 5

Hearing

Listen carefully to this sound on the Standard American Diction CDs.

Jaw

Open your jaw about a finger width. (For speech and much of your singing, your jaw floats open about one finger width. But sometimes you need to open your jaw wider, so it's best to practice with a wide jaw.)

Soft Palate

Feel your soft palate open, so that you can breathe through your nose.

Lips

Feel your lips relaxed open as you say this sound.

Tongue

Without closing your jaw, touch the edge of the blade of your tongue to your upper gum ridge.

Feel the edges of your tongue touching your upper teeth all the way around.

Feel the middle of your tongue relaxed down, not touching the roof of your mouth.

Start the vocal sound.

Feel the vibrations strongly on your tongue, on your palate, and across the bridge of your nose.

After you say the sound, relax your tongue down to the floor of your mouth.

Say the sound out loud, sustaining it for two counts.

[n]... relax tongue, [n]... relax tongue.

[n]... relax tongue, [n]... relax tongue.

Now sing the sound at a medium volume, on a comfortable pitch. Sustain it for two counts.

[n]... relax tongue, [n]... relax tongue.

[n]... relax tongue, [n]... relax tongue.

Resonant Feel

Pay particular attention to the resonant feel of [n]. The character of its resonance is different from all the other phonetic sounds. Learn to love it and look forward to saying it.

Mirror Exercise

Watch yourself in a mirror as you say [n].

For a clear, resonant [n], your jaw should stay open with your teeth approximately a finger width apart.

Your tongue should move to your upper gum ridge in a relaxed way.

Say the sound out loud, sustaining it for two counts.

[n]... relax tongue, [n]... relax tongue.

[n]... relax tongue, [n]... relax tongue.

Now sing the sound at a medium volume, on a comfortable pitch. Sustain it for two counts.

[n]... relax tongue, [n]... relax tongue.

[n]... relax tongue, [n]... relax tongue.

Possible Problems

There are two potential problems with saying this sound:

(1) Closing your jaw as you say the sound. Be sure to leave your jaw open approximately a finger width.

(2) Touching too much of the top of the front portion of your tongue against your teeth and hard palate. Be sure to touch only the front edge of the blade of your tongue lightly to your gum ridge. Feel as though the middle of your tongue is relaxed down from the roof of your mouth.

Saying Consonants in Words

When saying [n] in words, do not hold on to it. Say it quickly, but clearly, and move immediately to the vowel.

Start the vowel as soon as you release your tongue. Think of the consonant as a springboard that bounces you powerfully into a clear, open vowel. You can feel the [n] well forward in your mouth, imagine bringing the vowel into that position as well.

Practice Words

In the following practice words, say [n] clearly and strongly, but without any extra tension.

Speak the words out loud, then sing them on a comfortable pitch.

no... no...	*and... and...*	*fan... fan...*
net... net...	*dinner... dinner...*	*main... main...*
name... name...	*panel... panel...*	*dine... dine...*
never... never...	*many... many...*	*scorn... scorn...*
natural... natural...	*morning... morning...*	*began... began...*

Practice Sentences

In the following practice sentences, feel your articulators moving and feel the resonance of each individual sound as you say the words.

Say them slowly at first, then faster. Right now accuracy is more important than speed.

Speak them out loud, then sing them on a comfortable pitch.

No one knew it was nonsense.

The next announcement was funny.

Nine nimble noblemen nibbling nettles.

Nina needs nineteen knitting needles tonight.

Daily Exercises—Consonant #24 [n]

(1) Practice saying this sound and the other phonetic sounds you have learned with the Standard American Diction CDs.

(2) Read aloud from a newspaper, magazine or book until you feel and hear yourself say the [n] sound five times. Underline the words.

(3) Speak the following reading out loud, slowly at first, then faster. Right now accuracy is more important than speed. Underline the words with [n].

> *Not from the stars do I my judgement pluck,*
> *And yet methinks I have astronomy;*
> *But not to tell of good or evil luck,*
> *Of plagues of dearths, or seasons' quality;*
> *Nor can I fortune to brief minutes tell,*
> *Pointing to each his thunder, rain and wind,*
> *Or say with princes if it shall go well,*
> *By oft predict that I in heaven find.*
> *But from thine eyes my knowledge I derive,*
> *And, constant stars, in them I read such art*
> *As truth and beauty shall together thrive,*
> *If from thyself to store thou wouldst convert;*
> > *Or else of thee this I prognosticate,*
> > *Thy end is truth's and beauty's doom and date.*
> > *SHAKESPEARE, Sonnet 14.*

(4) Sing a short passage from one of your songs or arias that has the [n] in it. Repeat it several times, concentrating on saying [n] correctly.

(5) Repeat the entire section for [n] three times today.

(6) And make sure you're saying [n] correctly as you speak during the day.

Consonant #25 [ŋ] "ki*ng*"

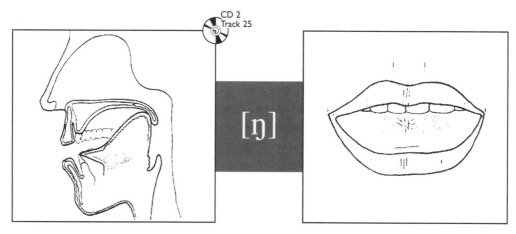

CD 2
Track 25

Hearing

Listen carefully to this sound on the Standard American Diction CDs.

Jaw

Open your jaw about a finger width. (For speech and much of your singing, your jaw floats open about one finger width. But sometimes you need to open your jaw wider, so it's best to practice with a wide jaw.)

Soft Palate

Feel your soft palate open, so that you can breathe through your nose.

Lips

Feel your lips relaxed open as you say this sound.

Tongue

Without closing your jaw, touch the back part of your tongue to your soft palate.

Leave the blade of your tongue touching the backs of your lower front teeth.

Start the vocal sound.

Feel the vibrations strongly across the bridge of your nose and where your tongue touches your soft palate.

After you say the sound relax your tongue down to the floor of your mouth.

Say the sound out loud, sustaining it for two counts.

[ŋ]... relax tongue, [ŋ]... relax tongue.

[ŋ]... relax tongue, [ŋ]... relax tongue.

Now sing the sound at a medium volume, on a comfortable pitch. Sustain it for two counts.

[ŋ]... relax tongue, [ŋ]... relax tongue.

[ŋ]... relax tongue, [ŋ]... relax tongue.

Resonant Feel

Pay particular attention to the resonant feel of [ŋ]. The character of its resonance is different from all the other phonetic sounds. Learn to love it and look forward to saying it.

Mirror Exercise

Watch yourself in a mirror as you say [ŋ].

For a clear, resonant [ŋ], your jaw should stay open with your teeth approximately a finger width apart.

The front edge of the blade of your tongue should remain touching the backs of your lower front teeth.

Say the sound out loud, sustaining it for two counts.

[ŋ]... relax tongue, [ŋ]... relax tongue.

[ŋ]... relax tongue, [ŋ]... relax tongue.

Now sing the sound at a medium volume, on a comfortable pitch.
Sustain it for two counts.

[ŋ]... relax tongue, [ŋ]... relax tongue.

[ŋ]... relax tongue, [ŋ]... relax tongue.

Possible Problems

Listen to yourself carefully as you say this sound. Make sure you do not add a [ə] sound at the end of [ŋ].

Saying Consonants in Words

When saying [ŋ] in words, do not hold on to it. Say it quickly, but clearly, and move immediately to the vowel.

Do not leave a breathy space between the consonant and the vowel, start the vowel as soon as you release your tongue. Think of the consonant as a springboard that bounces you powerfully into a clear, open vowel. Imagine bringing [ŋ] well forward in your mouth and imagine bringing the vowel forward as well.

Practice Words

In the following words, say [ŋ] clearly and strongly, but without any extra tension.

Speak the words out loud, then sing them on a comfortable pitch.

a**ng**le... a**ng**le...	ki**ng**... ki**ng**...
u**n**cle... u**n**cle...	lo**ng**... lo**ng**...
si**nk**... si**nk**..	ba**ng**... ba**ng**...
hu**ng**ry... hu**ng**ry...	si**ng**i**ng**... si**ng**i**ng**...
ki**ng**dom... ki**ng**dom...	wro**ng**... wro**ng**...

Practice Sentences

In the following practice sentences, feel your articulators moving and feel the resonance of each individual sound as you say the words.

Say them slowly at first, then faster. Right now accuracy is more important than speed.

Speak them out loud, then sing them on a comfortable pitch.

*The ki**ng** of E**ng**land sa**ng** a so**ng**.*

*The mo**n**key's u**n**cle swu**ng** in the ju**ng**le.*

*Si**ng**i**ng** and danci**ng** are part of romanci**ng**.*

*A sku**nk** sat on a stump.*

*The stump thought the sku**nk** stu**nk**.*

*The sku**nk** thought the stump stu**nk**.*

*The sku**nk** and the stump both stu**nk**.*

Daily Exercises—Consonant #25 [ŋ]

(1) Practice saying this sound and the other phonetic sounds you have learned with the Standard American Diction CDs.

(2) Read aloud from a newspaper, magazine or book until you feel and hear yourself say the [ŋ] sound five times. Underline the words.

(3) Speak the following reading out loud, slowly at first, then faster. Right now accuracy is more important than speed. Underline the words with [ŋ].

> *When in disgrace with fortune and men's eyes,*
> *I all alone beweep my outcast state,*
> *And trouble deaf heav'n with my bootless cries,*
> *And look upon myself and curse my fate,*
> *Wishing me like to one more rich in hope,*
> *Featured like him, like him with friends possessed,*
> *Desiring this man's art, and that man's scope,*
> *With what I most enjoy contented least;*
> *Yet in these thoughts myself almost despising,*
> *Haply I think on thee, and then my state,*
> *(Like to the lark at break of day arising)*
> *From sullen earth, sings hymns at heaven's gate;*
> > *For thy sweet love rememb'red such wealth brings,*
> > *That then I scorn to change my state with kings.*
> > SHAKESPEARE, *Sonnet 29.*

(4) Sing a short passage from one of your songs or arias that has the [ŋ] in it. Repeat it several times, concentrating on saying [ŋ] correctly.

(5) Repeat the entire section for [ŋ] three times today.

(6) And make sure you're saying [ŋ] correctly as you speak during the day.

Review of Semi-Vowels and Nasals

Let's do a quick review of **Semi-Vowels** and **Nasals**.

Speak the sounds and words out loud, then sing them on a comfortable pitch.

Semi-Vowels

(21) [l] *lake... laugh... all...* [l]
(22) [r] *rule... rain... are...* [r]

Nasals

(23) [m] *me... man... came...* [m]
(24) [n] *no... name... bin...* [n]
(25) [ŋ] *young... king... angle...* [ŋ]

Congratulations! You've learned to recognize and say all the **Consonant** sounds of **Standard American Speech**.

Review of Consonants

Let's do a quick review. Say the sounds and the words out loud.

Fricatives

(1) [v] *van... veil... live...* [v]
(2) [f] *fun... far... if...* [f]
(3) [ð] *the... that... other...* [ð]
(4) [θ] *thank... thing... booth...* [θ]
(5) [z] *zoom... zip... buzz...* [z]
(6) [s] *song... sail... voice...* [s]
(7) [ʒ] *Asia... rouge... garage...* [ʒ]
(8) [ʃ] *she... shore... dash...* [ʃ]
(9) [h] *has... help... who...* [h]

Plosives

(10) [b] *ball... about... web...* [b]
(11) [p] *pull... apple... pop...* [p]
(12) [d] *dean... door... lad...* [d]
(13) [t] *tall... tend... lot...* [t]
(14) [g] *got... give... dog...* [g]
(15) [k] *can... call... look...* [k]

Affricatives

(16) [dʒ] *jar... joke... fudge...* [dʒ]
(17) [tʃ] *chair... chum... church...* [tʃ]

Glides

(18) [w] *will... were... awake...* [w]
(19) [ʍ] *while... when... what...* [ʍ]
(20) [j] *yes... yacht... loyal...* [j]

Semi-Vowels

(21) [l] *lake... laugh... all...* [l]
(22) [r] *rule... rain... are...* [r]

Nasals

(23) [m] *me... man... came...* [m]
(24) [n] *no... name... bin...* [n]
(25) [ŋ] *young... king... angle...* [ŋ]

Notice how much more clearly and easily you can say these sounds.

If you're still having touble with any of the consonant sounds, listen to the demonstrations on the Standard American Diction CDs.

Repeat the exercise for that sound until you can say it clearly and easily.

Notes:

vowel #2 eɪ "ai"

vowel #7 ə "uh"

consonant #8 ʃ "sh"

consonant #22 l "l"

16 Pronunciation

Pronunciation is the way you say a word, with regard to:

Speech Sounds

Linking

Syllable Stress

Four Elements of Good Pronunciation:

(1) Saying clear, distinct speech sounds

(2) Saying the right sounds in the right places

(3) Connecting, or linking, the sounds together

(4) Placing correct syllable stress on the word

You can learn to pronounce words in two ways:

(1) Listen to good speakers and imitate the way they say their words

(2) Look up the pronunciation in a dictionary

Listening and imitating is the best and easiest way. Remember, that is the way we first learned to pronounce words.

But looking up a word in a dictionary is the only way you can learn how to say a word that you have never heard spoken. If you are not quite sure what vowel to say in a word, a dictionary will have the answer.

Two Surprising Obstacles to Good Pronunciation

There are two obstacles to good pronunciation that have nothing to do with your voice:

(1) Spelling

(2) An aversion to dictionaries

Spelling vs. Pronunciation

Don't let the spelling fool you.

In the *Introduction* and in the chapter on *Speech Sounds*, we noted in some detail how the spelling of a word is not always a good guide to the way it is said. Review those chapters, if you need to.

Use a Dictionary

If you are not quite sure how to pronounce a word, always take the time to look it up in a dictionary.

You should never be too embarrassed or too lazy to use a dictionary.

Intelligent and educated people use dictionaries frequently. Even experienced speakers of Standard American Speech, look up pronunciations of words. Radio and television announcers use pronunciation dictionaries regularly and have pronunciation guides in the scripts they read on the air. No one knows how to say every word.

The noted news commentator and professional speaker, Edwin Newman, in his introduction to the *NBC Handbook of Pronunciation*, advises looking up words for their correct pronunciation. He says,

> *There is, of course, no harm in asking how something is pronounced, or in looking it up. That is why books of this kind exist.... It is for anybody who speaks in public, habitually, occasionally, or once in a great while.... In fact, it is for anyone who engages in conversation, or even in interior monologues. There is no reason to be wrong just because you're talking to yourself.* (p. 10)

Pronunciation for Singing

Sing your words with the same pronunciation they have in speech.

Singers frequently change the vowels in words they sing. They have various reasons:

Sometimes they think a different vowel is more correct or formal.

Sometimes a different vowel is easier for them to sing.

Sometimes they think a different vowel will help them to sing a note better.

And, sometimes excessive tension forces them into singing a wrong vowel.

But changing the vowel when you sing a word makes it more difficult for your listeners to understand you.

Take the vowel [ɪ], as in *big*, for example. Frequently, singers sing the [ɪ] as an [i] and the audience hears the word as *beeg*. An unfamiliar English word, indeed.

Often the [æ] vowel, as in *fast* and *back*, is changed to [ɑ], creating two more unfamiliar words.

The number of examples could be expanded, but you get the idea: **You should sing the words as they are normally pronounced in good Standard American Speech.**

There are two exceptions to the above rule:

(1) When you are singing a note in your extreme high range (see the discussion on page 23 of the *Introduction*)

(2) When you sustain a nonstressed syllable

In speech, the vowel in a nonstressed syllable is often changed either to [ɪ], as in *receive* [rɪsiv] and *delight* [dɪlaɪt], or to [ə], as in *alone* [əloʊn] and *melody* [mɛlədɪ].

If the music calls for you to sustain one of these nonstressed syllables, it is sometimes acceptable to pronounce the vowel as it is said in a stressed syllable. For example, the vowel in the nonstressed syllable of *receive* may be sustained as [i] and the vowel in the nonstressed syllable of *melody* as [oʊ].

Changing the vowel to a stressed-syllable pronunciation sometimes makes the word easier to recognize.

Say the Right Sounds in the Right Places

Singing sounds that are indistinct makes it difficult for your listeners to understand you, but singing wrong sounds really confuses them.

How do you know when you should change the spoken pronunciation? Sometimes it is difficult to decide. You base your choice on the music and what other singers do in the same style. Then, between you and your vocal coach, you decide what sounds best.

Saying the Right Sounds

In general, Standard American Diction calls for more careful pronunciation than does less

disciplined, or more casual speech. For example, in Standard American Speech *fer* is not an acceptable substitution for *for*. Nor should you say *git* for *get*, or *dem* for *them*.

Such colloquialisms would probably still be understood, but they sound out of place in a trained voice.

Sometimes the wrong sound changes a word to an entirely different word, which changes your meaning.

Saying, *Write it with a pin*, creates a much different image and meaning for your listener than, *Write it with a pen*. *He is a bat boy*, is entirely different from, *He is a bad boy*.

Usually such pronunciation slips are made clear by the context in which they are said, but for a brief moment, your audience is confused by them.

Do Not Add Extra Sounds

You must also be careful to say only the sounds that should be said in a word. *Business* is pronounced *bus'ness*, not *business*, and *athlete* should not be pronounced *athelete*.

You should guard against singing unnecessary vowel sounds between words. Occasionally, you may hear a singer sing, *bad'a' man*, instead of *bad man*, or *deceive'a' me*, instead of *deceive me*.

Such additions make the words more difficult to understand, as well as giving the impression that you have an accent.

Say All of the Sounds

It is also important to say all of the sounds that are supposed to be said in a word.

Commonly, untrained singers and speakers drop the ends of words—*comin'* instead of *coming*, or *tha'* instead of *that*. Dropping sounds makes it very difficult to understand what you're saying and singing. (However, in some styles of Pop singing dropping the ends of words is part of the style. See the chapter on *Pop Pronunciation*.)

Good pronunciation makes it easy for your audience to understand you. The less they have to work at trying to figure out what you're saying, the more they're going to enjoy your singing.

Linking

Linking is connecting speech sounds together:

(1) You link sounds together to form words

(2) You also link words together to form phrases and sentences

Linking Speech Sounds In Words

There is an imaginary ideal position for each speech sound. When you say the sound in speech or singing, your articulators need to come close enough to that position to make pretty much the same sound each time. If they don't, then, of course, the sound is not recognizable.

You can think of the ideal speech sound as the bulls-eye on a target. Hit it right in the center and the sound is ideal. The further away you get from the bulls-eye, the less recognizable the speech sound.

When you practice a speech sound by itself, it's a simple, controlled process:

(1) Your articulators come from a position of rest. They move more slowly than in normal speech and are in place before you begin the sound. It's easy to hit the bulls-eye.

(3) You take the time to say the sound correctly.

(2) Then your articulators return to a position of rest.

When you combine, or link, sounds together to form words, the sounds normally change slightly from the way you say them by themselves. But the change is not so great that it makes the sound unrecognizable. It is only a slight modification.

There are two reasons for the change in pronunciation.

(1) When you say the sound in a word, your articulators move very fast and they are in almost continuous motion, sliding from one sound to another. It's not always possible to accurately place your articulators in the exact position for each speech sound.

(2) When you connect sounds together, your articulators begin and end each speech sound differently than when you say the sound by itself. At the beginning of the sound they do not start from a position of rest, they begin their move from the final position of the previous sound. And at the end of the sound they don't just relax, they begin their move to the position for the next sound.

This fast, continuous motion puts the articulators a little off target and changes the ideal speech sound slightly.

Luckily, for a speech sound to be recognizable, your articulators do not need to be in exactly the same position or touch exactly the same place each time you say the sound. That is an impossible goal. But you should try to place your articulators as close to that ideal target position as possible.

Three Phases of Articulation in Linking

There are three phases in the articulation and linking of each speech sound:

(1) The movement to the position.

(2) The holding in place while you say the sound.

(3) The movement away from the position.

   Feeling these three phases as you link the sounds together will help you to learn to say the sounds accurately.

   See the movements of your articulators in your mind.

   Listen to the sound you make to make sure it is right.

An Effective Method of Improving Pronunciation

There are four steps to learning how to easily link speech sounds together in a word:

(1) Break the word up into its component sounds.

(2) Learn how to say each sound individually.

(3) Connect the sounds smoothly together into syllables.

(4) Connect the syllables smoothly together into words.

For example, if you want to sing the word, *lovely*, break the word down into its five component sounds:

$$[l], [ʌ], [v], [l], [ɪ]$$

(Don't let the spelling fool you into thinking the word has more sounds than it actually has.)

Follow these steps, using the three phases of articulation. Use **feeling**, **seeing** and **hearing**.

Say the sounds out loud.

(1) Say each sound slowly by itself, being careful to get the articulation right.

$$[l], [ʌ], [v], [l], [ɪ]$$

Again...

$$[l], [ʌ], [v], [l], [ɪ]$$

(2) Say the sounds a little faster, one after the other, but still separately.

$$[l], [ʌ], [v], [l], [ɪ]$$

Again...

$$[l], [ʌ], [v], [l], [ɪ]$$

(3) Let the sounds connect to one another to form a complete syllable. Feel the articulators moving smoothly from the position for one sound to the position for the next sound.

$$[lʌv] [lɪ]$$

Again...

$$[lʌv] [lɪ]$$

(4) Link the syllables smoothly together.

$$[lʌvlɪ]$$

Again...

$$[lʌvlɪ]$$

(5) Gradually bring the pronunciation up to normal speaking speed.

lovely

Again...

lovely

(6) Now sing the exercise, starting with step (1).

Notice how much easier it is.

Articulator Movement

Standard American Speech flows easily and naturally. It's not in any way overarticulated or laborious.

When you practice, move your articulators far enough to reach the right positions for the sounds, but don't move them more than you need to to make the sounds you want.

That is, don't round your lips too much, or draw them back too far. Don't stick your tongue out between your teeth. And don't open and close your jaw excessively.

Also, move your articulators in a relaxed way, not tensely.

Watch good speakers, in person or on television, and notice how clear their speech is with minimum articulator movement.

The more you practice saying words clearly, easily and in a relaxed way, the more natural sounding they become.

Linking Syllables, Words and Phrases

Syllables and words are linked together in the same way you link speech sounds. That is, the last sound of the syllable flows into the first sound of the following syllable.

We'll demonstrate this with the sentence, *His arm is up*. All the words are single syllables so you'll see how the concepts apply to both syllables and words.

Say the words out loud and notice how they are connected.

His arm is up.

Notice that the last sound of *his*, [z], is connected to the first sound in *arm*, so that it sounds almost like you're saying **z**arm. The [m] of *arm* is connected to *is*, so that it sounds almost like **m**is. And the [z] of *is* is connected to *up*, so that it sounds almost like **z**up.

But you must also be careful not to slur the words together. To keep the words distinct, think of each word as a complete unit as you're connecting, or linking, it to the next word.

Of course, when you take a pause between words, they do not link together.

Four Possibilities of Linking

There are four possible combinations of linking.

(1) *A Consonant Linking to a Vowel.*

The last sound in a word may be a consonant and the first sound in the next word a vowel, as in, *come on*. The last sound of *come*, [m], is connected to the first sound of *on*, [ɒ].

Practice Words

Say these practice words slowly at first, then faster.
After you practice them speaking, sing them on a comfortable pitch.

Say the words out loud.

come on... come on...	*leave it... leave it...*
still up... still up...	*am I... am I...*
this is... this is..	*love it... love it...*
these are... these are...	*song of... song of...*
far away... far away...	*read it... read it...*

(2) *A Consonant Linking to a Consonant.*

The last sound of a word may be a consonant and the first sound of the next word may also be a consonant, as in, *call me*. The last sound of *call*, [l], is connected to the first sound of *me*, [m].

When connecting consonants to consonants you must be careful not to say a vowel in between, like this, *call'a'me*. Connect directly from one consonant to the next.

Practice Words

Say these practice words slowly at first, then faster.
After you practice them speaking, sing them on a comfortable pitch.

Say the words out loud.

call me... call me...	*duck soup... duck soup...*
this time... this time...	*down there... down there...*
tell tale... tell tale...	*clear day... clear day...*
sing this... sing this...	*dig down... dig down...*
time for... time for...	*over there... over there...*

Shared Consonants

When the same consonant both ends and begins two linked words, like this, *time may*, (don't let the spelling fool you — the *e* is not pronounced) the consonant is shared between the two words. That is, you don't separate the sounds and say two distinct consonants. You share the sound, so that it sounds like you are saying only one consonant.

Be sure you feel like you're putting the final consonant on the first word. If you don't, it will sound like you've dropped the consonant from the first word, like this, *ti' may*.

Think of putting the consonant on the end of the first word and also on the beginning of the second word. This may lengthen the linking consonant slightly, but don't purposely try to make it longer.

When the shared consonant is a plosive, as in *duck quick*, don't separate the words and say the plosive twice. Say only the one plosive.

Practice Words

Say these practice words slowly at first, then faster.
After you practice them speaking, sing them on a comfortable pitch.

Say the words out loud.

duck quick... duck quick...	*time may... time may...*
lost time... lost time...	*gone now... gone now...*
good deal... good deal...	*long gone... long gone...*
top pocket... top pocket...	*this song... this song...*
dog goes... dog goes...	*real love... real love...*

Shared Position

Linked words may also end and begin with consonants that don't sound the same, but are articulated in the same place, or almost the same place, like this, *dog **k**ennel*. The difference here is that [g] is a voiced plosive and [k] is a voiceless plosive. Say the ending sound and change smoothly to the second consonant to begin the next word. Don't make an obvious pause between the words.

Say the words out loud and feel your articulator movements.

fog creeps... fog creeps...
real time... real time...
same place... same place...

There are times when your articulators move in an unexpected way to link sounds together.

In the word *ge**ntl**e*, for example, the last three sounds, [n], [t], [l], all share the same front of the tongue position. When you're speaking, you can't release the edge of the blade of your tongue to articulate each sound. There is not enough time.

So from the position of [n], your soft palate raises to close off the passage to the nasal cavity, so that some breath pressure can build up to say [t]. Then the sides of your tongue release to give you a sound that sounds like [t]. When the sides of your tongue release, you are saying [l]. It's all very efficient, fast—and surprising. (If you release the front of your tongue to say [t], you will add an [ə] between [t] and [l].)

Say the word out loud and feel your articulator movements.

*ge**ntl**e... ge**ntl**e...*

Words that have a contraction of *not*, like *did**n't**, would**n't**, could**n't***, also have an unusual articulator movement.

From the position of the final [d], your soft palate drops to open up the nasal passages for the [n]. Then your soft palate closes to build up breath pressure for the [t].

When the soft palate does not drop, you hear an intrusive [ɛ] or [ə] between the [d] and [n], which sounds adolescent and uneducated.

Practice Words

Say these practice words slowly at first, then faster.
After you practice them speaking, sing them on a comfortable pitch.

Say the words out loud.

would not...	*wouldn't... wouldn't...*
could not...	*couldn't... couldn't...*
did not...	*didn't... didn't...*
have not...	*haven't... haven't...*
cannot...	*can't... can't...*

(3) *A Vowel Linking to a Consonant.*

The last sound of a word may be a vowel and the first sound of the next word may be a consonant, as in, *t**o** **b**e*. The last sound of *t**o**, [u], is connected to the first sound of *b**e*, [b].

Practice Words

Say these practice words slowly at first, then faster.

After you practice them speaking, sing them on a comfortable pitch.

Say the words out loud.

to be... to be...	*I know... I know...*
lie down.. .lie down...	*you can... you can...*
see them... see them...	*the team... the team...*
do not... do not...	*slow dance... slow dance...*
hey you... hey you...	*toy truck... toy truck...*

(4) A *Vowel Linking to a Vowel.*

The last sound of a word may be a vowel and the first sound of the next word may also be a vowel, as in, *go on.* The last sound of *go*, [oᵁ], is connected smoothly to the first sound of *on*, [ɒ].

Practice Words

Say these practice words slowly at first, then faster.

After you practice them speaking, sing them on a comfortable pitch.

Say the words out loud.

you and... you and...	*ado about... ado about...*
they are... they are...	*do you... do you...*
go away... go away...	*happy hour... happy hour...*
so on... so on...	*free apple... free apple...*
see all... see all...	*who asked... who asked*

Intrusive Sounds

Intrusive sounds are caused by your articulators sliding through the positions of sounds that you don't intend to say. As you're sliding from one sound to the next you may accidentally say sounds that are not supposed to be part of the word. For example, between the words *I am*, you may say the glide [j], like *I'y'am.*

When your articulators are moving from one position to the next, they can't help moving through positions for other sounds. But you should minimize unwanted sounds as much as possible.

You avoid intrusive sounds by moving quickly and directly from one sound to the next. This way you avoid the unwanted sounds altogether or you slide through their positions so fast that they are not noticed.

In particular, be careful of intrusive sounds in these combinations:

Did you, not *did'**j**'you.*

Got you, not *got'**ch**'you.*

Practice Words

Say these practice words slowly at first, then faster.

After you practice them speaking, sing them on a comfortable pitch.

Say the words out loud.

Did you... did you... did you... did you...

Got you... got you... got you... got you

When Not To Link

Occasionally, linking of words may create confusion. For example, if you're not careful, *see love* could sound like *seal of*, or *I scream* could sound like *ice cream*.

To avoid misunderstanding, you may have to take a slight pause to separate the words. Always keep in mind that you want your audience to understand what you are saying or singing.

Of course, you don't always link words. When you speak, you occasionally pause in your speech. Pauses naturally occur between thoughts and phrases or any time you need to take a breath. You can't link words over a pause.

However, when you pause, don't fade off on the ends your thoughts or phrases. Make sure the final word and the final sound in the final word is said clearly and distinctly. Your goal is to be understood.

Syllable Stress

Syllable stress, (sometimes called **emphasis** or **accent**) is easy to recognize when you hear it. It's as though the stressed syllable bounces out with a little more energy and power than the other syllables.

Why is Syllable Stress Important?

Syllable stress is an organic part of pronunciation in English. Every English word of two or more syllables has one syllable that is spoken with greater emphasis than the other syllable(s) in the word.

Learning how to control syllable stress helps to make the word recognizable. When you put stress on the wrong syllable, you make the word sound strange and difficult to understand and, in some cases, a different word altogether, i.e., **con**tract: an agreement; con**tract**: to get smaller.

Understanding how to control syllable stress is especially important in distinct and expressive singing.

How to Give Stress to a Spoken Syllable?

Many people think emphasis is achieved by saying the syllable louder. But listen to someone speaking. Do you hear any obvious and frequent changes in volume, as you would if volume change was the primary element of stress?

No.

The volume stays relatively constant. But other indications of emphasis are obvious.

Syllable stress in normal conversational speech is created by four interrelated voice changes.

(1) **Pitch/Resonance Change:** The pitch/resonance makes a noticeable slide up or down on the stressed syllable. (Pitch/resonance is explained below.)

(2) **Duration:** The stressed syllable takes longer to say than the other syllables in the word.

(3) **Volume:** The stressed syllable is said slightly louder than the other syllables in the word.

(4) **Force:** The stressed syllable is given a little extra energy in the sound, by putting extra firmness into the support muscles.

Some of these voice changes are more obvious stress characteristics than others.

Studies have shown that our ear most easily picks up changes in **pitch/resonance**. That is, a pitch/resonance change gives the most obvious emphasis to a syllable.

Next, our ear is most sensitive to a **durational** difference. A slight change in duration is easily heard as syllable emphasis.

Our ear is least sensitive to a change in **volume**. A sound must have a large volume change to give noticeable emphasis. (When we are speaking conversationally, the volume change on a single syllable is practically undetectable.)

Force is easily recognized, but it is difficult to establish what it actually is. It seems to be a combination of a little extra firmness in the support muscles, which pushes the air out of your lungs with a little more force, which, in turn, creates a more resonant sound (that is, a less breathy sound). The extra support also results in a change in pitch (usually higher), duration (longer) and volume (louder). So what we recognize as force appears to be the combined effect of changes in pitch/resonance, duration, volume and a more clear vocal tone.

For listeners, these heard changes may also be coupled with an empathic awareness of the extra physical exertion used by the speaker to give emphasis (see also, Peter Ladefoged, *A Course in Phonetics*, p. 104).

Feeling and Hearing Spoken Syllable Stress

Adding stress to a syllable does not take much extra physical effort. But, if you pay careful attention as you give stress to a syllable, you can feel a **little extra firmness** in the support muscles.

You can also hear the **pitch** slide up or down on the stressed syllable.

And you can hear and feel the difference in **resonance** on the stressed syllable.

The vocal changes that create syllable stress are most noticeable on the vowel in the syllable. The **pitch/resonance** change usually happens on the **vowel**, although a voiced consonant also changes pitch/resonance before or after the vowel.

When you create emphasis with **duration**, or sustaining, of the syllable, you usually lengthen the **vowel**—generally you don't sustain a consonant.

An increase in **volume** is also most noticeable on the **vowel**.

If the consonant is a voiced consonant, you may change its pitch/resonance with the vowel. However, the consonant pitch/resonance change is not as noticeable as the vowel pitch/resonance change.

Note: to make sure the consonant is heard clearly, you may increase its loudness to make it match the volume of the vowel.

At first, as you practice syllable stress, **overemphasize the stress**. This will help you to feel and hear syllable stress more easily. Then, as you become more aware of syllable stress and gain more control over it, you can be less obvious with the emphasis and allow it to be more natural and subtle.

Pitch/Resonance

The term pitch/resonance may not be familiar to you. It means a combination of pitch and the vocal resonance qualities (chest, mouth, mask, head).

Resonance qualities are different from registers, or head and chest voice. They are vocal qualities, not pitch ranges.

You are probably used to thinking of your voice changing pitch as you speak. But you may not be aware that when your voice goes up and down in pitch, the pitch change is also accompanied by a change in resonance quality.

That is, when your pitch goes up, more head resonance, or a lighter sound, comes into your voice, and when your pitch goes down, you add more chest resonance.

Say, *Are you?*, and let your pitch go up on *you*. Say the words out loud.

Are you?... Are you?

Notice your voice quality change to a lighter, more heady resonance as you go up in pitch on you.

Now go down in pitch on *you*. Say the words out loud.

Are you?... Are you?

Notice your voice quality change to a deeper, more chesty resonance as you go down in pitch.

This pitch/resonance change is natural in normal speech.

Listen for the pitch/resonance change in the voices of your friends and other speakers. Once you are aware of it, you can hear it easily and clearly.

Resonance changes give variety and interest to your voice. If you always spoke with the same resonant quality, your voice would sound dull and monotonous, even if you changed pitch.

Direction of Pitch/Resonance Change

A pitch/resonance change means that the pitch/resonance moves either up or down on the stressed syllable.

When you say a word by itself, the pitch/resonance change on the stressed syllable is almost always up. But when you say words as part of a phrase, the pitch/resonance change may be either up or down, depending on the subtleties of your meaning. (We discuss the relationship of pitch/resonance and meaning, or sense, in the chapter, *Inflections and Intonations*.)

Pitch/Resonance and Duration in Speech and Singing

The primary indicators of syllable stress in speech are pitch/resonance and duration. These are the voice changes most easily picked up by human hearing.

Pitch and duration changes also occur in singing, but with a difference.

In speaking, the different pitch changes and durations are established by the normal pronunciation of the word and by the meaning and emotion of the speaker. The pitch changes and duration are not set, they are flexible and improvisational.

In singing, pitch and duration are strictly controlled by the musical notes. That is, in singing, you sing a syllable up or down in pitch and sustain it according to what the composer has written. And the resonance you use depends on the quality, or color, you want in your singing at any given moment.

Good composers and lyricists attempt to match up correct syllable stress with the music. They try to have pitch changes coincide with stressed syllables and they try to place a sustained note on a stressed syllable. But they are not always successful, especially in translations.

You, as a singer, must be aware of the natural syllable stress of the word and combine your vocal emphasis with the musical emphasis. When you do, your words become more distinct and recognizable to your audience.

Since pitch and duration in singing are controlled by the music, how does a singer give vocal emphasis to the words?

Controlling Syllable Stress in Singing

In a song, pitch and duration emphasis is controlled by the composer. You sing the melody written for you and automatically certain syllables receive emphasis as a result of the pitch and duration changes in the melody.

But you also have a certain amount of control over syllable and word stress. You can:

(1) vary your volume

(2) change the quality or resonance of your voice

(3) use more or less voice.

You have control over the volume you give to your voice. You can sing louder on stressed syllables and words or softer on nonstressed syllables and words. (But don't forget that all words have to be heard clearly.)

Often pop singers change resonance to give emphasis to the stressed syllable or word, just as speakers do. Pop singing is much closer in sound to the spoken voice.

Classical singers, however, generally maintain their resonant quality, so they **emphasize syllables and words by giving more voice to the stressed syllables and words and less voice to the nonstressed syllables and words.**

As a singer, you change your voice to enhance the musical line and to incorporate personal interpretations of meaning and emotion. [I am indebted to John DeMain, Musical Director for the *Houston Grand Opera*, for pointing this out to me.]

If the composer has not matched the music to the natural syllable stresses in a word, then it is up to you to try to reestablish as much of the normal syllable stress as possible. If you don't, your audience will have great difficulty understanding you.

As an illustration, suppose a composer has written the music so that the first syllable of *receive* is sustained longer than the second syllable,—which is contrary to normal syllable stress. To help reestablish the normal syllable stress, you could sing the first syllable lightly and quietly and the second syllable with more voice and volume. The greater volume and stronger resonance emphasizes the second syllable more than the first and reestablishes the normal syllable stress.

According to Elisabeth Howard, coauthor of *Sing Like a Pro* and *Born to Sing*, when you are singing, the accented syllable generally needs a little more volume. She also suggests that where notes are written for equal duration, you may shorten the duration of the note for the nonstressed syllable. Such licence is allowable to make the word more understandable or the meaning of the lyric more clear.

She recommends this practice particularly in operatic recitative, which is speech-like, and which is usually sung *colla voce* or *rubato*. The composer writes the duration of the notes which seems most desirable to his mind, but often, for emotional effect or meaning, the singer sings the words with different durations than those given by the composer.

Be alert for these possibilities of interpretation in your music. We will discuss this further in the chapter on *Expressive Singing*.

Practicing Syllable Stress

When you practice syllable stress, clap your hands or pat something as you say the stressed syllable. The physical action helps you to feel the difference between the stressed and nonstressed syllables.

When you practice syllable stress, overemphasize the stress. Feel the vocal sensations that accompany the emphasis. The physical sensations will help you to be aware of syllable stress and to control it in your speaking and singing.

As you become more familiar with the feeling and sound of stressed syllables, decrease the amount of emphasis you use until your syllable stress matches that of good Standard American speakers.

The following exercises give you practice in each element of syllable stress separately, so that you more easily feel it and hear it. But, remember, when you are speaking, natural syllable stress is created by a combination of these voice changes.

Pitch/Resonance Change

(1) Speak the following words with the stressed syllable (**bold** & **underlined**) on a higher pitch and resonance than the nonstressed syllable(s).

Clap on the stressed syllable.

a**bout**... a**bout**...	**al**most... **al**most...	**for**tunate... **for**tunate...
ca**reer**... ca**reer**...	**rather**... **rather**...	**ad**vertise... **ad**vertise...
sup**pose**... sup**pose**...	**sim**ple... **sim**ple...	ac**cep**table... ac**cep**table...
be**tween**... be**tween**...	**open**... **open**...	oppo**si**tion... oppo**si**tion...
per**form**... per**form**...	**rea**son... **rea**son...	po**li**tical... po**li**tical...

(2) Speak the following words with the stressed syllable (**bold** & **underlined**) on a lower pitch and resonance than the nonstressed syllable(s).

Clap on the stressed syllable.

a**bout**... a**bout**...	**al**most... **al**most...	**for**tunate... **for**tunate...
ca**reer**... ca**reer**...	**rather**... **rather**...	**ad**vertise... **ad**vertise...
sup**pose**... sup**pose**...	**sim**ple... **sim**ple...	ac**cep**table... ac**cep**table...
be**tween**... be**tween**...	**open**... **open**...	oppo**si**tion... oppo**si**tion...
per**form**... per**form**...	**rea**son... **rea**son...	po**li**tical... po**li**tical...

(3) Now sing the words, with the stressed syllable on a higher pitch than the nonstressed syllable(s). Sing the nonstressed syllable lightly and sing the stressed syllable with a more full resonance.

Clap on the stressed syllable.

a**bout**... a**bout**...	**al**most... **al**most...	**for**tunate... **for**tunate...
ca**reer**... ca**reer**...	**rather**... **rather**...	**ad**vertise... **ad**vertise...
sup**pose**... sup**pose**...	**sim**ple... **sim**ple...	ac**cep**table... ac**cep**table...
be**tween**... be**tween**...	**open**... **open**...	oppo**si**tion... oppo**si**tion...
per**form**... per**form**...	**rea**son... **rea**son...	po**li**tical... po**li**tical...

(4) Sing the words, with the stressed syllable on a lower pitch that the nonstressed syllable(s). Sing the nonstressed syllable lightly and sing the stressed syllable with a more full resonance.
Clap on the stressed syllable.

a**bout**... a**bout**...	**al**most... **al**most...	**for**tunate... **for**tunate...
ca**reer**... ca**reer**...	**rath**er... **rath**er...	**ad**vertise... **ad**vertise...
sup**pose**... sup**pose**...	**sim**ple... **sim**ple...	ac**cep**table... ac**cep**table...
be**tween**... be**tween**...	**o**pen... **o**pen...	oppo**si**tion... oppo**si**tion...
per**form**... per**form**...	**rea**son... **rea**son...	po**lit**ical... po**lit**ical...

Duration Change

(1) Speak the following list of words out loud slowly. Sustain the stressed syllable (**bold** & **underlined**) obviously longer than the other syllable(s). As you become more aware of the durational difference, say the words faster, until you reach normal speaking speed.

re**deem**... re**deem**...	**ac**tion... **ac**tion...	**tel**evision... **tel**evision...
ca**reen**... ca**reen**...	**con**tract... **con**tract...	**ap**titude... **ap**titude...
pre**pare**... pre**pare**...	**south**ern... **south**ern...	dis**cus**sion... dis**cus**sion...
con**tract**... con**tract**...	**fur**ther... **fur**ther...	oc**ca**sion... oc**ca**sion...
dis**turb**... dis**turb**...	**bas**ket... **bas**ket...	po**si**tion... po**si**tion...

(2) Now sing the words out loud. Stay on the same pitch for each syllable in the word. Sing the non-stressed syllable(s) quickly and sustain the stressed syllable.

re**deem**... re**deem**...	**ac**tion... **ac**tion...	**tel**evision... **tel**evision...
ca**reen**... ca**reen**...	**con**tract... **con**tract...	**ap**titude... **ap**titude...
pre**pare**... pre**pare**...	**south**ern... **south**ern...	dis**cus**sion... dis**cus**sion...
con**tract**... con**tract**...	**fur**ther... **fur**ther...	oc**ca**sion... oc**ca**sion...
dis**turb**... dis**turb**...	**bas**ket... **bas**ket...	po**si**tion... po**si**tion...

Volume

(1) Speak the following list of words out loud slowly. Say the stressed syllable (**bold** & **underlined**) obviously louder than the other syllable(s).

re**deem**... re**deem**...	**ac**tion... **ac**tion...	**tel**evision... **tel**evision...
ca**reen**... ca**reen**...	**con**tract... **con**tract...	**ap**titude... **ap**titude...
pre**pare**... pre**pare**...	**south**ern... **south**ern...	dis**cus**sion... dis**cus**sion...
con**tract**... con**tract**...	**fur**ther... **fur**ther...	oc**ca**sion... oc**ca**sion...
dis**turb**... dis**turb**...	**bas**ket... **bas**ket...	po**si**tion... po**si**tion...

(2) Now sing the words out loud. Stay on the same pitch for each syllable in the word. Sing the non-stressed syllable(s) quietly and sing the stressed syllable more loudly.

re**deem**... re**deem**...	**ac**tion... **ac**tion...	**tel**evision... **tel**evision...
ca**reen**... ca**reen**...	**con**tract... **con**tract...	**ap**titude... **ap**titude...
pre**pare**... pre**pare**...	**south**ern... **south**ern...	dis**cus**sion... dis**cus**sion...
con**tract**... con**tract**...	**fur**ther... **fur**ther...	oc**ca**sion... oc**ca**sion...
dis**turb**... dis**turb**...	**bas**ket... **bas**ket...	po**si**tion... po**si**tion...

Force

(1) Speak the following list of words out loud slowly. When you say the stressed syllable (**<u>bold</u>** & **<u>underlined</u>**) give it a little more support with the support muscles. On the stressed syllable, you will probably go slightly up in pitch, get a little louder and increase your resonance.

re**deem**... re**deem**...	**ac**tion... **ac**tion...	te**le**vision... te**le**vision...
ca**reen**... ca**reen**...	**con**tract... **con**tract...	**ap**titude... **ap**titude...
pre**pare**... pre**pare**...	**sou**thern... **sou**thern...	dis**cus**sion... dis**cus**sion...
con**tract**... con**tract**...	**fur**ther... **fur**ther...	oc**ca**sion... oc**ca**sion...
dis**turb**... dis**turb**...	**bas**ket... **bas**ket...	po**si**tion... po**si**tion...

(2) Now sing the words out loud. Stay on the same pitch for each syllable in the word. Sing the stressed syllable using a little more support. On the stressed syllable, you will hear yourself get a little louder and hear and feel a little more resonance.

re**deem**... re**deem**...	**ac**tion... **ac**tion...	te**le**vision... te**le**vision...
ca**reen**... ca**reen**...	**con**tract... **con**tract...	**ap**titude... **ap**titude...
pre**pare**... pre**pare**...	**sou**thern... **sou**thern...	dis**cus**sion... dis**cus**sion...
con**tract**... con**tract**...	**fur**ther... **fur**ther...	oc**ca**sion... oc**ca**sion...
dis**turb**... dis**turb**...	**bas**ket... **bas**ket...	po**si**tion... po**si**tion...

Dictionary Stress Marks

All dictionaries mark the syllable stress as part of their pronunciation guide for each word.

For primary stress they usually place an accent mark ['] above the line and in front of the syllable to be stressed, like this, **be 'cause**.

Sometimes a word of three or more syllables has what is called a **secondary stress** on a syllable. Secondary stress means that a syllable has a little more stress than the other syllables, but not as much as the stressed syllable. The secondary stress mark [ˌ] is placed below the line and in front of the syllable.

For example, in the word **advertise**, the first syllable is stressed, **'advertise**. But the third syllable also has a slight stress **adverˌtise**.

You don't need to be overly concerned with the secondary stress. If you get the stressed syllable correct, the word will be easily recognizable.

When you look up the pronunciation of a word, always take note of the stressed syllable and practice saying it with the correct syllable stress.

Pronunciation of Difficult Words

If you have a problem pronouncing a word, you can learn how to say it easily by following these simple steps:

(1) Look up the pronunciation.

(2) Articulate each sound separately.

(3) Feel how your articulators move to say the speech sounds.

(4) Picture the movement of your articulators as you say the speech sounds.

(5) Link the individual sounds into syllables.

(6) Link the syllables in the word.

(7) Listen carefully to how you are saying the word.

(8) Say the word slowly at first, then gradually faster and faster.

(9) Say and sing the word out loud ten times.

Of course, it also helps to hear someone say the word correctly.

These steps make the pronunciation familiar to your articulators and your ear. Making it familiar makes it a habit. Then you don't have to consciously think about it any more. As soon as you think of the word, your articulators automatically say it the right way.

Of course, you still have to be aware of how you're saying and singing the words, and correct yourself if you make mistakes.

Pronunciation Exercises

(1) Record good speakers, listen to them word by word and phrase by phrase and copy the patterns of syllable stress they use.

(2) Obtain recordings of good singers, listen to them word by word and phrase by phrase and copy the patterns of syllable stress they use.

(3) Write down words that have pronunciations unfamiliar to you and practice speaking and singing them out loud.

(4) Use the dictionary to look up the words and learn their pronunciation.

(5) Four times every day, say one new word out loud at least ten times, paying attention to saying the correct sounds, syllable stress and linking.

(6) Four times every day, sing one new word out loud at least ten times, paying attention to singing the correct sounds, syllable stress and linking.

(7) Record yourself as you do the above exercises and listen to the way you pronounce the words. Correct yourself, if you hear mistakes.

Notes:

vowel #3 ɔ: "ai"
vowel #7 ə "uh"
consonant #9 ʃ "sh"
consonant #21 l "l"

17 Pop Pronunciation

by Elisabeth Howard

"*Why don't I sound pop?*" moans the classically trained singer. "*I always heard that with a solid foundation in classical technique you can sing anything.*"

Well, this simply is not so. It's true that if you have a good basic foundation in vocal technique, you probably have the potential to sing Pop. But, just as a concert pianist with the technique to play a Mozart piano concerto cannot automatically play a jazz piece of Eroll Garner's, neither does good vocal technique automatically make you a Pop singer.

Surprisingly, learning to sing Pop can be as challenging as learning to sing Mozart.

First of all, you should like and listen to the music you sing, whatever style you choose and be able to relate emotionally to the lyrics and music in order to bring your own personal interpretation to the song.

If you never listen to Pop music and only learn a Pop song for a friend's wedding, chances are you will sound stilted or "old-fashioned." Would you try to sing lieder without listening to some good examples?

Singing Pop is different from Classical singing in a number of ways, including the use of registers, vocal color, phrasing and vibrato.

Here we are going to look at the element of Pop style called **Pronunciation**.

Pop vs. Classical Pronunciation

I am using the term Pop in a very broad sense, to mean music that is nonclassical. Not all non-classical music falls under the general heading of Pop, but it is a convenient way for us to indicate nonclassical styles, without having to refer to each one specifically and individually.

Classical pronunciation is careful Standard American pronunciation. Pop pronunciation is not necessarily less careful, but it is more colloquial.

Although some styles of Pop may be sung with Standard American pronunciation, generally Pop pronunciation has more regional dialect and street pronunciation.

You'll even hear some individual Pop artists with their own idiosyncratic pronunciation of words, which in many cases becomes part of that artist's personal style, or trade mark.

Obviously, it's not possible to cover every potential difference between Classical, or Standard American, pronunciation and Pop pronunciation. But, hopefully, the following guidelines will be helpful to you in discovering and developing your Pop style.

Keep in mind two things: Pop pronunciation is not bad or wrong because it is not Standard American and your pronunciation must fit the style of the music you are singing.

Vowels

[i], as in *see*, is usually pronounced as the Standard American [i]. Sometimes it is sung closer to the [ɪ] sound, as in *it*. This softens the vowel sound and prevents it from becoming strident. On higher notes, especially, [i] tends to move toward the [ɪ].

Lowered [i̯], as in *truly*, is usually pronounced as the Standard American Lowered [i̯]. But it may be changed to [i], [ɪ] or [ə].

[ɪ], as in *sit*, is usually sung as the Standard American [ɪ]. However, sometimes, in Country music the singer might change it to [ɛ], "*Set right there.*"

[eᴵ], as in *ache*, is sometimes pronounced as [ɛᴵ]. These two pronunciations are so close that it is difficult to tell the difference between them. At the end of a word, like *way*, it is often sung as the vowel [e] or [ɛ], without the slide to [ɪ]. For example, a Country singer might use a pure [e] sound all the way through the sustained tone, [weee]. And, frequently, instead of sustaining the first part of the diphthong, the second part of the diphthong is sustained, often as an [i], [weiiii].

[ɛ], as in *yet*, is usually sung as the Standard American [ɛ]. But in some styles of music, such as Country or Rock, [ɛ] is often changed to [ɪ]. For example, get may be pronounced as *git*, "*Git* down!"

[æ],   as in *ask*, is usually sung as the Standard American [æ].

[a],   the "Boston" pronunciation is frequently heard in Pop, as a substitute for [ɑ].

[ɑ],   as in *far*, usually stays the same. Occasionally, it will be changed to the brighter vowel, [a]. For example, *got* may be pronounced [gat].

[ɒ],   as in *jaw*, is generally sung more towards the [ɑ], as in *far*. It is used in words where [ɔ] would be used in Standard American Speech, even in the *o*, *r* combination. For example, *for*, [fɔr], may be sung as [fɒr] or [fɑr].

[ɔ],   as in *organ*, is not generally heard in Pop music. It is changed to [ɒ] (see [ɒ], above).

[oᵁ],   as in *go*, is usually pronounced with less lip rounding, so that the beginning sound is closer to [ʌ], as in *under*.

[ʊ],   as in *look*, is made with less lip rounding than for Standard American pronunciation.

[u],   as in *soon*, is sung with less lip rounding than in Standard American Speech and the tongue may raise slightly toward the [ɪ] position. A true [u] vowel with the lips slightly protruding would most likely smack (pardon the pun) of the Classical or Musical Theater approach.

[ʌ],   as in *love*, often moves toward the [ɑ] vowel.

[ɝ]   and [ɚ], as in *learn* and *ever* are very relaxed. The "retroflex *r*" is only used in music that is sung with a dialect, such as Country or Hillbilly. Frequently, [ɝ] and [ɚ] are changed to the [ʌ] sound, as in *heard*, [hʌd] and *ever* [ɛvʌ]. But, there are some singers who sing [ɝ] most of the time and even sustain the tone on the [ɝ] sound, [hɝɝɝɝɝd].

[ɜ],   as in *were*, is sung with less lip rounding than in Standard American pronunciation. And frequently the [ɜ] is changed to [ʌ]. For example, *were* [wʌ], *world* [wʌld].

Diphthongs

When singing diphthongs, the general rule is to hold the first vowel sound for nearly the full duration of the tone and tag on the second vowel sound at the end.

But frequently that rule is broken and a singer will hold the final sound of the diphthong for a portion or even for most of the sustained tone.

[aɪ],   as in *my*, is usually sung as a Standard American [aɪ]. Some singers substitute [i] (*see*) for the final sound and even hold the [i] longer than the [a], i.e., *whyeeeee*. Often, you will hear a Pop singer sing only the first vowel sound of the diphthong, as in *mah*, eliminating the [i] sound altogether. For example, *Mah heart*. The sustained vowel may be either the "Boston" [a] or [ʌ], as in *up*.

[aᵁ],   as in *how*, is often pronounced with a beginning sound of [æ], as in *at*, [æᵁ]. Some singers substitute the [u], of *soon*, for the final sound, [aᵘ], and even sustain the [u] longer than the first sound. For example, *now*, [nauuu].

[ɔɪ],   as in *boy*, is sung with the beginning sound closer to the [ʌ], as in *us*.

[jᵘ],   as in *beauty*, is often changed to [ɪᵘ]. Often the [u] sound is substituted for the diphthong. For example, *new* might be pronounced [nu]. The word *you* is often pronounced *yuh* [jʌ], *Miss yuh*.

[ɪᵘ],   as in *few*, is sung as in Standard American Speech, except when the [u] sound is substituted. For example, *June* would probably be pronounced [dʒun].

Consonants

Consonants in Pop music are generally pronounced the same as in Standard American Speech.

However, frequently, the consonant on the end of a word is dropped or barely pronounced and there are some substitutions, as we point out below.

[s] is sometimes changed almost to a [ʃ] sound by some Country singers, in words like *speak* [ʃpik] or *some* [ʃʌm].

[h] is frequently dropped in <u>h</u>e, <u>h</u>im, <u>h</u>is, <u>h</u>er. But if the word is emphasized, the [h] is not dropped, i.e., *What's 'e doin' with* **<u>her</u>**.

[t] is sung closer to the [d] sound, when it is between two vowels. For example, *be<u>tt</u>er, la<u>t</u>er*. Don't go by the spelling, go by the sound. For example, in *bough<u>t</u> (h)er* and *go<u>t</u> (h)im* the [t] is between two vowels.

[ʍ] is not used in Pop music. [w] is always substituted.

[l] is always sung as a "front *l*" at the beginning of a word. But sometimes it is sung as a "back *l*" in the middle of a word, *si<u>l</u>k, a<u>l</u>ways*, or at the end of a word, *midd<u>l</u>e, ca<u>ll</u>*. For example, in the phrase, *I'<u>ll</u> a<u>l</u>ways <u>l</u>ove you*, *I'll* and *love* would probably be sung with a "front *l*" and always with a "back *l*."

[r] is always sung when it is the initial letter in the word or before a vowel in the middle of a word, for example, <u>r</u>ain, pa<u>r</u>ade, t<u>r</u>y.

[r] may be dropped:

(1) before a consonant, as in *ha(r)d, ha(r)mony, hea(r)d*;

(2) before a consonant in the following word, as in *Befo(r)e the..., Ca(r)e fo(r) me...*;

(3) before a pause at the end of a phrase, *I'll always ca(r)e, Look at a sta(r)*.

When the [r] is dropped, it is sometimes changed to a [ə], *ev<u>er</u>*, [ɛvə], *our*, [aᵁə]. (Also see p. 209, *Dropping the r.*)

[r] is not usually sustained in Pop singing. The vowel is held and the [r] is tagged on at the end, *I'll be thee<u>eeeere</u>*. But sometimes, in Country or Hillbilly, it is sustained, *I'll be the<u>rrrr</u>*.

[m] and [n] in Pop pronunciation are often sustained with or without vibrato, particularly at the end of a word, as in *ti<u>m</u>e*, or *mea<u>n</u>*. Holding the final [m] or [n] with vibrato is a common stylistic feature in Jazz.

Dropped Sounds

One of the most common characteristics of Pop pronunciation is dropping the endings of words, such the *g* in the *ing* ending. For example, *I'm getting closer to you* would be changed to *I'm gettin' closer to you*. and *What are you doing now* to *What are you doin' now*.

Typical words that drop the *g* are:

loving... lovin'
being... bein'
doing... doin'
making... makin'
trying... tryin'
seeing... seein'
moving... movin'
going... goin'
driving... drivin'
knowing... knowin'
believing... believin'
taking... takin'
sending... sendin'
falling... fallin'
telling... tellin'

Pop singers often drop the beginning sound of pronouns.

let him... let 'im
let them... let 'em
knew he... knew 'e
can his... can 'is
let her... let 'er

Often the *d* on the end of a word is dropped.

ground floor... groun' floor
kind of... kin' uh
used to... use' tuh

Often the *t* on the end of a word is dropped.

don't you... don' chuh or don' choo
won't you... won' chuh or won' choo

Contractions

Writers of Pop songs use contractions to give the lyrics an informal, conversational tone. Usually the sheet music has the contractions written in, but, occasionally, it doesn't. To get the right feel, you might have to decide yourself when to use a contraction and when not to.

As a general guideline, if the second word falls on a sustained tone, don't contract it—or if each word of a possible contraction is on a separate note, don't contract it.

The following words are typical contractions in Pop pronunciation.

I am... I'm
I have... I've
he is... he's
you have... you've
she is... she's

she has... she's
you are... you're
he has... he's
we are... we're
we have... we've
they are... they're
they have... they've
you will... you'll
he will... he'll
she will... she'll

Sometimes the vowel sound in the contraction is changed to *uh*.

some have... some'uv
some of... some'uh
kind of... kind'uh
sort of... sort'uh
out of... out'uh
going to... gonna
got to... gotta

Added Sounds

Frequently a [tʃ] sound is added between a word that ends with *t* and the word *you*. For example, *want'**ch**'you, get'**ch**'you, but'**ch**'you, didn't'**ch**' you.*

Likewise, a [dʒ] sound is added between a word that ends with *d* and the word *you*. For example, *did'**j**'you, made'**j**'you.*

Sound Changes

In Pop singing, it is common for pronunciations to be different from Standard American Speech. Usually, the changes reflect the dialect in which the song is sung. For example:

When you drop the *th*, (*let **th**em... let 'em*) the vowel in *th**e**m* is often changed to [ʌ], let *'**uh**m*.

The vowel in *t**o**, [u], is often changed to [ʌ], *int**o**... int**uh*** *t**o** me... t**uh** me have t**o**... have t**uh***.

The vowel of *o**f*** is often changed to *uh*.

Frequently, *you* is changed to *y**uh***.

Don't feel that these pronunciations are wrong or sloppy. You need these pronunciations to give the song the right feel, or style.

Here are some phrases as they might appear in the printed music, followed by the Pop pronunciation singers would use.

This waiting around is killing me...
This waitin' 'round's killin' me.

We've got each other... We got each othuh.

I'll let him be what he wants to be...
I'll let 'im be what 'e wants tuh be.

But you don't want to hear it...
But'ch'uh don' wanna hear it.

Because I'm begging you, baby...
'Cause I'm beggin' yuh, babeh.

The best way to work on a Pop song is to listen to the commercial recording and copy the pronunciation. With time and practice Pop pronunciation will become more familiar to you and will feel more natural. And, if you practice enough, you'll develop your own personal style.

It is important to note that learning Pop pronunciation and diction will in no way change your pronunciation or diction for Standard American Diction, used in non-pop music. Your ear will guide you once you are aware of your options.

Have fun with it!

Notes:

18 Inflections and Intonations

The Melody of Speech

Inflections and **intonations** are the **pitch/resonance** changes in your voice.

Inflections and intonations are often explained simply as pitch changes, but as we discussed in the chapter on *Pronunciation*, under *Syllable Stress*, when your voice goes up and down in pitch, it also changes resonance. So the term **pitch/resonance** is more descriptive of the vocal change that actually takes place.

Intonations and **inflections** pertain primarily to speech. You have little opportunity to use your own inflections and intonations in singing. We are including a discussion of them in this book so that you will have a well-rounded understanding of Standard American Diction.

Defining Inflections and Intonations

Both inflections and intonations refer to **pitch/resonance** changes and are frequently used interchangeably. However, we generally use the term **inflection** when we have in mind the pitch/resonance change on a **single syllable or word**, and we use the term **intonation** when we refer to **a pattern of pitch/resonance changes over a whole phrase or sentence**.

Inflection: the pitch/resonance changes on a single word or syllable.

For example, *yes,* *yes.*

(⌣) means a rising pitch/resonance.

(⌒) means a falling pitch/resonance.

Intonation: the gradual rise or fall of pitch/resonance over a whole phrase or sentence.

For example, *Are you going?*

Yes; I'm going.

(⌒) means a generally rising pitch/resonance pattern.

(⌒) means a generally falling pitch/resonance pattern.

What Do Inflections and Intonations Do?

Pitch/resonance changes affect your expression in four ways:

(1) They help give meaning to your words.

(2) They express emotion.

(3) They give emphasis to words.

(4) They make your speech more pleasant and interesting to listen to.

Words and phrases can mean different things, depending on the inflection or intonation with which they are spoken.

For example, a rising inflection is generally interpreted as a question—and a falling inflection as a statement.

Say the following words out loud, with the inflection marked.

Yes...(question)   *Yes...*(statement)

Benefits of Pitch/Resonance Changes

- Pitch/resonance changes make your voice more expressive.
- Pitch/resonance changes give nuances of meaning to your speech.
- Pitch/resonance changes give your voice dynamism and interest.
- Pitch/resonance changes make your voice more pleasant to listen to.
- Pitch/resonance changes give your voice a compelling attraction.
- People stop and listen to voices that have a wide variety of pitch/resonance changes.

The Melody of Speech

Pitch/resonance changes are an important element of what is called, the **melody of speech**. This is the pattern of pitch/resonance changes in speech. (The melody is also affected by duration and emphasis, but we are concerned here only with pitch/resonance.)

Listen to a good speaker. You hear his or her pitch/resonance moving continually up and down. The voice never stays the same from one word to the next. Charismatic speakers always have a wide range of pitch/resonance.

Pitch/Resonance Exercise

To clearly hear and feel the pitch/resonance change in your voice, alternate between a higher and lower pitch/resonance on each of the following words.

Listen for the change in pitch and resonance quality.

Say the words out loud.

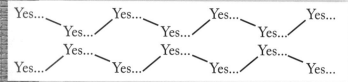

Inflections

Inflection refers to a change in the pitch/resonance of the **syllable** or **word**. That is, you start the syllable or word on one pitch/resonance and slide to a higher or lower pitch/resonance.

Exercises

(1) Say the following word out loud, with a rising pitch/resonance.

Yes...   Yes

(2) Now say the word out loud, with the pitch/resonance going down.

Yes...   Yes

Meaning and Emotion

Inflections do more than give variety and interest to your voice, they also give **meaning** and **emotion** to your words.

There are so many possible nuances and shades of human meaning and emotion

expressed by inflections that it would be foolish to even try to list all of them. But we can make some broad generalizations that will be helpful.

Rising Inflection

In general, a word with a rising inflection may indicate:

(1) Uncertainty or tentativeness
(2) That something else is going to be said
(3) Happiness

Falling Inflection

In general, a falling inflection may indicate:

(1) A definite, strong statement
(2) The end of a statement or thought
(3) Sadness

Exercises for Inflections

In the following exercises, say the word out loud, with the inflection marked, and listen for the different meanings or emotions.

(1) A rising inflection.

Yes...(question)

Yes...(tentative)

Yes...(happy)

(2) Now a falling inflection.

Yes...(statement)

Yes...(end of statement)

Yes...(sad)

(3) Say the following words out loud, with their indicated inflections.

now... now...   now... now

open... open...   open... open

about... about...   about... about

again... again...   again... again

always... always... always... always

(4) Now say the following sentences out loud with the indicated inflection on the last word.

This is the end? (question)

This is the end. (definite statement)

Call me at home? (question)

Call me at home. (definite statement)

Circumflex Inflection

The inflection placed on a word can sometimes be more complex than a simple upward or downward movement.

You can also give what is called a **circumflex** inflection to a word or syllable. That is, the pitch/resonance may fall then rise (⌣), or the pitch/resonance may rise then fall (⌢), or it may even rise then fall then rise (∿).

Say the following words out loud, with the marked inflection.

Yes... *Yes...*

Yes... *Yes...*

Yes... *Yes...*

Inflections and Pauses

A rising inflection with a pause may also indicate that you're going to add something to what you've just said.

Put an upward inflection on the word *beginning* in the following sentence and pause slightly before continuing. It will sound like you haven't finished what you want to say.

Say the words out loud.

This is the beginning... and the end.

Pay close attention to the inflections of good speakers among your friends and professional associates, as well as, public speakers on radio, television, film and stage. When your ear gets used to hearing a wide and expressive variety of inflections, you will find it easier to use them yourself.

Intonation

Intonation is the overall rising or falling pattern of pitch/resonance as you say a phrase or sentence.

Meaning and Emotion

Pitch/resonance change helps give meaning to a sentence, just as it helps give meaning to a word.

Rising Intonation

When the intonation is rising it generally indicates:

(1) Uncertainty or doubt

(2) A question

(3) An incomplete statement

Falling Intonation

When the intonation is falling it generally indicates:

(1) A definite, strong statement

(2) A completed statement

Exercises for Intonations

(1) Say the following sentence out loud, with a rising intonation. (The symbol (⌣) indicates a rising intonation.)

This is the place.... This is the place.

(2) Now say the following sentence out loud, with a downward intonation. (The symbol (⌢) indicates a falling intonation.)

This is the place.... This is the place.

(3) Say the following sentences out loud, with the indicated intonation.

I am.... *I am.*

Are you going.... *Are you going.*

Is this the book.... *Is this the book.*

This is the book.... *This is the book.*

Intonations for Questions

Usually a question has a rising intonation, as in,

Are you home?

But a question does not always have a rising intonation. If the meaning is clear from the words, the intonation may drop down, like this,

Are you home?

Exercises

Say the following sentences out loud, with the indicated intonation.

Where are you?...　Where are you?

What is this?...　What is this?

Complex Intonational Patterns

There can be more than one intonation pattern in a sentence. For example,

This is the beginning and the end.

Notice that the pitch/resonance rises on *this is*, drops down and rises again on *the beginning*, and drops down on *and the end.*

Now you say it out loud.

This is the beginning and the end.

How to Avoid Monotony

Good speakers use a variety of inflections and intonations to give meaning, emotion and interest to their speech.

Poor speakers often have what are called monotonous voices. These are voices that have very little, if any, pitch/resonance change.

Monotony can take two forms:

(1)　Very little pitch/resonance change in the speaking voice

(2)　A frequently repeated pattern of inflections and intonations

No one wants to listen to speakers that stay on one pitch/resonance.

They sound boring.

We may lay the fault on poor pitch variety. But usually the problem is that the speaker has little resonance change. He or she stays in chest resonance or head resonance or nasal resonance most of the time. The combination of little or no pitch change and the same resonance quality gives the voice (and the speaker) a flat, dull quality.

Likewise, a pattern of repeated pitch/resonance changes, such as going down on the end of every phrase or up on the end of every phrase, can also make your listeners bored and even irritated by the sound of your voice. When that happens, you might as well not be speaking, because your listeners have stopped listening.

Exercises

Here is an exercise to help you feel and hear the difference between monotonous speech and expressive speech.

(1)　Say the following sentence out loud, with no pitch/resonance change.

Today I speak better than I did yesterday.

(2)　Now with more pitch/resonance change.

Today I speak better than I did yesterday.

*Natural Sounding Inflections
and Intonations*

One last point. **Your inflections and intonations must follow your meaning and emotion.**

You should not take wide pitch/resonance changes just for the sake of variety. If you do, it will interfere with the sense of what you're saying and sound phoney to your listeners.

The more you listen to good speakers and the more you practice using a variety of inflections and intonations the more your speech will have a natural and pleasing Standard American melody.

Once you become used to speaking with free and expressive pitch/resonance, don't pre-plan your inflections and intonations. Let them happen automatically as a result of the meaning and emotion of the thought you are communicating.

Exercises for Inflections and Intonations

(1) Practice the following exercise to expand your pitch/resonance range and to accustom your ear to hearing you use a wide pitch/resonance range.

Speak the following words out loud, gradually rising and then falling in pitch/resonance.

Expand your range to its maximum by going higher and lower each time you do the exercise.

```
                        TEN
                  NINE      NINE
               EIGHT          EIGHT
             SEVEN              SEVEN
           SIX                    SIX
          FIVE                     FIVE
        FOUR                        FOUR
     THREE                           THREE
   TWO                                TWO
 ONE                                   ONE
```

(2) Practice the following exercise to improve your range of inflections and intonations and to familiarize your ear with the characteristic melody of Standard American Speech.

Record one or two minutes of good speakers from the radio or television.

Listen to them phrase by phrase.

Record yourself copying the inflections and intonations speaking the same words and phrases.

Compare your recording with the original recording.

Record yourself again, matching the inflections and intonations even more closely.

Notes:

vowel #8 eɪ "aɪ"
vowel #7 ə "uh"
consonant #8 ʃ "sh"
consonant #22.1 T

19 Expressive Singing

Putting Meaning and Emotion Into Your Words

You must imagine some basis for the words as a justification for saying them.... In brief, you have to invent a whole film of inner pictures, a running subtext... of the words given you to speak.... These inner images will create a mood and that in turn will stir feelings in you.... This is not done for the sake of realism, naturalism, per se, but because it is necessary for our own creative natures, our subconscious. For them we must have truth, if only the truth of imagination, in which they can believe, in which they can live...

(Constantin Stanislavski, *Building a Character*, p. 114)

Expressive singing is singing with the full meaning and emotion of the words and thought, as well as singing beautifully and accurately.

Why Is Expressive Singing Necessary?

The quote at the head of this chapter, from the most famous and influential acting coach the world has known, applies to singers, as well as to actors.

Great singers agree, to be a great singer, you must sing the music accurately, with a beautiful vocal sound, and you must also sing expressively, with feeling. That is, with the meaning and emotion of the words and thoughts in your voice.

Though probably no singer would question the importance of expressive singing, much of the time they do not give it the attention its importance warrants. Frequently you hear singers concentrating so much on the music and their vocal quality that they cut themselves—and their audience—off from their meaning and emotions.

The legendary singer, Lotte Lehmann, in her book, *More Than Singing, The Interpretation of Songs*, noted:

I have listened to many young singers, and have found with ever increasing astonishment that they consider their preparation finished when they have developed a lovely voice, a serviceable technique and musical

accuracy. At this point they consider themselves ready to appear before the public... (p. 10)

But, she reminded us, the final polish of a great performance is emotional expression.

That fine God given instrument—the voice—must be capable of responding with the greatest subtlety to every shade of each emotion. But it must be subordinate, it must only be the foundation, the soil from which flowers true art. (p. 10)

For her, true art was the expression of the meaning and emotion found in both the words and the music.

"Learn," she wrote, *"to feel as a whole that which is a whole in complete harmony: poem and music. Neither can be more important than the other."* (p. 12)

The Art of Acting In Singing

When you sing with expression, or interpret a song, you combine the art of acting with the art of singing.

The full scope of the craft and art of acting is beyond what we can present in this book. However, we can take a brief, insightful look at one aspect of acting—analysis of the words and lines in the script, libretto or lyrics, to discover our character's images, thoughts and emotions.

By **character**, we mean the person singing the song. In opera and musical theatre, the character is the role you are playing. In an art song you may decide the character is the poet who wrote the lyrics or you may decide to be the character yourself. But whether you feel you are playing someone else or you are yourself singing the words, the same basic acting principles apply. **You must find the meaning and emotion of the words in yourself first, then communicate them to the audience.**

Words are more than just sound. They carry *images*, *meanings* and *emotions* that affect both you, as a singer, and your audience.

But neither you nor your audience receive the full emotional effect of words automatically.

The words must first be analyzed by you, the performer. You must find out what they mean to you, then you can express them to the audience.

As Lord Laurence Olivier put it, in *Great Acting*,

> If somebody asked me to put in one sentence what acting was, I should say that acting was the art of persuasion. The actor persuades himself, first, and through himself, the audience. (p. 23)

It is not unusual when listening to a Shakespearean play to hear the words clearly, but not know what the actor is saying. Not because the words are unfamiliar, but because the actor is speaking without any sensitivity to the subtleties of expression in the text. All the words come out with the same energy and emphasis. Or, just as bad, with a rhythmical rise and fall of emphasis that pays no regard to the meaning and emotion of the lines.

Strangely, such a performance can sound very exciting. But the poor audience is left with no idea, or, at best, very little idea, of what, specifically, the actor is saying and what the words mean. (Probably the actor also has little idea of what, specifically, he is saying.)

The result is a frustrating paradox of enjoyment and irritation. You love hearing the words and voices, and seeing the costumes and scenery, but you feel something essential is missing. In the final analysis, you find the performance disappointing.

The same thing can happen with a singer's performance. Frequently we hear a voice that rings out with beauty and strength, but we are not moved emotionally, because there is no expression in the singing. All the words sound beautiful, but they all sound alike and we don't know what they mean.

There are reasons why this may happen. Perhaps the singer is not paying attention to the emotional nuances in the lyrics and sings everything with the same general feeling. Or perhaps the singer is concentrating so hard on vocal quality or correct pitch that he or she doesn't think of what the words and thoughts mean.

But an audience is not interested in why a singer does not sing expressively. They just feel that something is missing in the performance. **The audience expects a good singer to sing emotionally.**

Let's take a look at what you can do to put emotional expression into your voice.

Your Voice is the Sound of Your Soul

Just as your eyes are the windows to your soul, **your voice is the sound of your soul.** It reflects whatever you are thinking and feeling.

If you concentrate only on tone and pitch, your singing will be technically correct, but not necessarily expressive. And it will leave the audience cold.

But, if, while you are producing a beautiful sound, you also experience the meaning and emotion of the words and thoughts, your voice will be expressive and the audience will love you.

You need both a beautiful voice and expression in your voice to give a totally satisfying performance.

Words and Images: Reflections of Emotion

Your voice and the words you sing create pictures and images that reveal to your listeners your innermost thoughts and feelings.

They stimulate your audience into having similar thoughts and feelings of their own.

This communion is one of the basic ingredients of good acting.

How does this happen? What magical quality is there in your voice and the words that stimulate tears and happiness, hope and despair just by their utterance?

Of course, it's not the words themselves that stir emotions. To someone who doesn't understand English, the word *love* is just a jumble of sounds. It arouses no passion, no joy, no desire, no hope.

A word's meaning and its ability to stimulate emotion resides in the images and experiences that each of us associate with the word.

Images are what touch our souls and rouse our passions.

Sensuous Imagery

We experience imagery through our five senses:

Seeing

Hearing

Touching

Tasting

Smelling

We experience life through our five senses.

And we also experience our memories through our five senses.

Recall a wonderful moment in your life— the sights, sounds, smells, tastes and touches. Is there anything that is not connected to your five senses?

When you describe the moon, what do you *see*? When you remember the ocean, what do you *hear*? When you dream of your lover's caress, what do you *feel*? When you reminisce about a delicious meal, what do you *smell* or *taste*?

These are all images—memories of your experiences—stored away in your mind. All of these images are sensuous. That is, you reexperience them through your five senses.

Although sight appears to be the most accessible and most frequently used sense in our memory of things, the other four senses— hearing, touching, tasting and smelling— frequently play a powerful part in our images, or memories.

These sensory memories have a kind of magical power. At times, it seems that the mind cannot tell the difference between something that is actually happening and something that we strongly imagine.

Dreams are an illustration of the power of imagery. How many times have you awakened panting and terrified from a bad dream or laughing and delighted from a beautiful one and said to yourself, *"It seemed so real!"*

The same thing happens in daydreaming. It is possible to imagine something so strongly that, for a moment, it seems to be actually happening.

In acting, this magical power leads to a believability that emotionally affects both yourself and your audience.

With it you can enter into the life of your character and imagine into reality things that you know are only make-believe.

Sensuous Imagery and Emotions

Sensuous imagery has an extraordinary connection to your emotions.

When you recall experiences, or images, your emotions are affected, just as they were with the original experience.

Remember what it was like last time you were at your favorite vacation spot.

Say the name of the place out loud...

Think of your most enjoyable time there...

Describe it out loud, in detail...

How does remembering it make you feel? Happy? Sad?

Did you feel your emotion change as you recalled the details of the images? What caused the change? It had to be the images you remembered.

Through your sensuous imagery, you influence your emotions.

This concept is of paramount importance for actors and singers. It gives you a way of tapping into the emotions of a role and of being able to recreate the emotion whenever you need to.

The technique of using imagery to establish a sense of reality and to stimulate your emotions is natural. You use it unconsciously every day. You only need to learn how to use it consciously, to create the emotions of an aria, a song or an entire a role.

The Meaning of Words: Imagery and Emotion

Most of the time our associations with words are unconscious associations. We don't remember how we first learned their meaning or why we feel the way we do about what they signify.

But there is a natural process by which we all associate meanings and emotions with words.

How did you first find out the meaning of the word house?

When you were little, someone said, *"This is your house."*

You **saw** something with four walls, a roof, windows, doors, etc.

You **smelled** what the house smelled like.

You **heard** the sounds of the house.

You **touched** various things in the house.

And **felt** the floors as you walked, climbed stairs, and so on.

Maybe there was even a **taste** to your first house.

In short, you learned what house meant through your five senses. Your image of your house was a composite of all the sensory impressions you had experienced in the house.

All of these sensuous impressions gave you a specific, personal meaning for the word house. And, simultaneously, through these impressions you also developed an emotional attitude about your house—you liked it and felt safe there. Love and security was in the house.

With words that represent tangible things—*house, cat*— it's easy to see that we use our five senses to experience them.

But how do we learn the meaning of words that represent things we cannot touch and see—like *love* or *loyalty*?

We learn the meaning of words that represent nonphysical things the same way we learn the meaning of words that represent physical things.

How did you learn what the word *love* meant when you were a child?

By hearing someone say, *"I love you."*—and at the same time **seeing** the look on the person's face, **feeling** the touch of the person, **tasting** what the person fed you, and **smelling** the scent of that

person. You found all these sensory experiences pleasurable—and you associated them with the word love.

We learn the meanings of all words the same way. Of course, the specifics of the sensuous experiences are different for each of us, but they are enough alike that when you say a word your listener knows what you are talking about.

I may not have had a drink of the same water as you have, but when you say, *"I drank some water,"* the word water evokes in me sensuous memories similar to your experience with water and we understand each other.

This is the way we communicate. Language is based on the principle that people experience similar things.

Most words have a complex set of physical, sensuous associations for each person—particularly the following kinds of words:

object words—*house, horse, me, you*
action words—*run, hold, arrive, sing*
emotion words—*happy, love, anger, frustration*

(Other words, such as *are, for, the* and *and*, do not necessarily have sensory associations. But they are important for the smooth flow of the language and must be said clearly.)

Two Kinds of Meanings for Words

For most words we have two kinds of meanings:

(1) **A specific, sensual meaning**—with strong emotion.
(2) **A general, intellectual meaning**—with very little or no emotion.

Specific Meaning

When you were a child, with little experience of things outside of your immediate seeing, touching, tasting, smelling and hearing, your meanings for words remained associated with your direct sensory experience. Your awareness of things was specific.

General Meaning

But as you grew older and experienced more of the world outside your house you found that words had other, less specific, meanings.

For example, you found that there were a lot of houses in the world. They all had the same general characteristics in common, so you could recognize them as a house.

This more universal experience gave you a generalized, intellectual meaning that was different from your specific, sensuous meaning.

With this general meaning you could have a conversation about a house without personally experiencing it.

However, you lost something that was connected to the specific meaning—the emotional attachments. **You could feel no liking or disliking for something for which you had no personal, specific imagery.**

Both kinds of meanings are useful. **But for actors and singers, whose stock-in-trade is emotions, the specific, sensuous meaning of a word, with its emotional attachments, is much more valuable.**

Expressing Your Own Thoughts with Imagery and Emotion

When we want to express our own thoughts (as opposed to a thought given to us in a script or libretto), we go through three stages:

(1) **We have a mental, sensuous image.**

(2) **We search around in our store of words for a word that has those images attached to it.**

(3) **We speak the words.**

The act of searching for the word is usually so fast that we don't even realize we are doing it. In fact, the imaging and speaking appear to be simultaneous, even identical acts.

But the sequence becomes clear when you think of how you tell someone about your vacation.

Without any effort on your part, the images run through your mind like a motion picture: packing, saying good-bye, travelling, arriving, seeing new things, doing new things, eating, sleeping, returning. The whole experience is all there all at once—the sensuous images and the emotions—before you have the words to express them. And automatically and unconsciously your brain goes to work and finds the words—fast!

How wonderful it would be if the scripts, librettos and lyrics you work on could automatically evoke such a flood of creative images in you.

It is possible!

Every script or libretto has abundant imagery. Remember that the words have images attached to them—the author's (or character's) images and your images. All you have to do is let yourself become aware of them.

Finding Sensuous Imagery and Emotion in a Script or Libretto

As a singer you are given a libretto and expected to say and sing the words and thoughts as if they were your own.

The problem is, saying the words in a script is contrary to the way you speak in real life.

In real life, you have the **images first**, then you find the **words** to express them.

But with a script, you have the **words first** and no images.

So you need to take an extra step and find the images for the words.

At this point, you need to be aware of a danger in reading a script or libretto.

You will have no problem understanding the words the first time you read them. If your character says, **"This is my house,"** of course, you will know what the line means and you will be able to say it, because you have a **general, intellectual understanding** of what a house is.

The danger is that you may accept just the intellectual understanding, not realizing that you are not fully experiencing the imagery in the line and, therefore, not fully experiencing the emotion.

But general meanings lead to general and unemotional acting. Or, just as bad, to acting with a wrong or a made-up emotion. Both of which mean death for a performance.

To avoid general acting, you must find the specific, sensuous images attached to the words, so that you can speak them as though they were your own.

How can you experience specific, sensuous images that will make someone else's words real to you?—By using your own set of specific, sensuous and emotional experiences that you have attached to every word. All you have to do is let the word in the script trigger your own sensory recall.

Finding the sensuous imagery in a text is a two phase process:

(1) **Look at each word and remember your own sensuous images for it.**

(2) **Create a detailed sensuous memory for that word in the context of the scene.**

Once you have created your own imagery, it is as though you have created personal memories. Speaking or singing the lines becomes just like the natural process of talking.

You go through the same three steps that you do when you talk about your own experiences:

(1) **You remember the sensuous imagery in the line.**

(2) **You let the imagery remind you of the word you want to say.**

(3) **You speak or sing the word.**

How does this work in practice? Let's take one of Juliet's lines in Romeo and Juliet,

> *...That which we call a rose*
> *By any other word would smell as sweet,*

Use your five senses on every word that you can.

That, the first word, refers to *rose*, so we will wait until we analyze *rose* and then come back to it.

Which doesn't really have any sensory images, so we can skip it. (Although, like all words, it must be spoken clearly in performance.)

We is meant to be spoken in its general sense, but even so, it has some sensory imagery. Who do you mean by *we*? Your father, your mother, your teacher, your friends? The images are yours—who do you see?

Call has some sensory imagery. Possibly you might see a mouth moving. You may also hear a loud sound, but that is not appropriate to this context, so don't dwell on it. *Call* also refers to giving something a name. Do you remember naming something? Like your favorite doll or your first puppy?

A has no sensory imagery.

Rose is rich with imagery. Go into it in detail. Find a real rose. (A garden one that has scent, not one of the commercial, scentless, street corner kind.)

Look at it, **smell** it, **feel** its petals and its stalk. Does it have a thorn? You may even **taste** it.

A real, specific rose inspired Juliet's comparison. You must have that kind of specific imagery and emotion before you can say the word as Juliet does. (Now you can go back and apply your rose imagery to the first word, *that*.)

By, any and *other* don't have any particular imagery. (Maybe *other* has some imagery. Do you think so?)

Word has a certain amount of imagery. How do you know what a *word* is? You see a group of symbols on a page, you hear a group of sounds connected together. Again the images are yours.

Would does not have any imagery.

Smell, in this context, has the scent of *rose*. Can you remember its scent?

As has no imagery.

Sweet has an abundance of imagery. How do you know what *sweet* is? Candy? Jam? What was the dessert you really liked when you were a kid? In this instance, the pleasure in the taste of sweetness is transformed into the pleasure in the scent of the *rose*—or perhaps Juliet is remembering the scent of Romeo and the *sweetness* of his lips when they kissed. Remember, your images are your own.

You can and should go into much greater detail than we have room for here. Your images can be any images that come up for you when you think of the word. And your images are private. You don't have to tell anyone what they are, unless you want to. Sometimes, in fact, the images are more potent if you don't tell anyone what they are.

The only restriction on your imagery is that it should fit the context of the scene in some way. The word *call*, for example, in Juliet's line above, could have the association of shouting to someone, but in the context of the line and the scene, *yelling* is not an appropriate image for the word. Perhaps you can't avoid thinking about *yelling* because it is one of the images you have for *call*,—that's all right, just don't dwell on it and let it become a primary image.

Not All Words Have Imagery

It's probably not necessary to point it out, but in case it escaped your attention, not every word has sensuous imagery attached to it. Concentrate on finding the imagery in those words that have strong sensory associations. Those are the important words, the words that open up your thoughts and emotions to your audience.

However, the other non-sensory words are necessary for grammatical correctness and they must be said clearly. Otherwise, you will confuse your audience.

Memorizing is Easy With Imagery

A fortunate side effect of this kind of sensory exploration of the text is that you memorize the words very easily, almost automatically. You make the images your personal images. You create memories for yourself and then attach the same words the character uses to describe them.

In fact, they are not the character's words any more, they are **your** words. They are the words **you** use to describe **your** images.

Singing and Speaking Complete Thoughts

Up to this point we have been analyzing individual words.

But we don't generally communicate in single words. We communicate by putting groups of words together to form logical, coherent thoughts.

The character you are playing also speaks and sings whole thoughts. As a singer/actor, you analyze the character's thoughts, to find their sensuous imagery and emotion.

All thoughts in scripts and librettos can be analyzed in a simple, straightforward manner. They are made up of images that are familiar to us (otherwise we wouldn't be able to communicate with each other).

The images are contained in **image phrases**, or groups of words which describe a single image.

Each image phrase has one or more **key words** which contain the essence of the image.

In your beginning, creative analysis of your character's lines you should clearly identify these three elements:

(1) **Thoughts**
(2) **Image phrases**
(3) **Key words**

Contained within these three elements are the imagery, logic and emotion that your character is feeling and expressing.

As you explore these elements you will find your own matching imagery and emotion for the lines—and, along the way, the essence of a great performance.

The Logic In the Lines

As an actor, the first thing you have to find in your lines is the logic—the sense of what you are saying.

The logic tells you what you are doing or what your objectives are as the character. Once that is clear to you, your emotions can take over.

Stanislavski stressed to his actors that the logic comes first and out of that flows the emotion. In *Building a Character*, he said,

> *Don't you know that the power* [emotional effect] *lies in the logic, the coherence of what you are saying?... So for the very sake of the powerful effect you seek you must learn in the first instance to speak logically, coherently with proper spacing.* (p. 138)

The logic of the lines comes from connecting your images together to create a thought.

An Actor's Description of a Thought

Generally speaking, we communicate in complete thoughts—that is, in thoughts that make logical sense.

In our English grammar classes we are taught to think of complete thoughts as sentences, with a noun, a verb and other parts of speech. But for the creative work we do as singers and actors, rather than analyzing a thought in terms of its grammar, it is more natural and effective to think of a thought in terms of its imagery.

In this sense, **a complete thought is composed simply of two parts, or images:**

(1) **The thing you are talking about and**

(2) **What you are saying about that thing.**

These two images together form a complete, logical and coherent thought.

This approach has the advantage of focusing on imagery, which is what you work with as a performer and what you want to get across to your audience.

The concept of two parts of a sentence is not new to you—you know that a sentence has a subject and predicate. But thinking about them as sensuous images may be new to you. (You may experience a little puzzling resistance to this simplified approach, at first. But it is only because our school training in grammatical analysis continues to exercise a powerful influence on us.)

As you get used to working with the imagery in the thoughts, you'll find it opens up a whole new world of creativity and spontaneous imagination.

Analyzing a Thought Through Imagery

Let's look at how to analyze a thought through its imagery.

If we say,

The cat is in the corner.

The thing we are talking about is *the cat* and *is in the corner* is what we are saying about it.

Both parts, or images, are necessary for the thought to make sense.

If you say just

the cat...

and stop....

You leave us with a sense of expectancy. What about the cat?

Likewise, if you just say

...is in the corner.

We don't know what you're talking about.

And both images must be clear in **your** mind when you say the thought or **you** don't know what you are talking about.

Of course, the two images may be embellished. *The cat* may be *the brown and white cat.* And *the corner* may be *the corner by the door.*

But no matter how we build them up, the whole, sensible thought is basically composed of only two images—the thing we are talking about and what we are saying about that thing.

This approach focuses attention on the specific and personal imagery in the thought. It actually requires that you bring your own imagery to the thought, which, in turn, makes the thought your own.

Don't be confused if the sequence of the two parts is reversed in the lines, as they frequently are.

In one of Hamlet's famous soliloquies he says,

O, what a rogue and peasant slave am I!

What is the thing he is talking about? *Rogue and peasant slave?*

No.

He is talking about himself, *I.*

Am a rogue and peasant slave is what he is saying about *I.*

Two complete thoughts may also be placed closely together, as if they were one thought.

King Lear connects two thoughts with:

They flattered me like a dog, and told me I had white hairs in my beard ere the black ones were there.

The first thought is *They flattered me like a dog.* The second is *[they] told me I had white hairs in my beard ere the black ones were there.* (Notice that some words, like *they,* apply to more than one image phrase, though they are only said once.)

In the first thought, the thing he is talking about is *They.* (We are not told who they are, so you must use your creativity and imagination to see them and hear them.) What Lear is saying about they is *flattered me like a dog.*

In the second thought he is still talking about *they.* What he is saying about *they* is *told me I had white hairs in my beard ere the black ones were there.*

A thought may also be stated as a question.

Macbeth has two thoughts closely combined when he asks:

Is this a dagger which I see before me, the handle toward my hand?

The first thought is *I see a dagger before me.* (It might also be restated as, *Do I see a dagger before me?*) The thing he is talking about is himself, *I.* What he is saying about himself is *see a dagger before me.*

(At first, you might think the thing Macbeth is talking about is *dagger.* But then what is *I?* I can't be what he is saying about *dagger.* And *I,* himself, is who he is concerned about.)

The second thought is *the handle toward my hand.* The thing he is talking about is *the handle,* what he is saying about it is *toward my hand.*

In your analysis of your lines, it doesn't matter if you change the sequence of the images in a thought. Also, it is better if you separate compound thoughts into simple thoughts.

But, of course, when you actually say or sing the lines, you say them the way the author wrote them for the character.

When you break thoughts down into their two simple parts, or images, thoughts that appear to be complex, become easier to analyze and, as an extra benefit, easier to remember.

The purpose of your logical analysis is to clearly establish for yourself the imagery in the lines. You have to find out what the character is imaging and establish strong, specific imagery for yourself before you can communicate it to your audience.

The Image Phrase

An image phrase may be thought of as having two characteristics:

(1) **It is a sensuous image.**

(2) **It is not a complete, logical thought by itself.**

For example, Portia, in *The Merchant of Venice,* expresses the thought,

The quality of mercy is not strained.

What is the first image phrase?—*The quality of mercy.*

This is also the thing we are talking about— but it does not make sense by itself. If you say *the quality of mercy...* and stop, you leave us waiting for more.

What is the second image phrase?—*is not strained.*

This is what you are saying about *the quality of mercy*—but it also does not make sense alone. If you say *is not strained* by itself, it doesn't have any logical meaning.

The two parts of the thought may be composed of more than one image phrase.

Portia's next thought is,

It droppeth as the gentle rain from heaven upon the place beneath.

Here we can pick out at least three images— one in the first part and two in the second part.

The first image is *It,* which refers to *the quality of mercy* and is the thing that she is talking about.

In the second part the image phrases are *droppeth as the gentle rain from heaven* and [*droppeth*] *upon the place beneath.* Each is a specific image that stimulates your sensuous memories and emotions. (Notice again that some words, like *droppeth,* play double duty in image phrases.)

Let's take another example, this time a thought of Oberon's, from *A Midsummer Night's Dream*:

I know a bank where the wild thyme blows,
Where oxlips and the nodding violet grows.
Quite over-canopied with luscious woodbine.
With sweet musk-roses and with eglantine.

What is the thing Oberon is talking about?

At first glance it would appear to be the *flowered bank* and, certainly, the images of the flowers are the most powerful and obvious.

But, if you look again, you'll see that it is *I*— himself—that he is talking about. *Know a bank...* etc., is what he is saying about himself.

If Shakespeare's imagery for the character at this time was only the bank of flowers, he could have written, *There is a bank...*etc.. This line still fits the meter, but it leaves Oberon out of the picture. Having Oberon say *I* adds a subtle, but significant, note of egotism to Oberon's character and gives a dramatic, human dimension to what would otherwise be merely a beautiful, poetic description.

If the actor says the line without paying any attention to the *I* image, as many actors do, he misses part of what Shakespeare wrote into the lines for him and, consequently, part of the genius of a great performance.

The next image phrase is *know a bank.*

Then come the embellishments—the brilliant images of flowers.

Where the wild thyme blows is a single image.

Where oxlips and the nodding violet grows has two images, but, because they are closely connected by *where* and *grows*, it is probably best to say them as one phrase.

Quite over-canopied with luscious woodbine is also one image phrase.

With sweet musk-roses is a single image phrase, as is *and with eglantine.*

How do you know where the image phrase starts and ends?

There is no cut-and-dried formula. Basically, an image phrase contains a single image. But you also need to feel the flow of the words and use your sense of rhythm to determine whether a long image phrase should be handled as two images (*with sweet musk-roses / and with eglantine*) or whether two images should be connected together to form one image phrase (*where oxlips and the nodding violet grows*).

Three Kinds of Words

There are three kinds of words in an image phrase:

(1) **Key words**
(2) **Support words**
(3) **Connecting words**

Key Words: The Essence of the Image

The key word expresses the essence of the image. Without it there would be no image. This makes key words the most important words in an image phrase.

Usually there is only one key word in an image phrase, but sometimes there may be two and less frequently three.

The following thought is composed of two image phrases:

> *The moon / rises over the ocean.*

The first image phrase is the thing we are talking about, *the moon.*

What is the most important word? Naturally, *moon.* Without that word we would have no image.

In the second image phrase what words are essential to the image?

Rises tells us what the *moon* does and it could be a key word, particularly if you are trying to communicate a feeling of movement or the passage of time. (You would be expressing a different image if you sang, *The moon hangs over the ocean.*)

Ocean certainly is another key word—we are not picturing a country town or a forest.

Emphasize Key Words: You emphasize, or stress, key words more than the other words in the image phrase.

Exercise

(1) Say the following thought out loud, emphasizing each word equally.

> *The moon rises over the ocean.*

(2) Now sing the thought, emphasizing each word equally. (Improvise a melody.)

> *The moon rises over the ocean.*

Notice how undramatic and stiff the line is when you give equal stress to all the words.

(3) This time say the thought out loud, emphasizing only the key words. (You may or may not emphasize *rises*.)

> *The **moon** **rises** over the **ocean**.*

(4) Now, sing the thought out loud, emphasizing only the key words. (Improvise a melody.)

> *The **moon** **rises** over the **ocean**.*

Notice how much more dramatic the thought is when you emphasize key words.

In expressive singing and speaking, you give primary emphasis to the key words.

Support Words

Support words give information about the essential image you are communicating. They are important words because they provide additional details about the basic image, but they are not so important that we would lose the primary image if the words were not there.

Let's embellish the thought we used above with some support words:

The languorous, silver moon rises over the dark, stormy ocean.

We still have a *moon* image and an *ocean* image, but we have added some specific details that influence our picture of the scene.

In the first image phrase, *languorous* and *silver* are support words, telling us more about the basic image.

In the second image phrase, *over*, *dark* and *stormy* are support words, guiding us to picture a certain kind of *ocean*.

Give Less Emphasis to Support Words. You don't give the support words as much emphasis as key words, but they are emphasized more than connecting words.

Exercise

(1) Speak the following thought out loud. Give the key words the strong emphasis and the support words just a little emphasis.

*The **languorous**, **silver** <u>moon</u> <u>rises</u> over the **dark**, **stormy** <u>ocean</u>.*

(2) Now, sing the thought out loud, the same way. (Improvise a melody.)

*The **languorous**, **silver** <u>moon</u> <u>rises</u> over the **dark**, **stormy** <u>ocean</u>.*

Notice that if you are thinking of the imagery your voice naturally gives the support words a little emphasis.

Connecting Words

Connecting words are necessary for the smooth flow of thought when you sing or speak, but they don't add anything to the basic image.

Look at our example, again.

The languorous, silver moon rises over the dark, stormy ocean.

The word *the* in both image phrases is simply a connecting word. It has no sensuous imagery.

No Emphasis on Connecting Words. Connecting words must be said clearly and distinctly, but they do not receive any emphasis.

Exercise

(1) Say, the thought out loud. Hear and feel that *the*, does not receive any emphasis,

although it is said clearly.

The languorous, silver moon rises over the dark, stormy ocean.

(2) Sing the thought the same way. (Improvise a melody.)

The languorous, silver moon rises over the dark, stormy ocean.

Word Emphasis

When you sing or speak the thought:

(1) **Key words are given the most emphasis.**

(2) **Support words are given less emphasis than key words.**

(3) **Connecting words are given no emphasis, but they must be clearly said and heard.**

These three degrees of emphasis are merely general guidelines. You cannot consciously think of and control all the subtle degrees of emphasis required for expressive singing and speaking. However, you can and should keep in mind the images and you can emphasize the key words that symbolize the images.

One of the laws controlling speaking and singing is that your voice automatically expresses whatever you are thinking and feeling. Your voice is the sound of your soul. As long as you concentrate on communicating the image and thought through the key words, the degrees of emphasis will fall in place.

The Problem of Wrong Emphasis

Frequently, you hear speakers or singers emphasize words that are not important to the thought. Sometimes, this is because they have not carefully analyzed the thought and picked the right key words. Their emphasis is more or less random. Or, if they have analyzed the thought, they have picked the wrong key words or too many key words.

But, often, incorrect emphasis is simply the result of not keeping the images and key words in mind while you are speaking or singing.

You must think about what you are singing as you are singing.

You must be aware of where you are placing your emphasis.

Inexperienced speakers and singers often place emphasis on connecting words without realizing it. When it is pointed out to them, they easily correct it. You have to develop the ability to emphasize the words you want to emphasize and to not emphasize the words you don't want to emphasize.

In your analysis, you must be crystal clear about what your images are and about which words convey their essence. Part of the art of acting in singing is making sure that you pick the right key word and that you get it across to your audience.

Logical and Emotional Emphasis

Analyzing your lines for key words and support words forces you to make choices. You can't say, *"Well, maybe I mean this."* You have to be specific.

Choosing key words establishes your essential image and consequently your meaning and emotion. In this way, choosing key words helps guide you in your creation of your role.

There are two kinds of key words:

(1) The logical key word

(2) The emotional key word

The Logical Key Word

As we have discussed, the logical key word is the word that contains the essence of the image.

Logical emphasis is also determined by the point you are trying to make. Let's take an obvious example,

The black cat is in the corner.

Of course, the two logical key words are *cat* and *corner.*

Black is a support word.

But if you have two cats, one *black* and one *white*, and if you wanted to be clear about which cat was in the corner, you might say,

*The **black** cat is in the corner.*

You must be sure you are making the point you want to make.

The Emotional Key Word

The emotional key word is also determined by the point you are trying to make.

The logical and emotional key words in an image phrase may be the same word.

But if the logical and emotional key words are different, the emphasis always goes to the emotional key word.

For example, in the thought, *It is the truth*, the logical key words are *it* and *truth*.

But, if someone has insisted that what you have said is **not** *the truth*, you would probably say the line with the strongest emphasis on *is*:

*It **is** the truth!*

Emotional emphasis always takes precedence over logic.

In a more subtle thought, in *Richard III*, Richard says,

I would to God my heart were flint,
like Edward's.

Between *my* and *heart* the logical key word is *heart*.

*I would to God my **heart** were flint,*
like Edward's.

But if the actor wanted to more strongly point up the comparison between himself and Edward, he could emphasize *my* more than *heart*.

*I would to God **my** heart were flint,*
like Edward's.

Your choice of key words is decided by your intention.

The logical analysis has to be done first. If you don't know what point you are trying to get across, you can't know what you are being emotional about.

Stress New Information

Once an image has been established in the minds of your listeners it is not necessary to continue to stress that image each time you mention it.

It is more interesting to stress new information about the image.

If you say, **He** *is my* **brother**, you establish that you are talking about your brother. Then you might say, *He is my* **big** *brother*, in which you emphasize the new information.

But if your first statement is, *He is my big* **brother**, you need to emphasize *brother* to establish the essential image.

The same holds true if the image is established by someone else.

In *Henry V*, Gower asks Fluellen,

*How now, Captain Fluellen, **come** you from the **bridge**?*

Fluellen answers,

*I **assure** you, there is very **excellent services** committed at the bridge.*

Gower first mentions the *bridge*, so he will emphasize the word. Then Fluellen can emphasize the image of excellent services.

If Fluellen also emphasizes *bridge*, there will not be a natural flow of ideas, as there is in normal conversation. To emphasize *bridge* again would be confusing to the audience.

Of course, there are moments of great emotion in which the same word, or image, is stressed repeatedly. In the sleepwalking scene in *Macbeth*, Lady Macbeth cries,

Out, *damn'd **spot**! **out**, I say.*

and emphasizes *out* each time.

But, generally, the normal flow of conversation gives emphasis to the new ideas that come up.

Congratulations! You have learned how to sing with **meaning** and **emotion**—the basics of **expressive singing**.

Exercise

(1) Find the recording you were asked to make at the end of Chapter One.

(2) Rerecord the same material.

(3) Compare your pronunciation now with your pronunciation then.

(4) Give yourself some pats on the back. You have done a good job.

Notes:

Appendix
Additional Readings

Say these readings out loud, slowly at first, then faster. As you become familiar with the words, see how fast you can speak them without losing clarity.

When you're lying awake with a dismal headache, and
    repose is taboo'd by anxiety,
I conceive you may use any language you choose to indulge
    in without impropriety.
For your brain is on fire, the bedclothes conspire of
    usual slumber to plunder you.
First your counterpane goes and uncovers your toes and
    your sheet slips demurely from under you.
Then the blanketing tickles, you feel like mixed pickles,
    so terribly sharp is the pricking.
And you're hot and you're cross and you tumble and toss
    till there's nothing 'twixt you and the ticking.
Then the bedclothes all creep to the ground in a heap and
    you pick 'em all up in a tangle.
Next your pillow resigns and politely declines to remain
    at its usual angle!
Well, you get some repose in the form of a doze, with hot
    eye-balls and head ever aching.
But your slumbering teems with such horrible dreams that
    you'd very much better be waking.
For you dream you are crossing the Channel and tossing
    about in a steamer from Harwich,
Which is something between a large bathing machine and a
    very small second-class carriage,
And you're giving a treat (penny ice and cold meat) to a
    party of friends and relations.
They're a ravenous horde and theyd all come on board at
    Sloane Square and South Kensington stations.
And bound on that journey you find your attorney (who
    started that morning from Devon);

He's a bit undersized and you don't feel surprised when
    he tells you he's only eleven.
Well, you're driving like mad with this singular lad (by
    the by, the ship's now a four-wheeler)
And you're playing round games and he calls you bad names
    when you tell him that "ties pay the dealer."
But this you can't stand, so you throw up your hand and
    you find you're as cold as an icicle,
In your shirt and your socks (the black silk with gold
    clocks), crossing Salisbury Plain on a bicycle;
And he and the crew are on bicycles too (which they've
    somehow or other invested in);
And he's telling the tars all the particulars of a
    company he's interested in.
It's a scheme of devices to get at low prices all goods
    from cough mixtures to cables
(Which tickles the sailors), by treating retailers as
    though they were all vegetables.
You get a good spadesman to plant a small tradesman
    (first take off his boots with a boot tree),
And his legs will take root, and his fingers will shoot,
    and they'll blossom and bud like a fruit tree.
From the greengrocer tree you get grapes and green pea,
    cauliflower, pineapple and cranberries;
While the pastrycook plant cherry brandy will grant,
    apple puffs, and three-corners, and Banburys.
The shares are a penny and ever so many are taken by
    Rothschild and Baring,
And just as a few are alloted to you, you awake with a
    shudder despairing.
    You're a regular wreck, with a crick in your neck,
    and no wonder you snore, for your head's on the floor,
    and you've needles and pins from your soles to your shins,
    and your flesh is a-creep, for your left leg's asleep,
    and you've cramp in your toes, and a fly on your nose,
    and some fluff in your lung, and a feverish tongue,
    and a thirst that's intense, and a general sense
    that you haven't been sleeping in clover.
But the darkness has passed and it's daylight at last,
    and the night has been long — ditto, ditto my song —
    and thank goodness they're both of them over!

W. S. Gilbert

To sit in solemn silence
In a dim dark dock,
Awaiting the sensation
Of a short, sharp shock
From a cheap and chippy chopper
On a big black block.

W. S. Gilbert

Here's a first-rate opportunity
To get married with impunity,
To indulge in the felicity
Of unbounded domesticity.
You shall quickly be personified,
Conjugally matrimonified,
By a doctor of divinity,
Who resides in this vicinity.

W. S. Gilbert

You can take a tub with a rub and a scrub in a two-foot
      tank of tin.
You can stand and look at the whirling brook and think
      about jumping in.
You can chatter and shake in the cold black lake, but the
      kind of bath for me,
Is to take a dip from the side of a ship, in the trough
      of the rolling sea.

W. S. Gilbert

A complicated gentleman allow me to present,
Of all the arts and faculties a terse emodiment.
A great arithmetician, who can demostrate with ease,
That two and two are three or five, or anything you please.
An eminent logician, who can make it clear to you
That black is white — when looked at from the proper point of view.
A marvelous philologist, who'll undertake to show
That "yes" is but another form of "no."

W. S. Gilbert

I am the very model of a modern Major-General,
I've information vegetable, animal and mineral,
I know the kings of England and I quote the fights historical,
From Marathon to Waterloo, in order categorical.
I'm very well acquainted too with matters mathematical,
I understand equations, both the simple and quadratical.
About binomial theorem I'm teeming with a lot o'news,
With many cheerful facts about the square of the hypotenuse.
I'm very good at integral and differential calculus,
I know the scientific names of beings animalculous.
In short, in matters vegetable, animal and mineral,
I am the very model of a modern Major-General.

I know our mythic history, King Arthur and Sir Caradoc's,
I answer hard acrostics, I've a pretty taste for paradox.
I quote in elegiacs all the crimes of Heliogabalus,
In conics I can floor peculiarities parabolous.
I can tell undoubted Raphaels from Gerard Dows and Zoffanies,
I know the croaking chorus from the Frogs of Aristophanes.
Then I can hum a fugue of which I've heard the music's din afore,
And whistle all the airs from that infernal nonsense "Pinafore."
Then I can write a washing bill in Babylonic cuniform,
And tell you every detail of Caractacus's uniform.
In short, in matters vegetable, animal and mineral,
I am the very model of a modern Major-General.

In fact, when I know what is meant by "mamelon" and "ravelin,"
When I can tell at sight a chassepot rifle from a javelin,
When such affairs as sorties and surprises I'm more wary at,
And when I know precisely what is meant by "commissariat."
When I have learnt what progress has been made in modern gunnery,
When I know more of tactics than a novice in a nunnery;
In short, when I've a smattering of elemental strategy,
You'll say a better Major-General has never sat a gee.
For my military knowledge, though I'm plucky and adventury,
Has only been brought down to the beginning of the century.
But still, in matters vegetable, animal and mineral,
I am the very model of a modern Major-General.

W. S. Gilbert

Selected Bibliography

Appelman, D. Ralph. **The Science of Vocal Pedagogy**. Bloomington: Indiana University Press, 1967.

Berry, Cicely. **Voice and the Actor**. New York: Macmillan Publishing Co., Inc., 1973.

Buchanan, James. **Linguae Britaaicae Vera Pronunciatio or A New English Dictionary 1757**. Vol. #39 of **English Linguistics**. Edited by R. C. Alston. Menston, England: The Scolar Press Limited, 1967.

Burn, John. **A Pronouncing Dictionary of the English Language 1786**. Vol. #173 of **English Linguistics**. Edited by R. C. Alston. Menston, England: The Scolar Press Limited, 1969.

Christy, Van A. **Foundations in Singing**. Revised by John Glenn Paton. Dubuque: Wm. C. Brown Publishers, 1990.

Caruso, Enrico and Tetrazzini, Luisa. **Caruso and Tetrazzini on the Art of Singing**. New York: Dover Publications, Inc., 1975.

Dobson, E. J. **English Pronunciation, 1500-1700**. Oxford: At the Clarendon Press, 1968.

Eisenson, Jon. **The Improvement of Voice and Diction**. New York: The Macmillan Company, 1958.

Forward, Geoffrey G. **Power Speech**. Los Angeles: Forward Company, 1987.

Giles, Howard and Powesland, Peter F. **Speech Style and Social Evaluation**. London: Academic Press, 1975.

Giles, Wilkeson Gray and Wise, Claude Merton. **The Bases of Speech**. New York: Harper & Brothers Publishers, 1934.

Hagen, Uta. **Respect for Acting**. New York: Macmillan Publishing Co., Inc., 1973.

Howard, Elisabeth and Austin, Howard. **Born To Sing**. Los Angeles: Vocal Power, Inc., 1991.

Johnston, William. **A Pronouncing and Spelling Dictionary 1764**. Vol. #95 of **English Linguistics**. Edited by R. C. Alston. Menston, England: The Scolar Press Limited, 1968.

Jones, Daniel. **Everyman's English Pronouncing Dictionary**. New York: E. P. Dutton & Co. Inc., 1956.

Jones, Daniel. **The Pronunciation of English**. Cambridge: Cambridge University Press, 1980.

Kenyon, John Samuel. **American Pronunciation**. Ann Arbor: George Wahr Publishing Company, 1950.

Kenyon, John Samuel and Knott, Thomas Albert. **A Pronouncing Dictionary of American English**. Springfield: G. & C. Merriam Company, Publishers, 1953.

Kokeritz, Helge. **Shakespeare's Pronunciation**. New Haven: Yale University Press, 1953.

Krapp, George Philip. **The English Language in America**. New York: Frederick Ungar Publishing Co., 1960.

Kraus, Michael. **The United States to 1865**. Ann Arbor: The University of Michigan Press, 1959.

Kurath, Hans. **A Word Geography of The Eastern United States**. Ann Arbor: University of Michigan Press, 1949.

Ladefoged, Peter. **A Course In Phonetics**. New York: Harcourt Brace Jovanovich, Inc., 1975.

Lamperti, Giovanni Battista. **Vocal Wisdom Maxims of Giovanni Battista Lamperti**. Transcribed by William Earl Brown. Edited by Lillian Strongin. New York: Taplinger Publishing Company, 1957.

Lessac, Arthur. **The Use and Training of the Human Voice**. New York: DBS Publications, Inc., 1967.

Linklater, Kristin. **Freeing the Natural Voice**. New York: Drama Book Specialists (Publishers), 1976.

Machlin, Evangeline. **Speech for the Stage**. New York: Theatre Arts Books, 1966.

Marckwardt, Albert H. **American English**, 2nd edition. Revised by J. L. Dillard. New York: Oxford University Press, 1980.

Marshall, Madeleine. **The Singer's Manual of English Diction**. New York: Schirmer Books, 1953.

Mathews, M. M., ed. **The Beginnings of American English**. Chicago: Phoenix Books, University of Chicago Press, 1963.

Meisner, Sanford and Longwell, Dennis. **Sanford Meisner on Acting**. New York: Vintage Books, 1987.

Mencken, H. L. **The American Language**. New York: Alfred A. Knopf, 1937.

Miller, Richard. **The Structure of Singing.** New York: Schirmer Books, 1996

NBC Handbook of Pronunciation. Revised and updated by Eugene Ehrlich and Raymond Hand, Jr. New York: Harper & Row, Publishers, 1984.

Norman, Barry. **The Story of Hollywood**. New York: New American Library, 1987.

Pyles, Thomas. **The Origins and Development of the English Language**. New York: Harcourt Brace Jovanovich, Inc., 1971.

Sheridan, Thomas. **A General Dictionary of the English Language 1780**. Vol. #50 of **English Linguistics**. Edited by R. C. Alston. Menston, England: The Scolar Press Limited, 1967.

Skinner, Edith. **Good Speech for the American Actor**. New York: Drama Book Specialists, 1980.

Skinner, Edith. **Speak with Distinction**. New York: Applause Theatre Book Publishers, 1990.

Stanislavski, Constantin. **An Actor Prepares**. Translated by Elizabeth Reynolds Hapgood. New York: Theatre Arts Books, 1948.

Stanislavski, Constantin. **Building a Character**. Translated by Elizabeth Reynolds Hapgood. New York: Theatre Arts Books, 1949.

Stanislavski, Constantin. **Creating a Role**. Translated by Elizabeth Reynolds Hapgood. New York: Theatre Arts Books, 1961.

Turner, Clifford J. **Voice and Speech in the Theatre**. London: Pitman Press, 1970.

Vennard, William. **Singing, the Mechanism and the Technic**. Boston: Carl Fischer, Inc., 1967.

Walker, Alexander. **The Shattered Silents, How the talkies came to stay.** New York: William Morrow and Company, Inc., 1978.

Walker, John. **A Critical Pronouncing Dictionary 1791**. Vol. #117 of **English Linguistics**. Edited by R. C. Alston. Menston, England: The Scolar Press Limited, 1968.

Webster, Noah. **Dissertations on the English Language**. Boston: Printed for the author by Isaiah Thomas & Co., 1789. Facsimile reproduction Menston, England: The Scolar Press Limited, 1967.

Webster, Noah. **The American Spelling Book**. Middletown: Published by William H. Niles, 1831 (first printed 1817).

Webster, Noah. **A Compendious Dictionary of the English Language**. Facsimile of the first (1806) edition. New York: Crown Publishers, Inc., 1970.

Webster, Noah. **The Elementary Spelling Book**. New York: American Book Company, 1908.

Index

About the Author

Geoffrey G. Forward has conducted seminars for and spoken before numerous groups and organizations, including **Toastmasters International, The John Caffey Society, The Huntington Library, The Optimists Club, UCLA School of Law, The English Speaking Union, The National Association of Teachers of Singing, United Teachers of Los Angeles** and the **National Association of Accountants-Orange Coast Chapter**, among others.

Voice Building and Standard American Diction

Geoffrey G. Forward is the founder of **SpeechMasters of America** and has taught voice and speech for over twenty years, including 7 years for the American Academy of Dramatic Arts. His clients include actors, lawyers, business executives and other professionals who want to improve their voice, their image and their persuasive power.

He was one of the first authors to publish voice and speech books with audio cassettes, *"Because,"* he said, *"you can't learn to speak from a book."* His **American Diction for Singers**, was given high praise by the National Association of Teachers of Singing (NATS) Journal, which called it *"a remarkable book, a significant contribution to the literature,"* and *"highly recommended for use in all voice studios."*

He has also written, **ProSpeech**, for business-people and other professionals who want to improve their diction, and his **Power Speech** audio cassettes have been selling world-wide since 1986.

Actor / Director

Geoffrey G. Forward is also an accomplished actor and director. He has appeared in numerous film, television and stage roles and is the Founder and Artistic Director of **The Los Angeles Shakespeare Company.**